MORE PRAISE FOR *MERGE LEFT*

"I've been working to change the political system for years. I have believed that what is needed is a movement strong enough to unite both people of color and white working-class people. I have scratched my head about how best to frame this. Then *Merge Left* arrived. Finally, we have the how-to manual for dismantling a system of division that hurts everyone."
—Jane Fonda

"Racism is a weapon against the working class and cross-racial solidarity is the linchpin to creating an energized and empowered movement for restaurant workers and beyond. In *Merge Left*, Haney López explores a powerful strategy and path forward where working people and families can win—not just in the next election, but into the future."
—Saru Jayaraman, president, Restaurant Opportunities Centers United

"Frankly, this approach connecting race to class and calling for unity is the most important work I've been involved with in twenty years of polling."
—Celinda Lake, Democratic pollster and strategist

"Having presented and implemented winning campaigns based on this research, I can't imagine a clearer or more long-overdue playbook for progressives than *Merge Left*. Haney López moves us from diagnosis to cure."
—Anat Shenker-Osorio, research director for the Race-Class Narrative Project

"We all lose if the only people talking about race are the people trying to divide us against each other. That's why [*Merge Left*] is so pivotal in our fight for an economy and democracy that works for everyone."
—Gerry Hudson, secretary-treasurer, SEIU

"Ian Haney López has established himself as one of the most prescient and insightful voices on how race and racism have shaped and continue to reshape American society. Here he asks the toughest question facing strategists of the left. How do we unite those on the losing end of both the nation's racial divide and its rampant class inequality? . . . This is an important read for anyone hoping to build a meaningful workers' coalition on the left."
—Gary Segura, dean, Luskin School of Public Affairs, UCLA

"*Merge Left* makes clear that major progress on racial justice will follow from defeating dog whistle politics once and for all. For all of us seeking to end state violence against communities of color, this book is powerful, timely, trenchant, and practical."
—Kimberlé Crenshaw, executive director, African American Policy
    Forum, and faculty director, Center for Intersectionality and
    Social Policy Studies, Columbia University

"*Merge Left* is the essential handbook for everyone who is standing up to xenophobia and fighting for humane immigration policies. And it is so much more than that. *Merge Left* is for every activist and progressive committed to building a broad, diverse and dynamic movement that actually delivers on the promise of both racial and economic justice."
—Frank Sharry, executive director, America's Voice

"Solidarity is the crucial ingredient in the fight against the ever-more-dangerous plutocracy. Ian Haney López helps explain where that solidarity might come from, even in our strained and divided society. Epically helpful!"
—Bill McKibben, environmentalist and author of
    Falter: Has the Human Game Begun to Play Itself Out?

MERGE LEFT

Fusing Race and Class, Winning Elections,
and Saving America

IAN HANEY LÓPEZ

THE
NEW
PRESS

NEW YORK
LONDON

Requests for permission to reproduce selections from this book should be made through our website: https://thenewpress.com/contact.

"Old Man Trump." Words by Woody Guthrie, music by Ryan Harvey. © Woody Guthrie Publications, Inc. (BMI) & Ryan Harvey (ASCAP). All rights reserved. Used by permission.

Published in the United States by The New Press, New York, 2019
Distributed by Two Rivers Distribution

ISBN 978-1-62097-564-0 (hc)
ISBN 978-1-62097-565-7 (ebook)

CIP data available

The New Press publishes books that promote and enrich public discussion and understanding of the issues vital to our democracy and to a more equitable world. These books are made possible by the enthusiasm of our readers; the support of a committed group of donors, large and small; the collaboration of our many partners in the independent media and the not-for-profit sector; booksellers, who often hand-sell New Press books; librarians; and above all by our authors.

www.thenewpress.com

Composition by dix!
This book was set in Garamond Premier Pro

Printed in the United States of America

10 9 8 7 6 5 4 3 2 1

To Debbie,
for the better part of my life
my wife and partner

Contents

Competing Narratives

Preface

The question from the floor signals that the wheels are off the unity bus.

In my day job, I'm a law professor at the University of California, Berkeley, but this Hilton meeting hall is no ivory tower seminar room. In 2014, I published *Dog Whistle Politics*. That book explained how the economic royalty and the politicians they fund have been twisting American politics for decades by manipulating racial resentment. After that, rather than continue conversing only with scholars and students, I resolved to do what I could to discuss this widely with people and groups dedicated to fighting back.

Now it's early 2016, and this hotel conference room is full of union officials who have come together for their annual retreat. The union's national leadership has brought me to Fort Lauderdale, Florida, to lead a day-long workshop on racism and economic hardship for their state representatives. The unions I've worked with have been further along than most liberal institutions in seeing how race and class interact, so this is an audience that should be open to my analysis. Still, even before the unnerving question, the pressure of the looming day weighs on me.

Partly the weight comes from the significant risk that the union's top leadership is taking. They've ordered the fifty state leaders into stackable chairs in a windowless room. I look around. With a handful of exceptions, everyone is white. There are just a very few women. Really? This room full of big white guys who came up through labor is going to listen to a Latinx professor with soft writer's hands pontificate on racism for eight hours? The national leadership has gone out on a limb, and then handed me the saw.

Even more, though, the weight pressing on me comes from the seeming absurdity of my goal. I think there's a way to move whites toward a pragmatic commitment to racial justice. I also believe doing so provides a fulcrum to build economic justice for all racial groups, whites included.

It sounds good in theory, my academic comfort zone. But this morning as I survey the faces looking at me, the audacity of it seems delusional. The practical reality of actually moving the solid bodies sitting around the large U-shaped conference table racks my nerves.

I start by asking if they think they have a racism problem in their union. Some volunteer spontaneously, oh yes, we have racism. But it's not a problem, others laughingly rejoin. They're half talking to themselves and half responding to me. There's some chuckling around the room. Then someone calls out to explain: sure, there's some racism among a few of our members, but it's not really a big deal.

That's when I get the question that really unsettles me. "Why can't I say the n-word?"

I struggle to understand where the question is coming from. Is it asked in good faith, in a space perceived as safe? Maybe, but this early in the conversation, I doubt it. Rather, it seems more confrontational, some sort of taunt.

Answering a question you're unsure about with a return question is a trick of the trade among professors. So I query the room regarding how they would respond to their union brother. No help there. Over the clink of water glasses there's an overlay of murmurs and low laughter, as people turn to their neighbors to joke. The only direct responses I get are more voices repeating the challenging question, and making clear what had only been implied before: *They get to say it, they call each other that all the time, it's everywhere in their rap music, so why can't I say the word?*

Maybe they're feeling like there's a double standard that only criticizes whites for stuff everybody supposedly does—like prefer-ring the company of their own group or saying the n-word. Or maybe they're bristling at what they perceive as preaching from a brown person with lots of degrees after his name. Maybe it's some combination. I'm not sure.

But I do know that the longer the n-word conversation goes on, the more the faces looking at me start to harden, eyes narrowing and mouths pressing thin. Arms cross and men lean back in their chairs, their chests rising. The room seems to be letting me know they're not going to lie down for another mini-sermon on their racism.

I reach for another teaching trick: turn your answer in the di-rection you want to go. All people should be treated the same, I acknowledge. The statement is abstract enough that those in the room can fill it with their own meanings, perhaps finding in it confirmation that they are being treated unfairly. But then I add that when society puts groups in very different positions, some-times the same actions carry very different meanings. Chairs scuff over the industrial carpet patterned in muted blocks of contrast-ing colors. I can feel people pushing further away as I seem to jus-tify what they see as a double standard.

Let me explain, I quickly interject. Let's talk about what's hap-pened in society since the civil rights movement in the 1960s made uttering the n-word broadly unacceptable.

I have ulterior motives. First, I know from experience that dis-placing hard conversations about racism onto the past can smooth the discussion. Pointing at distant others slows people from deaf-ening their ears to defend themselves.

Second, I really do want to describe what's happened to the country since the 1960s, in a way that connects racism and surg-ing wealth inequality—including, most relevant in this context, labor union decline.

Addressing the incendiary question from the floor, I start:

The n-word is one of the most violent terms expressing white supremacy, and for generations in this nation it permeated public life. But in the 1960s, the civil rights movement succeeded in driving this word out of polite conversation. In turn, that cultural change set the groundwork for laws prohibiting white supremacy from operating openly in voting, jobs, schools, housing, and union halls as well.

But the word still carries a terrible potency, I say. Sometimes groups contesting ugly beliefs about them seek to strip vile words of their power by claiming those words for themselves. Think about how some in the gay rights movement adopted and thereby transformed the term "queer." In the same way, those of us who are not Black should understand when some in the Black community seek to take ownership of the n-word to redefine it in ways that shift its meaning to them.

But the truth is, I state, it's still a word tied to a bloody history and a revolting set of views. When whites use this word today, it strikes many as suggesting at best an indifference to hard-won advances in racial equality, and possibly a persistent attachment to dehumanizing beliefs about racial supremacy. It furthers the kind of racial divisions that we are gathered here to discuss.

Then I pivot to take the group beyond abstract piety to focus on the consequences of racial division. This is not just a moral issue, I tell them. At stake is the future of their union. This is where I want to go. My goal is to transform the racism conversation by connecting it to their self-interest.

I walk them through a slide show I've prepared with photos, campaign videos, and maps of electoral results that tell a dismal tale. In the presentation, Richard Nixon strides into the conference room in images from 1968, pushing back against civil rights by calling for "law and order" and claiming to represent "the silent majority." These are dog whistles, I explain. A literal dog whistle sounds at such a high frequency that human ears cannot hear it but canines can. As a metaphor, it points to political language that operates at two levels, one silent about race, the other provoking sharp racial reactions.

Nixon wins in 1968, and then wins reelection in 1972 in a

landslide that colors the whole electoral map red. Ronald Reagan then appears, warning the union leaders about "welfare queens." These racial dog whistles, I say, are how the party of big business has been winning support from working families for decades. Democrats, I explain, eventually decided their best answer was imitation. The supposed hero of the white working class Bill Clinton pops up to ask for their votes by repeating Republican dog whistles, promising to "end welfare as a way of life" and to "crack down on crime."

A sharply rising graph shows wealth inequality surging higher decade by decade from the Reagan years onward. The government policies that leave working people choking on dust emerge as familiar bullet points:

- Tax cuts for the rich
- Slashed social spending
- Corporations writing the rules
- More police than jobs in poor communities of color
- Government hostility toward unions

Here's the biggest mystery, I say: Why in the midst of increasing economic hardship are so many white working families voting for this? Because they've been convinced to fear and resent people of color. Big money interests and the politicians and media outlets they bankroll have been selling the same basic lie for fifty years: *Distrust liberals and government for coddling rather than controlling people of color. Demand that government start punishing dangerous and undeserving people, by slashing social spending, launching a war on crime, and a war on immigrants, too. Punish government itself, by cutting taxes to starve it and gutting its regulations. Trust yourself to the marketplace. The party of big business and the working man are on the same team.* Basic numbers flash on the screen showing the GOP's 2012 presidential candidate drawing more than 90 percent of his support from white voters, while 98 percent of the GOP's elected officials are white.[1]

I close the morning by asking whether they see a future for

their own children in their union. Many admit with frustration that they do not. Among the immediate crises facing unions are hostile politicians and the judges they've appointed. The underlying problem is the racially charged elections that have put those politicians in power. Like a lawyer going for the jugular in a closing argument, as they prepare to file out for lunch I ask these mostly white union leaders a final question: *Isn't it true that racism against people of color is the biggest threat your own families face?*

They come back from the buffet trending toward the verdict I hoped they would reach. Using ideas and terms we've been discussing, they start asking questions that demonstrate an evolving mindset. What is unconscious bias and what is strategic racism? How can we effectively communicate to our members the critical importance of building strength across racial lines? What are the best practices for integrating a union? Not all of them, of course, are sold on this new perspective. But most seem to have made a major shift—from early questions about their prerogative to use a racial slur to earnest inquiries about how to build cross-racial solidarity.

I don't mean to oversell the moment. The about-face in the conference room was not my doing alone, not nearly. Union leaders have been pushing a related analysis for decades, making it easier for the people in the room to grasp arguments about racism as a divide-and-conquer tactic. And while I hope some of the leaders in that room put the lessons they learned into practice, I really don't know what, if anything, changed on the ground after our meeting.

For me, the day's conversation was hopeful but also discouraging. It confirmed as sound the basic strategy of connecting the fight against racism to economic self-interest. But it also underlined the difficult part: how to actually do that. Eight-hour lectures could not be scaled up.

For decades, the Right has been pushing a core narrative about undeserving people of color, government betrayal, and the saving power of the marketplace. It's now widely accepted as common sense. How could unions create a concise counterstory? How could they fashion a narrative so compelling and so frequently repeated it became its own version of common sense? And what about nonunion audiences: How could a new progressive story be made into common sense outside of the strong institutional support some unions provide?

All of this was a tall enough order just by itself. But in practice another mountain also loomed. I was meeting rejection from racial justice activists.

I had assumed that the main stumbling block to urging cross-racial solidarity would be convincing a majority of whites. At least equally formidable, it turned out, was enlisting support from people directly focused on racial justice, overwhelmingly activists of color.

To some extent, I encountered this sort of skepticism within unions. But even more frequently, I met rejection from race-focused advocates in my lectures on university campuses. As I came to see cross-racial solidarity as the key to both racial justice and economic fairness, I began delivering the same lecture I gave to the unions at colleges across the country. In those progressive settings, much of the pushback came from the students most committed to racial justice. I felt I knew them well, even when I was meeting them for the first time. They were just like my Berkeley students.

As a general rule, racial justice student-activists are steeped in history. They've studied the country's founding decisions and subsequent patterns, allowing them to perceive contemporary injustices in a context that emphasizes these injustices' deep roots and also society's broad culpability. They also live in a present that has them battling every day. It's not just the scale of the challenges, nor the wrenching emotions of witnessing racism devastate particular lives and families, sometimes their own. They're also warring against indifference expressed as lukewarm support. Even within a progressive space like my famously left-leaning campus, the committed activists are relatively few in number. Most of them are women of color, fighting not only racism but patriarchy and often class hierarchy and other inequalities as well. A few white students also fervently take up racial justice—in the law school context, they often plan to work in criminal law, immigration, or human rights.

When I urge racial justice advocates to link racism to economic issues in order to enlist more whites, these committed activists react in a range of ways. Some say straight up that they would rather demand that society face the crimes of white racism—even if it means not much really changes on the ground—than to reframe whites as victims of racism, too. These students challenge the very heart of my approach.

I argue back by focusing on the goal most important to them, helping communities of color.

Since the civil rights movement, I tell them, many politicians have won votes through racially coded scaremongering. Every time they triumph, they ramp up state violence against communities of color to prove their mettle—if you promise to keep whites safe from violent people of color, prove yourself by funding more police and building more prisons; if you say you'll clamp down on welfare cheats, especially defund the government programs that serve communities of color; if you claim that terrorists pose a looming threat, launch major surveillance programs and jail people for minor immigration violations; if you describe human beings as illegal aliens, rip families apart, jail hundreds of thousands, and deport millions more.

Behind all that storm and drama, I explain, these politicians do yet more favors for their big money patrons. The resulting economic inequality devastates everyone, including already vulnerable communities of color. But people of color especially suffer, I argue, as targets of the massive state violence designed to prove just how dangerous and unworthy we are. The key to immediate relief—to ending mass incarceration and mass deportation and systemic neglect—is to build a cross-racial coalition that defeats politicians who campaign using dog whistle scare tactics.

Often I invoke the work of pioneering race scholar Derrick

Bell. Bell was the first African American to become a tenured professor at Harvard Law School, and a founder of what has become known as critical race theory. Bell knew that racial progress stems from what he termed "interest convergence." "The interest of blacks in achieving racial equality will be accommodated only when it converges with the interests of whites," he explained.[2] Bell certainly believed in moral suasion. But he also understood that most people move in the directions they think will benefit them.

Channeling Bell, I say to the racial justice students that while moral arguments are important and human beings often act altruistically, it is a losing battle to expect that most whites (or any group) will relinquish a key form of their power simply because it is the right thing to do. You cannot radically improve the lives of communities of color until you convince whites that your pain ultimately hurts them, too. I ask, is the point to fault society, or to seek a way forward?

This often sparks a different concern. Are they now, some activists wonder, supposed to stop talking about racism as a social dynamic of whites over nonwhites? These student-activists often believe that the key to racial justice is to broadly educate people about white-over-nonwhite racism. Some of them have done so full time before coming to law school, for instance as labor movement organizers or in their churches.

The point of framing racism as a class weapon is not to permanently displace discussions about racial hierarchy, I say. Instead, it's to create added space for those exchanges as well as a greater inclination to participate. When more people see that cross-racial solidarity provides the best way forward for themselves and their families, they should be increasingly willing to engage in and sustain uncomfortable but necessary conversations. Educational work about racial hierarchy is hugely important to racial justice as well as to the project of building robust cross-racial solidarity. It's just that *starting* with conversations about white dominance feels unwelcoming and overwhelming to many. Ultimately, however, framing racism as a class weapon and as white-over-nonwhite hierarchy are complementary rather than competing ways to promote racial justice.

Even if they come to agree that genuine cross-racial solidarity would be beneficial in theory, many remain skeptical about what it would look like on the ground. They particularly worry that an interest-convergence approach offers little more than another opportunity for white folks to put themselves at the center. Will "cross-racial solidarity" in practice mean a coalition that responds to anti-Black racism only to the extent doing so helps white people? The racial justice activists also want proof. If they're going to risk having the racism conversation hijacked, they want to see some evidence that large numbers of whites might really endorse and work for racial justice for communities of color.

These were the sorts of challenging conversations I was already having when Donald Trump launched his presidential run with broadsides against Mexican rapists.

It's important to understand that Trump did not invent the larger pattern of political racism harnessed to rule by the rich. It's even more important to recognize this dynamic will continue long after Trump departs the scene, until the country actively defeats it.

Nevertheless, Trump's campaign and then his election catalyzed a sense of acute urgency. Trump was stomping on the accelerator of a democracy already headed toward a cliff because of rising racial divisions and surging wealth inequality. The little time left to avert catastrophe was burning up in clouds of choking fumes and plumes of spinning hate.

I knew by then that new frames and story lines were needed to solidly and consistently connect racism and plutocracy in the public mind—ideally, messages that communicated this reality quickly and that could be repeatedly reinforced. At the same time, it was obvious that any new approach could only be promoted with hard evidence. People needed proof a big departure might actually work. But how to actually craft and test these messages? I'd spent my career researching, writing, and teaching about how racism evolves, but when it came to effective political messaging, I was way out of my depth.

I needed someone like the Republican political consultant Frank Luntz. Luntz is perhaps the preeminent wordsmith for the party of corporate America. His mantra: "It's not what you say, it's what people hear." [3] By this he means that whether in politics or in branding toothpaste, it's not enough to announce attractive selling points. At least as important, you have to figure out what people actually hear, remember, and react to. Luntz extensively uses focus groups and public polling, and with their help has concocted terms like "death taxes" for the inheritance taxes many of the very rich seek to abolish.

Luntz also contributed to GOP race-baiting around immigration. In 2005, he wrote a then-confidential memo to Republicans titled "Words that Work"—work, that is, to build politically potent animus toward undocumented immigrants. He advised that Republicans should say over and over to voters, "This is about the overcrowding of YOUR schools. This is about emergency room chaos in YOUR hospitals. This is about the increase in YOUR taxes. This is about crime in YOUR communities." [4] These themes contradict the facts of immigration, but no matter. They work as dog whistles by triggering racial anxiety without directly naming race. Schools, hospitals, taxes, community—and especially the emphasized "your"—communicate a basic message of ownership, scarcity, and racial division. The tactic has played well for Republicans for years and become a routine rallying cry for Trump. "The Democrats don't care what their extremist immigration agenda will do to your neighborhoods or your hospitals or your schools," Trump said at a 2018 rally in Houston. [5]

Immediately after Trump's inauguration, a mutual friend put me in touch with Anat Shenker-Osorio as a potential partner. Shenker-Osorio is an expert on progressive messaging around the economy and immigration, with extensive experience helping unions domestically and abroad. [6] With the Right resorting to focus groups, polling, and careful message testing to hone their dog whistles, we would do the same to neutralize their weaponry and seek a basis for cross-racial common ground.

Shenker-Osorio had good relationships with pollsters, and we eventually partnered with Celinda Lake and Cornell Belcher, pre-eminent researchers and Democratic strategists. I was close with Heather McGhee, a former standout student at Berkeley Law and someone also focused on the destructive power of dog whistling. As the president at the time of Demos and Demos Action, think tanks geared toward connecting racial and economic justice, Mc-Ghee also brought an initial institutional home for the project.

In addition, the Service Employees International Union, with almost two million members, was on the cusp of launching their own research on how to meld anti-racism and pro-labor organizing. Through contacts with several of us, SEIU joined our core working group.

There was early thought given to expanding beyond race and class. The searing experience of an extraordinarily competent woman losing to a man who boasted on tape of sexually assaulting women made anti-sexism seem especially promising for progressive mobilizing. The millions who marched in the women's protests the day after Trump's inauguration—perhaps the largest day of protests in US history—added to this sense that fighting patriarchy could be as powerful an organizing tool as anti-racism.[7] But the culture wars around gender bisect race in complex ways. Many white women support patriarchy and do so in a manner that closely connects to support for continued white dominance, the sort of mindset that contributed to more white women voting for Donald Trump than Hillary Clinton.[8] Recognizing that our project was just a first step, it seemed best to focus on the already daunting task of shifting how progressives talk about race and class.

Together and with the help of many others, in 2017 and 2018 we ran a large research project interviewing activists, drafting potential messages, trying out early versions with multiple focus groups involving different racial communities all across the country, and testing the resulting messages in national as well as state surveys. We called the endeavor the race-class narrative project.

The result of all of this new research? We found encouraging evidence suggesting that racial dog whistling can be effectively defanged.

- Against the dominant consensus, most whites hold progressive views on race—though they also swing back and forth to reactionary ideas. This is good news. It suggests the Left does not need to tear down a mountain of white racism. Instead the task is to help the majority of whites connect their self-interest to the anti-racist values most already hold.
- Also contra the conventional wisdom, majorities of African American and Latinx voters find large parts of the Right's story convincing. This means that neutralizing the Right's narratives of racial fear and resentment is also key to turning out communities of color.
- A message urging joining together across racial groups to demand that government promote racial and economic justice consistently proved more convincing—to whites as well as to people of color—than the Right's racial fear story. The race-class message also proved stronger than the main progressive alternatives, either staying silent about race to focus on class, or leading with racial justice.

Bottom line: the race-class research suggests that merging race and class builds energy and excitement between core constituencies indispensable to a resurgent Left but typically seen as mutually hostile—the white working class and Barack Obama's coalition of nonwhite voters.*

---

* Copies of the race-class narrative project's public reports are hosted on the author's website, https://www.ianhaneylopez.com.

The book in your hands places the evidence, insights, and lessons of the race-class narrative project in a larger political and racial context. This includes:

- Detailing how dog whistle politics evolved in response to a Black president
- Exploring why liberals for five decades and still today distance themselves from racial justice
- Examining the limited power of colorblind economic populism to actually achieve economic populism, let alone racial justice
- Parsing why leading with racial justice for communities of color actually loses support from many in those very communities, not to mention from most whites
- Probing the ominous relationship between Trumpism and dangerous new trends in white identity

Ultimately, this book asks where we are in the long arc of a country struggling to overcome white supremacy. An enormous question, it nevertheless has immediate implications. Human societies take care of only those they see as worth caring for. This was America's founding insight—"with liberty and justice *for all.*" It has also been its enduring limitation. Decade by decade, though, with peaks and reversals, people fought to expand who truly belongs, who fully deserves dignified treatment. When the civil rights movement insisted that people of color should be included in the broad "we," many Americans agreed. But enough balked that their resentment could be harnessed by politicians beholden to economic elites. Through the purposeful encouragement of racial resentment and fear, the new plutocrats battered social solidarity and built popular support for their rule.

Today, every bold progressive vision depends on building cross-racial solidarity first. This is obviously important to assembling broad support for racial justice initiatives like abolishing mass incarceration and creating a humane immigration system. But it is also pivotal to enacting progressive legislation seemingly distant from racial issues, for instance publicly funded child and elder care, affordable and excellent healthcare, and a Green New Deal. Only a sense of linked fate across color lines seems likely to foster the supermajorities necessary to sweep away the politicians dog whistling on behalf of rule by and for the rich. The best response to divide-and-conquer is unite-and-build.

Our fates have always been bound together. For centuries, our greatest heroes—radicals like W. E. B. DuBois, Martin Luther King Jr., and César Chávez—have insisted that American salvation requires cross-racial alliances. Repeatedly, this insight has been suppressed, forgotten, and abandoned. Today, some of the wealthiest, most powerful forces in this country bend their will and money toward driving us apart so they can tighten their grip on government and the economy. Yet the very wreckage they have created—and the president they helped elect—open up another opportunity to build a broad cross-racial movement with the will and the political power to promote racial reform and shared economic prosperity.

This book explains the good evidence that cross-racial solidarity for racial and economic justice is possible, today.

Introduction: Matt and Tom

I'm in my office in Berkeley watching a live video feed from Cleveland. It's October 2017 and the race-class narrative project is under way. This is one of the first focus groups we've sponsored. On my desktop screen, I watch three youngish men enter a small conference room: interviewer Jonathan Voss accompanied by two recruits, "white non-college male friends, age 35–50." The space has the barren feel of a repurposed dentist's office. There's a translucent glass vase with white carnations on a white Formica table. The walls are gray above a waist-high perimeter band shaded toward Pepto-Bismol. Mini-blinds hide the windows. It's a low-budget sensory deprivation tank. Maybe the effect is supposed to be soothing, a fitting place for undistracted conversations. But as the interview topic turns to race, I feel like I'm getting my teeth drilled.

We've invited Matt and Tom—not their real names—to answer a series of questions about race, class, and government. We need to understand where people are starting from before we get too far along crafting messages about coded racism in American politics. Rather than recruiting groups of strangers, the typical approach to focus groups, we initially invite pairs of friends. We hope that when they know each other, people will be more honest in discussing the sensitive subjects of class inequality and racism.

Matt and Tom have been friends for years, since they worked together on maintenance jobs. Tom left when he earned enough to support himself as a self-described "starving artist"; he shows up with a buzz cut and a long gray beard that drapes his black T-shirt.

Matt, in a button-down blue oxford and wire-rimmed glasses, moved up from maintenance into management.

Getting them to talk about race turns out not to be a challenge. It's what they say that sets me worrying.

"At least where we live, it is hard *not* to be prejudiced," Tom says, "because bad things happen to you and it just happens to be a different race." Tom moved out of the city for a while, and racism seemed to disappear. "I lived out where no one was racist at all because everyone was the same," he explains. "I moved back to Cleveland, and you know you get jumped."

Matt admits that seeing past stereotypes can be challenging. To illustrate, he offers a story that suggests he believes some stereotypes are true. He describes encountering a hypothetical "you" who is the quintessential welfare recipient, living large while the working man struggles: "You go down to the store and you're filling your bag; your cart is overflowing and you whip out EBT. And I'm sitting there with five items wondering how I'm going to pay for it. Like, it's hard, you know?"

They're leery of speaking bluntly in racial terms, so they talk euphemistically about geography in a city racially divided by the Cuyahoga River. Still, every so often, the geographic façade crumbles. "Here it's the east side and the west, and the east side is falling apart," says Tom, the artist. "You don't cross the river. It is unspoken," Matt interjects. There's a pause, then Tom explains the pitiable state of the east side—and who is to blame for that. "There are giant, beautiful houses, but they have just been trashed. It just happens to be those are Blacks or Hispanics."

Years of mandatory busing to integrate the schools made things worse and amplified the racial tensions, they contend. "It destroyed the entire city," says Matt. He's the manager, so perhaps it's no surprise he would add that the busing orders made matters worse because "Americans don't like being told what to do."

Racism against whites is the problem these men see. They back it up with personal stories. "I had one of the highest scores for the police entrance exam, but I was not a minority and I was male," says Matt, talking about an earlier effort to move out of his maintenance job. "There's nothing I could've changed on that and so I got bumped down like six hundred slots because of how I was born. Like it didn't matter that I scored better than almost everybody. I wasn't the right color and gender."

Attuned to perceived racial limitations in their own lives, they resist seeing it in the lives of others. The conversation later turns to people of color and whether racism holds them back. Matt says no. "I think that it's an excuse that you fail because you're the wrong color, because I can think of hundreds of examples off the top of my head that will contradict you." For Matt, centuries of history aren't part of the equation. "But how many generations are we out of slavery? I had nothing to do with it."

Tom responds that Blacks need to get over slavery. "Using that is just a horrible crutch to not trying, not working, not fixing yourself."

It's easy to presume from their words that Matt and Tom voted for Donald Trump. After Trump's election rocked the nation, political researchers and journalists launched themselves with cameras, tape recorders, and binoculars into Trump's America. Motivating most of them was the widely shared assumption that Democrats would have to win back Trump Country voters in the next election go-round. With the race-class project, we started from a different premise. We were less focused on wooing those who voted for Trump than on activating Democrats and independents.

That's what made listening to Matt and Tom so disheartening—they were *not* Trump voters. Tom said he preferred Bernie Sanders, but with him out, voted for Hillary Clinton. Matt went third party, voting for libertarian candidate Gary Johnson.

Matt and Tom were supposedly the good guys. And yet the more they talked the clearer it became that they lived in a racially segregated environment where geography and stereotypes conspired to keep them separate from and suspicious toward people of color. How in the world could we convince people like this to enthusiastically join a multiracial progressive movement?

But as I kept listening, I learned something startling from Matt and Tom, something I simply did not know before. I was predisposed to hear stereotypes from a couple of white guys in Ohio, and they didn't disappoint. But as the conversation went on, they also expressed racial sentiments that were enlightened. They seemed both racially reactionary *and* racially progressive, jumping back and forth between conflicting ideas.

Listen as Matt and Tom talk about their lives and you'll hear them say things that contradict their earlier statements in remarkable ways.

"My profile picture for years was my son and his Black baby doll." Matt shrugs as he says this, his voice going soft. He seems to marvel at his child's innocence, giving a half laugh and explaining, "He had no idea. He loved that baby." Matt doesn't say what compelled him to use that photo to craft his public persona on social media, but it seems like the ideal of seeing people untainted by stereotypes holds a deep appeal.

From behind his gray beard, Tom chimes in: "Like my kids have friends all over the world that they talk to. They have no idea how they are different than us." In their children, they seem to see a more beautiful world free from racism.

Matt defines racism as "walls that need to be removed that shouldn't have been constructed in the first place."

"There's a lot of racism out there," Tom admits. "You go to get a job, they will pick the white guy. Even though they are not allowed to do that, it happens. Whereas, if you show up Black, you are already one point behind." It's better to be poor and white than poor and Black, he says. "Sadly, the white man has ruled the planet for thousands of years."

When it comes to the role of government, the men sound downright progressive. They are willing to work and pay taxes to fund a government that helps strangers meet the basic necessities of life—including, implicitly, strangers of different colors.

"I don't want anybody to starve in this country," says Matt, "like, ever."

"Yeah," Tom agrees.

"Everyone should eat," Matt continues. "And if part of my tax money goes to that, fine. Are there people who could have gotten jobs? Probably. But there are a lot of kids who need—"

"Education," Tom interjects.

"Education and food and shelter," Matt restarts. "And like if the government can provide that because no one else can, then it needs to be funded." That's the same Matt who had complained about welfare recipients on a binge in the grocery store.

Further into the conversation, interviewer Jonathan Voss asks Tom and Matt to make a list of words they associate with "racism," and then asks Tom what he included. "Trump," Tom says, because "he likes to shout racist stuff a lot." Matt lists "fear," "isolation," and "prejudice."

Strikingly, Matt has also written down "profit," "power," and "control." This was important, because we wanted to push the public to view manipulating racial resentment as a strategy. Overwhelmingly, the country thinks about racism in terms of individual malice, and also as whites versus nonwhites. The Right promotes this sort of thinking, telling whites they face mistreatment because the country is tilting toward people of color. The Left offers more nuanced definitions of the multiple forms taken by racism: interpersonal, unconscious, structural, cultural. But even so, all these different forms of racism are typically discussed in a white-over-nonwhite framework.

In the race-class narrative project, however, we suspected that defeating dog whistle politics required a new perspective on racism. The plan was to encourage people to see racism as a weapon of the rich—the sort of behavior undertaken in pursuit of profit, power, and control.

Because the truth is, racism's bottom line has always been more about money than hate.

"If you can convince the lowest white man he's better than the best colored man, he won't notice you're picking his pocket. Hell, give him somebody to look down on, and he'll empty his pockets for you." That's future president Lyndon Johnson in 1960, explaining to Bill Moyers, then his young assistant, the import of racial epithets they had seen scrawled on signs as they traveled by motorcade through Tennessee. Johnson understood the relationship between racism and rule by the rich: economic royalists exploit race to rile working people, while they rig the game for themselves. That's precisely the con that dog whistle politicians have been running for decades. It also fits Trump to a fake-gold T. His fiery attacks on people of color, lies about the dangers of unsecured borders, and budget-busting tax cuts for billionaires are not separate offenses but notes blown from the same whistle.

Could understanding the weapon provide the basis for fashioning a shield? Could it do even more than that, and actually provide a means to build political support for reclaiming government for working families? These questions impelled our focus groups and message testing. We wanted to know if we could shift the basic "us versus them" dynamic that is driving politics. Dog whistling pits whites against nonwhites. What if we could show voters that racism is *a class weapon*? Then the root conflict would become the rich versus the rest of us, white, Black, and brown, native and newcomer.

We were not looking to build a "class before race" frame—the sort of narrative that argues that class is more fundamental or universal than race and should replace race in political organizing. This framing too often presents those seeking racial justice as dividing the Left, rather than being a key and indispensable component of any progressive majority.

Nor did we seek to promote a "race and class" approach. In practice, many progressives argue for economic and racial justice while treating them as separate things that should both be addressed: *We need racial justice. We need economic justice. Let's do both.* This hasn't worked especially well. The do-both advice often leaves people unclear about how racial division connects to class war, and in turn uncertain why they should spend their limited energy on issues not primary to them.

Instead, we sought to develop a "race-class" strategy, race-hyphen-class. Race and class in the United States blend together like welded steel, fused by distant history as well as current politics. We believed the Left could prevail by turning this fusion to progressive advantage. Our theory was that the Left must simultaneously fight for racial justice and for economic fairness because they are inseparably connected.

The race-class narrative project talked to ordinary Americans, people of color as well as whites like Matt and Tom, to help us develop that merged approach. Throughout these conversations, we listened and learned, trying out and then honing initial formulations. Here's the message we asked Matt and Tom to react to. It's still an early effort to describe strategic racism in politics, but it hit important elements:

> Conservative politicians in this country go to great lengths to paint government services as handouts to Black and brown people. They have positioned government as a force that takes taxes from supposedly hardworking whites and gives them to supposedly lazy Black and brown people. This is how Republicans get whites of every income level to vote for them, even as their policies rig the economy for the very rich, hurting regular people regardless of their race or ethnicity.

I watch nervously as Voss asks the two men, "So, what do you think about this statement?"

"It's a great statement," Tom tells him. "My father-in-law, this is exactly . . . he spouts this stuff every day."

Matt quickly agrees. "You have a group of people who that's their card they want to play to remain in power. If they can create that sentiment, then they will get a group of people to follow them, no matter what craziness they end up doing," he says. "I can tell you that more white people receive government assistance than any other people group but they won't acknowledge that, I feel. As you said, they blame others."

To give Matt and Tom as much room as possible to disagree, Voss intentionally communicates skepticism. He's a partner in Celinda Lake's polling firm, and like Lake, keeps his pulse on views outside the Washington, DC, beltway by regularly conducting focus groups in person. Until this point, Voss has been a blank slate, but now he goes edgy to convey disbelief and draw the men out.

"Do you feel that the right wing actively works to demonize government doing this *intentionally?*" His voice rises on the last word to suggest hesitancy. As Matt starts to answer, Voss interrupts to push the issue:

"I mean does this seem like bullshit to you or does this seem like actual—"

Matt cuts him off, insisting, "That's what they do."

Were Matt and Tom exceptions in their receptivity to our race-class story? Not at all. Based partly on their reactions, we ultimately crafted nine slightly different takes of the race-class narrative. Some iterations stressed patriotism or unions or putting children first, but all told the basic race-class story offered to Matt and Tom, with one key addition. Matt and Tom heard an early version that focused on criticizing the Right for intentionally dividing us. We found the negativity of this message hampered its acceptance, and that it became far more energizing when we added a positive call for people to join together.

After shaping these messages, we poll-tested them. We ran a national poll with 2,000 respondents, and also did polling in four states and with union households. The poll asked respondents whether they found various messages convincing, using a scale of zero to one hundred. In addition to the race-class messages, we also offered a typical dog whistle narrative promoting racial fear. How did the race-class messages perform? They trounced the racial fear story. The Right's dog whistle narrative received an average convincing rating of 65. Every one of the nine race-class messages beat that, earning average convincing ratings ranging from a low of 68 to a high of 72.

We also tested a message designed to replicate the habitual Democratic response to dog whistle politics. Since the 1970s, the predominant response among liberals to dog whistling has been and remains to stay silent about it, out of concern that talking frankly about racism alienates white voters. Colorblind economics—ignoring race in favor of pocketbook issues—is standard liberal advice for how to beat the opposition. We tested a colorblind economic message, and it earned a mean convincing rating of 68. That meant that it tied the two worst-performing race-class messages, but was not as convincing as seven others. Our race-class messages largely outperformed the standard liberal message that superficially avoids race.

These results were especially encouraging given how new our messages were. Typically, people favor familiar arguments—stories that by their very repetition pervade their waking and sleeping minds. The dog whistle message very much has this characteristic. So too does today's colorblind economic populism. Republicans and Democrats bombard the public with these respective messages relentlessly.

Knowing the power of this "familiarity bias" from her communications experience, when Anat Shenker-Osorio and I first talked about testing race-class messages, she warned that the best we could hope for was that our innovative messages did not lose too badly. Their novelty, she cautioned, put them in a hole. But the very first time people heard the insurgent race-class messages, they found every version more convincing than the opposition's racial fear message and also found most more convincing than the colorblind economic populism approach. In the realm of message testing, this was a remarkably promising first showing.

What contributed to these messages coming across as convincing? After all, they were addressing topics typically considered taboo in American politics, including racism and class warfare.

Importantly, the race-class messages seemed to succeed not despite but because they broached these difficult conversations. From the very outset of the focus group conversations, it became immediately clear that most participants were keenly troubled by society's racial divisions and also by spreading economic hardship for most and vast wealth for a few. Participants *wanted* to talk about these things. But they felt betrayed in various ways by the existing approaches, and didn't know how to productively name what they deeply sensed. The race-class narratives seemed to provide the storyline they were already groping toward.

"Racism" in particular proved an emotionally volatile concept. Listen as Celinda Lake talks with a white woman probably in her late thirties, in a focus group the race-class project held in Denver. Lake asks, "How do you feel about racism?" There is a long pause as the woman, in jeans and Converse sneakers, thinks about the question. Then as she speaks, her comments stretch out with more pauses, as if she's carefully picking her way through thorns:

"I don't notice it like in my little world so much. . . . I don't . . . I don't get too involved in it because I don't want to . . . it freaks me out."

"So why does it freak you out," Lake gently inquires.

"It's overwhelming . . . It's a lot of energy . . . It's a lot of strong emotions. And it's a lot of heated stuff. And it just kind of overwhelms me." She stumbles phrase by phrase, pondering her explanations.

Then the dam seems to break and her words rush out as she describes how people "get worked up" and "in your face" when race is the subject. "It's like 'I can get bigger than you and I'm gonna get more intense and I'm gonna scare the crap out of you.' And nothing really beneficial happens."

This woman experienced conversations about racism as intense and scary, even physically threatening, and so she avoided them. Perhaps she recalled a particular and especially aggressive encounter. It's possible, though, that she was exhibiting what the sociologist and educator Robin DiAngelo terms "white fragility." Over her years as a racial justice trainer, DiAngelo has come to expect a range of strong defensive responses from whites when exposed to disorienting conversations about race. Among these reactions, whites frequently report feeling physically unsafe. "Whites often confuse comfort with safety and state that we don't feel safe when what we really mean is that we don't feel comfortable," DiAngelo observes.[1]

For some readers, that sort of discomfort may kick in with this book, or when contemplating whether to actively seek to build cross-racial solidarity. It might seem safer to stick with colorblindness—the norm of pretending, sometimes even to one-self, not to notice racial group membership or racial dynamics. But experience teaches that avoiding problems by sweeping them under the rug works poorly with issues any larger than grains of sand. It cannot possibly work with the boulders of racial division.

Still, to be fair, among many of those insisting that the Left must frontally address race and racism, there *is* a lot of anger. Re-call my students, steeped in the history of white supremacy and battling to make their justice claims heard. Their outrage is war-ranted. But it also makes conversations about racism more fraught. Those new to conversations about racism have to push through their discomfort. Those demanding attention to racism have to be thoughtful about when and how to call people in or out.

One potential trap involves the meanings of the words "rac-ism" and "racist." These terms carry tremendous social and politi-cal power because they communicate moral condemnation. But precisely because "racism" and "racist" carry so much power, they have been dumbed down to refer to only the narrowest range of conduct. The Right has especially promoted an impoverished conception of racism that is now accepted by broad swaths of the country. The result is that for many people, including many on the Left, "racism" does not extend past treating another person badly for reasons connected to their skin color, while "racist" exclusively identifies a bigoted culprit.

Like Tom, huge numbers of Americans already think that

"racist" describes Donald Trump. When polled the week before the 2016 election, 52 percent of registered voters agreed that word applied to him.[2] That was before Trump pursued his Muslim ban and before his "shithole countries" comment, his stripping of children from their parents at the border, and his description of immigrants as "animals" who "infest" our country.

But what does "racist" mean to most of those who apply it to Trump? If "racist" is limited to meaning only personal antipathy, many in the middle and on the Left may be mistaking as personal bigotry what at root is political strategy. Perversely, this may *help* Trump and politicians like him. In ways that will be explained, Trump has perfected the art of provoking liberal accusations of bigotry that offend and in turn build support from his base.

As far as messaging is concerned, because "racism" is explosive and subject to multiple meanings, depending on the audience, it may be good advice to drop the word. The term itself is not necessary. The race-class project found it more effective to focus instead on the actual form and function of the racial dynamics being challenged—for example, by pointing not at "racist" politicians, but at politicians who "deliberately distract us with fear mongering, especially along racial, ethnic, and religious lines."

As discussed in this book, "racism" takes many shapes. Of particular importance, racism often operates unconsciously as a set of attitudes and beliefs absorbed by osmosis, even by people firmly opposed to racism. Also, racism can be strategic: a calculated effort to exploit racial divisions for one's own ends. Both of these very different sorts of racism fuel the success of dog whistle politics.

Racism also easily works alongside other social dynamics, such as patriarchy, fear of crime, or job insecurity. To identify a likely racial component in political speech, voting decisions, or public policies is not to claim that race explains everything, only that it may contribute an important element.

How about "class"? In the race-class narrative project, we tested terms like "the wealthy few" and "powerful elites." They did not resonate as well as "wealthy special interests who rig the rules" and "the greedy few." What's the difference?

Terms like the wealthy few or powerful elites describe a class of people, a whole group. Many felt it was unfair to single out groups of people for blame. This felt a lot like simply a reverse of what the Right does. The pushback from many often took this form: *They say blame people of color, you say blame the rich. A pox on both of you and your blame games.* Beyond this, it's likely people especially resisted blaming the rich because being wealthy is a widely shared aspiration. When it comes to class consciousness, it seems many Americans believe they belong to the not-yet-rich class. Simply invoking the upper class as a threat proved unhelpful.

In contrast, respondents were far more comfortable faulting people for ill motives. To describe a villain required identifying threatening actors *plus* explaining why they acted as they did. "Wealthy special interests who rig the rules" implies a profit motive; the "greedy few" identifies actors by their selfish intentions. The fact that the merchants of division gain by dividing Americans resonates forcefully because it connects division to a common and easily understood human drive.

On a different level than messaging, in thinking about what's happening in society, motives both matter and don't matter. "There's class warfare, all right," said Warren Buffett, the billionaire investor and one of America's leading philanthropists. "But it's my class, the rich class, that's making war, and we're winning."[3] When Buffett said this in 2006, he could only anticipate what the investigative journalist Jane Mayer would uncover in *Dark Money: The Hidden History of the Billionaires Behind the Rise of the Radical Right.*

In the preface to the 2017 paperback edition, Mayer updated her reporting on the political ambitions of the billionaire brothers Charles and David Koch, who control a huge petro-chemical and industrial conglomerate. Their goal is to limit the potential tax burden on the very wealthy by opposing government efforts to help working people, and also to rewrite market and environmental regulations so that their industries can rake in barrels of money. Despite Trump's posturing as a populist, he appointed numerous political officers with deep ties to the Koch machine, not least his vice president, Mike Pence. "Amazingly, in 2016 the Kochs' private network of political groups had a bigger payroll than the Republican National Committee," Mayer wrote. "The tentacles of the 'Kochtopus,' as their sprawling political machine was known, were already encircling the Trump administration before it had even officially taken power." The Kochtopus, Mayer pointed out, is "sponsored by just four hundred or so of the richest people in the country."[4]

But the threat of great wealth to society goes beyond the selfish motives of identifiable culprits. Greed is not the central problem, nor, likewise, will the main solution come from the good intentions of progressive philanthropists. As the country's founders long ago recognized, democracy exists in tension with great riches. Democracy sets the conditions for competitive markets and entrepreneurial freedom, but is threatened by concentrated wealth and its tendency to capture government for its own benefit. Justice Louis Brandeis, one of the great jurists of the New Deal era, warned, "We may have democracy, or we may have wealth concentrated in the hands of a few, but we can't have both."

Or so those on the Left tend to think, while those on the Right typically disagree. I use the terms "Left" and "Right" to talk about competing constellations of ideas around race, class, and government. By their very nature, political labels can refer to many different ideas. The race-class narrative project especially focused on race, class, and government because those are the core elements of the Right's story, and in turn the Left must reweave these elements into a progressive counterstory. I also use "progressive" and "reactionary" as loose synonyms for Left and Right.

In contrast, I avoid the term "conservative." Today's Right has largely abandoned conservatism, understood as a commitment to protecting important social institutions, to a stable economy that works for the vast majority of the polity, and to a respect for tradition that nevertheless accepts that progress in human societies depends on evolutions in cultural and political norms. Promoting the interest of a new economic oligarchy in the face of enormous inequality is not conservatism. Neither is nostalgia for an imagined past of culturally sanctified hierarchy. Both of these can quickly lead to violence and the destruction of stabilizing social norms and institutions—the sorts of dynamics typically condemned by conservatism. Like the conservative commentator David Frum, I too would welcome "a conservatism that is culturally modern, economically inclusive, and environmentally responsible." Though they often seek to wrap themselves in the "conservative" mantle, this is not today's Right.[5]

Obviously, "Left" and "Right" can be too sweeping. Within the Right and, even more, the Left, are huge ranges of policy ideas, divergent priorities, and competing strategies. Right and Left do not exist as monoliths; they are not celluloid giants, Godzilla versus King Kong, battling each other while unified in their own thinking and completely coordinated in their actions. Left versus Right is more akin to clashing weather fronts that pack tremendous power yet are composed of millions of air particles and rain drops swirling in cross-cutting currents.

Equally important, many Americans are neither Left nor Right. Americans as a whole are only loosely committed to these contending belief systems about race, class, and government. About one out of five voters embrace Left views, and they are opposed by a similar number subscribing to the Right's story.

That leaves Matt and Tom in the majority, among the three in five people in the large convergence zone between weather systems. These are the people who must be brought along in big numbers to shift the country's direction. As individuals, Matt and Tom are unlikely heroes. But as stand-ins for the vast middle, they reflect the way many voters toggle quickly between contradictory notions, sometimes drawing on one way of seeing the world and then bouncing to conflicting ideas about society.

Encompassing so many Americans, this persuadable group roughly tracks the demographics of the country as a whole. It's especially critical to recognize that the persuadable middle is not simply code for "white voters." The dominant Democratic mindset immediately after the 2016 election was to win back "the working class," which implicitly coded as white. But most people of color fall into the variable middle, and altogether minorities account for one-third of this pivotal majority.

In discussing the race-class research, "people of color" serves as shorthand for the two largest nonwhite groups in the United States, African Americans and Latinxs.* Though there are attitudinal differences between the two groups, there's still a fair amount of overlap in their views. Beyond these two groups, a separate race-class narrative project survey in September 2018 found that there was also enough commonality to justify including Asian Americans, Pacific Islanders, and Native Hawaiians under the "people of color" umbrella.[6]

This book routinely refers to racial groups as if they're real—because they are. They're real not as biological entities, of course. There's no fixed sameness among "whites" or any other group, nor any characteristics found on only one side of some natural color line. But as large social groups, there are important differences associated with race, variations that connect to life experiences, opportunities, attitudes, and worldviews. Because the Right has

---

* Many young people, especially activists and those in higher education, prefer "Latinx" to synonyms like "Latino" or "Hispanic." The "x" signals that no gender is indicated by the term, in contrast to "Latino," which is gendered male. In addition, the "x" carries a nonwhite racial resonance, in contrast to "Hispanic," which is often used by persons who see themselves as white. "X" also echoes the prevalence of that letter in the Nahuatl language of the Aztecs, giving "Latinx" a pre-contact flavor. The "x" also gestures toward the name of the Black radical Malcolm X, a reminder that many in the Latinx community are Black. The poet and journalist Ed Morales offers a full discussion in his 2018 book, *Latinx*.

exploited racial division as its principal political weapon for five decades and counting, any practical conversation about American politics must name and discuss racial groups.

The crux for progress on both racial and economic justice is countering the Right's racial messages. The dark magic of dog whistling lies in convincing people that, to keep their family safe, they must elect politicians who will ban Muslims, build a wall against Mexicans, and double down on imprisoning African Americans—when in reality they are electing politicians indebted to, and often members of, a new oligarchy.

This is when most on the Left despair. They recognize that those in the broad middle accept reactionary views that dispose them to racial fears and resentments. How, then, to convince this large group that those beliefs are racist and wrong? The task seems akin to tearing down a mountain of racism with the small wooden spoons of public service announcements or anti-racist presentations.

But the challenge is not insurmountable. It's true that those in the middle—most whites and most people of color, too—filter the world through stereotypes and racist ideas. It's also true, though, that they simultaneously hold progressive racial ideals. The job ahead is not to start from scratch in educating the broad middle about racism, but to speak to the anti-racist convictions they *already* embrace. The dots are there. The task is to connect them. This is no walk in the park, but neither is it taking a spoon to Everest. Our research suggests that the Left can build a cross-racial movement for racial and economic justice by convincing the broad middle that voting their racial ideals rather than their racist phobias will help them take care of their families.

1

Yes, It's Still Dog Whistling. That's a Good Thing Because the Alternative is Far Worse

By 2018, liberals were routinely denouncing Donald Trump for racism. Paul Krugman in the *New York Times* condemned Trump for having "replaced racial dog-whistles with raw, upfront racism."[1] In the *Washington Post*, Greg Sargent said Trump had gone "full white nationalist, not with a dog whistle but with a clanging, blaring sound truck."[2] Nancy Pelosi, the Democratic House leader, criticized "the Trump Administration's unmistakable campaign to make America white again."[3]

To be sure, like a performer thickly applying stage makeup, Trump made racially charged themes central to his political persona. But was this really upfront and raw racism, a blaring sound truck of white nationalism, an unmistakable appeal to make the country white? Here's why this matters so much: If Trump and politicians like him really exchanged the dog whistle of coded racism for the bullhorn of white supremacy, it implies that the majority of whites must be rallying to a racist call to arms. A majority of whites, 54 percent, voted for Trump in 2016.[4] Three years later, 90 percent of Republicans still supported him.[5] Did these people hear a blatant endorsement of white supremacy and thrill to it, norms of equality be damned?

If dog whistling is yesterday's strategy and now the Right has shifted to upfront and plainly heard racism, we stand on the cusp of spreading bloodshed. If Trump is openly calling for white nationalism, then the millions who support him must themselves consciously recognize and embrace this racist creed. We've seen what this means in the lynchings and white race riots of America's bloody past. We see what this means today, when people espousing white supremacy massacre African Americans, Jews, and Muslims in Western democracies around the world, including here at home. Is this where we are? Do most whites consciously endorse notions of their racial supremacy even if not (yet) its violent methods?

No, this is not America today. It's true that the Right exploits racist appeals. But in the main it does not do so using raw and upfront racism. Rather, it's still dog whistling—the communication of racist stereotypes in a coded form that, crucially, allows the Right's base to reassure themselves that they are *not* racists.

Most Americans—including many who do not consistently vote Republican—are susceptible to coded messages about threatening or undeserving people of color but are not consciously committed to defending white dominance. Compared to the alternative that people are voting for white nationalism, this is good news. Because many voters are responding to dog whistling, then, though they may vote their racial fears, the vast majority still adhere to norms of human equality. This means there remains a reasonable chance to convince voters that the actual threats to their well-being come from somewhere other than nonwhites and that upholding their values and forging cross-racial alliances is the best way to achieve security.

Dog whistling has become uglier and also more central to the Right's political strategy over the last decade, primarily in response to the election of Barack Obama and the country's changing demographics. Indeed, part of dog whistling today involves a purposeful effort to outrage engaged critics in order to stimulate charges of bigotry that the Right can then harness to present itself as a victim of liberal snobbery and condescension. Trump in particular has honed the technique of eliciting accusations of racism that he then uses to rally his base. But the core of the Right's political strategy remains dog whistling. That means the Left cannot respond effectively until it understands how dog whistling has evolved, the techniques it uses to build support, and its strategies to defend itself.

Dog Whistling Gets Louder

"A young woman, gunned down by an illegal immigrant who should have been deported but was protected by a sanctuary city."[6] The voice in the ad is male, the tone authoritative and newscaster-objective but tinged with outrage. The scene shows a young white woman walking down a sidewalk through a suburban Florida neighborhood of clipped lawns and palm trees. She's checking her phone, smiling slightly, lost in her own world, oblivious as a brown-skinned man brushes past her going the other way. He turns as he passes, a thin-lipped scowl emerging between thick dark mustache and beard, his hawklike face shadowed by a gray sweatshirt hood. He pulls a gun. She turns, helpless fear flashing across her face. The voice-over stops, the scene jumps, the background music accelerates into staccato drumbeats. There's a gun directly in your face. It fills the screen. Then the camera pans back to the young woman, a gunshot explodes over the soundtrack, and she falls backward as the scene fades.

The next image we see is of the white politician promoted by the ad. He's facing the camera from a similar suburban sidewalk, dressed in a blue jacket, red tie against white shirt, his name and position as the speaker of the Florida House of Representatives in text across the screen. "I'm Richard Corcoran," he says. "When I heard Kate Steinle's story, I thought about my own daughter Katie and how this could have happened to any family anywhere." The scene shifts to show him dressed casually, walking with his arm paternally draped over the shoulder of a young brunette still in braces.

"Kate Steinle's story." Donald Trump told it repeatedly during his presidential campaign, some facts cast in klieg lights, others shrouded. Two weeks after Trump announced his candidacy in June 2015, Steinle, thirty-two, was walking with her father in San Francisco when she was struck by a bullet that ricocheted off the ground. Two hours later in the hospital, she died in her father's arms, her last words "Help me, Dad."

It was a dreadful tragedy. But a jury concluded it was also an accident, not murder or manslaughter. They accepted the defendant's argument that the famously hair-triggered .40-caliber SIG Sauer semiautomatic pistol he'd found wrapped in a T-shirt under a public bench had accidentally discharged when he picked it up. The gun had been stolen by persons unknown four days earlier from a federal officer's car, where it had been kept loaded in a backpack.

Trump might not have remarked on the case, but for this: Steinle was an attractive young white woman with a charming smile, while the defendant, José Ines García Zarate, had a face deeply lined by years of living on the streets and was an undocumented immigrant from Mexico with a rap sheet that included several deportations and three low-level drug possession felonies. San Francisco had recently released him from custody instead of handing him to federal immigration officials. Framed side by side, the stories and faces of Steinle and García Zarate suggested pale innocence versus a drug-wasted deep brown. "This man, or this animal, that shot that wonderful, that beautiful woman in San Francisco, this guy was pushed back by Mexico," Trump told CNN a week after her death. "Mexico pushes back people across the border that are criminals, that are drug dealers." The assertion that "this guy was pushed back by Mexico" was a lie, as was Trump's subsequent claim that García Zarate shot Steinle five times, as was the way Trump spun the entire sorry episode.

Trump kept talking about "beautiful Kate," and Fox News joined the chorus with Bill O'Reilly in the lead, linking her death to San Francisco's position as a sanctuary city—a jurisdiction that limits local cooperation with federal efforts to deport immigrants—and also to the Obama administration's supposed laxity in border enforcement. "The mayor and city supervisors of San Francisco are directly responsible for the murder of Kate Steinle and the Obama administration is complicit," O'Reilly declared. The city officials should be arrested, he told his audience. Then O'Reilly urged that a new law be written and enacted, a so-called Kate's Law, that would impose harsh and mandatory prison time for anyone who reentered the United States after having been deported.

Within three days, Republican representative Matt Salmon of Arizona introduced such legislation, and less than two weeks later, Trump's campaign rival, Senator Ted Cruz, sought to capitalize on the case, too, sponsoring a parallel bill in the Senate.[7] From personal tragedy to campaign talking point to national media story to potential legislation, Steinle's death exploded on the Right in July 2015. Over the course of that month, Trump went from seventh in the GOP presidential primary contest to first.

That Trump would capitalize on racial rage to propel himself to the top of the field was entirely predictable. After all, Trump briefly entered the 2012 GOP presidential primaries and managed to climb to a tie for first place using lies and innuendo about Obama's supposedly foreign birth.[8] If his racially fueled ascent was likely inevitable, though, the narrative he engineered about "beautiful Kate" killed by an "animal" provided the hot-burning accelerant he needed. "Something happened in July to send Trump's numbers soaring," wrote David Frum in *The Atlantic* at the end of the month. "That something may have been the murder of Kathryn Steinle."[9]

Richard Corcoran's ad came out almost three years later, in early 2018. "On my watch, Florida will *never* be a sanctuary state," Corcoran intoned at the ad's end. The last frame featured Corcoran and his five children and wife in a group hug, blondes and brunettes and bright smiles, a middle-class white family backlit by Florida sunshine.

The tactic was hardly new. "The exploitation of Ms. Steinle's death by Fox News and Donald Trump brings back memories of the exploitation of the story of Willie Horton by the George H. W. Bush campaign in 1988," observed law professor Christopher N. Lasch.[10] He offered an apt comparison. Bush ran a campaign ad tying his Democratic opponent to Horton, a convicted murderer released from prison on a weekend furlough, who then kidnapped a young couple, stabbed the man, and raped the woman. The grainy mug shot and arrest photos used in the campaign ad made clear that Horton was Black. The young white couple did not appear, their race left to the viewer's imagination. As it would in Corcoran's ad thirty years later, the appeal rang clear: vote for the candidate who protects innocent whites, not for the politician who coddles criminal people of color.

But the comparison also highlights how powerfully dog whistling has mutated. However outrageous, the Horton ad hewed to actual facts in the case and used real photos, while staying away from depicting the victims at all. In contrast, Corcoran's ad fabricated a racist nightmare in Technicolor, visually depicting a hooded brown man deliberately murdering a young white maiden in a suburban setting. Moreover, the ad transferred the supposed threat directly to the viewer. Watching the ad landed you in the victim's place, staring into the gaping black barrel of a gun wielded by a malevolent racial specter.

Corcoran spent nearly one hundred thousand dollars pushing out his ad, hoping to become Florida's governor. Yet he was insufficiently reactionary. Trump endorsed someone to Corcoran's racial right, House Republican Ron DeSantis, and Corcoran pulled out of the race by May 2018.[11] In August, DeSantis won the Republican primary, on the same evening that Democrats rallied behind an African American candidate for governor, Tallahassee mayor Andrew Gillum. The very next morning, DeSantis kicked off his general election campaign by going on Fox News to urge Florida voters not to "monkey this up" by voting for his Black opponent.[12] DeSantis won the election.

In the age of Trump, things are metastasizing into monstrous versions of what they used to look like. We can see the resemblance to past dog whistling, but we've also never seen anything this vitriolic before. In the run-up to the 2018 midterm elections, *USA Today* reported that Republican candidates for Congress were blanketing the airwaves with ads touting their toughness on immigration. "The GOP focus on immigration is particularly striking, given that it was not among the top 10 issues Republicans spent their ad dollars on at this point in the 2014 midterms," the paper said, adding, "now, immigration ranks second only to pro-Trump spots in GOP campaigns across the country—and just by a smidgen." [13] Many of these ads were egregious. The GOP candidate for governor in Georgia and eventual winner, Brian Kemp, described himself as a "politically incorrect conservative" and boasted in a campaign video, "I got a big truck, just in case I need to round up criminal illegals and take them home myself." [14]

But for however over-the-top they were, were these ads broadcasting open racism?

We can look to a candidate in Tennessee to help answer this question. Running for Congress as an independent in 2016, Rick Tyler rented a billboard and plastered it with block letters proclaiming MAKE AMERICA WHITE AGAIN. Around the slogan, he pinned images in each corner. Three were paintings: one depicting the arrival of the pilgrims on the eastern seaboard, another of George Washington, and the third of a little white girl kneeling in prayer next to a covered wagon. Rounding out this iconography of white-American destiny, valor, and piety, the fourth corner featured a photo of a beaming heteronormative family of five, sitting together in a grassy field, all pink cheeks and blond hair.

As if he needed to clarify, Tyler explained in a lengthy statement that "the 'Make America White Again' billboard is a takeoff on Donald Trump's slogan of 'Make America Great Again.' . . . In a nutshell, it is stating that the 'Leave It to Beaver, Ozzie and Harriet, Mayberry' America of old was vastly superior to what we are experiencing today. It was an America where doors were left unlocked, violent crime was a mere fraction of today's rate of occurrence, there were no carjackings, home invasions, Islamic

Mosques or radical Jihadist sleeper cells." Lest anyone miss the racial subtext, Tyler added: "The racial component of this phenomenon is all-important." He closed by advocating "a moratorium on nonwhite immigration and the abolition of policies that subsidize nonwhite birth rates." [15]

Did Tyler sum up Trump's campaign? On Twitter one critic posted: "make no mistake that the Make America White Again sign in TN is representative of the republican party this election." [16] But if so, the Republican response was curious. The GOP repudiated Tyler's outright racism. "There's no room for this type of hateful display in our political discourse," said Ryan Haynes, the Tennessee Republican Party chairman, adding, "racism should be rejected in all its heinous forms in the Third Congressional District and around the country." Tyler's Republican opponent, Representative Charles "Chuck" Fleischmann, echoed that sentiment: "I totally and unequivocally condemn the billboard and Mr. Tyler's message and will vigorously fight any form of racism in the 3rd district of Tennessee or anywhere else in the nation." Over Tyler's objection, the billboard company removed his ad in response to protests. [17] In the November 2016 election, voters in the district, which is more than 85 percent white, opined through their ballots. Tyler received less than 2 percent of the vote. Instead, two-thirds of the district supported Fleischmann, who would vote with Trump 98 percent of the time. [18]

Tyler's experience was shared by former Ku Klux Klan leader David Duke, who in 2016 ran for the Senate from Louisiana saying, "I'd be the only person in Congress openly defending the rights and the heritage of European Americans." [19] The Republican National Committee chair turned to Twitter to respond, proclaiming that Duke's "hateful bigotry [has] no place in the Republican Party & the RNC will never support his candidacy under any circumstance." [20] Duke went down to spectacular defeat with just over 3 percent of the vote—even as Trump swept his state in a landslide with support from 6 out of 10 voters. "Make America *Great* Again" is a winning message among a majority of white voters and some voters of color as well; "Make America *White* Again" is a loser's lament.

Part of dog whistling involves publicly posturing against racism. Sometimes, as in the GOP's response to Tyler and Duke, the Right obfuscates its basic racial strategy by issuing impassioned denunciations of blatant racism. It does so against right-wing extremists as well as the occasional Republican who strays too far into audible range, as when the House GOP leaders stripped Iowa representative Steven King of committee seats after he defended the terms "white supremacist" and "white nationalist."[21] Party officials often also condemn "racism" from Democrats, thereby polishing their credentials as anti-racists while also fostering the both-sides sense that the two parties are equally susceptible to occasional eruptions of racism. The Republican-led Senate effort to rebuke Representative Ilhan Omar, Democrat of Minnesota, for supposed anti-Semitism fits this mold.[22]

Other times, dog whistle politics defends itself by denying that its coded assaults refer to race at all.

"This has nothing to do with race. I've never said anything about race. This has nothing to do with race or anything else. This has to do with respect for our country, and respect for our flag."[23] That's how Trump explained his attacks on the Black football players who protested police violence by taking a knee during pregame recitals of the national anthem. Trump has also at various times declared "I'm the least racist person." His base chooses to believe him. In the week before the 2016 election, a poll asked voters, "Would you use the word 'racist' to describe Donald Trump?" Almost nine in ten Trump voters, 87 percent, said no. Only 5 percent said yes.[24]

Trump was not merely defending himself. He was also reassuring his base. On issue after dog whistle issue, he told them they were not racists, just good patriotic folks.

On Mexican immigrants: "If you want to have strong borders so that people come into our country, but they come in legally through a legal process, that doesn't make you a racist. It makes you smart. It makes you an American."

On the supposed Muslim Arab threat: "People who speak out against radical Islam and who warn about refugees are not Islamophobes. They're not. They are decent American citizens who want to uphold our value as a tolerant society and who want to keep the terrorists the hell out of our country."

On crime: "People who support the police and who want crime reduced and stopped are not prejudiced. They're concerned and loving citizens and parents whose heart breaks every time an innocent child is lost to totally preventable violence. There is no compassion in tolerating crime, and poisonous drug dealing, and the killings all over our streets in so many different cities."[25]

As in these quotes, Trump often recast racial fear as instead something noble and principled, not prejudice but patriotism and even tolerance and compassion. He also frequently presented expressions of racial resentment as a matter of free speech, a campaign against the political correctness preventing the country from speaking hard truths.[26] Either way, Trump avoided telling his base in plain, unmistakable language that they should rally to him to defend the white race. This has been the heart of Trump's dog whistle to his base: Be afraid—but also, be assured that your fear is common sense, not racial prejudice. Dog Whistle Politics 101.

Intentionally Provoking Charges of Racism

If Trump was still dog whistling, why did so many on the Left believe he was shouting through a racist bullhorn? Because, it turns out, this is what Trump wanted. Trump inherited a fifty-year tradition of dog whistling, but also remade it to suit himself and modern times.

"These Republicans want to unmistakably establish the party of Lincoln as the white man's party." That might sound like a critique of Trump's GOP. In fact, it's a quote that bubbles up from the depths of the civil rights movement, an observation from the late conservative journalist Robert Novak. When Novak attended the 1963 Republican National Committee meeting in Denver, he described it in a newspaper piece titled "Future 'White Man's' Party." He characterized the GOP this way: "Far from desiring to out-do Democrats as crusaders for racial equality, substantial numbers of party leaders from both North and South see rich political dividends flowing from the negrophobia of many white Americans." [27]

Novak stood witness to the birth of a new Republican strategy: the party would abandon its historic support for civil rights, and instead attempt to exploit white rancor over civil rights. It worked shockingly well. No Democratic candidate for president has won a majority of the white vote since 1964—not once, in the more than half a century that has elapsed since Republican dog whistling began in earnest. Trump did not assemble a new racial base. He drew roughly the same support from white voters as his 2012 predecessor. Even before Trump, the Republicans had built their white man's party.

But this does not mean dog whistling always sounds the same. It evolves. Princeton politics professor Tali Mendelberg studied the use of coded racism in politics, discussing at length the Willie Horton ad in her 2001 book, *The Race Card*. She found evidence, both from that ad campaign and from tests she devised, that coded racism in politics worked only so long as people did not recognize that the underlying conversation was about race. From this, she concluded that surfacing the racial subtext effectively neutralized its appeal. Dog whistling, it seemed, worked only so long as the racial aspect of the campaign—not just the racism, but the topic of race—was hidden from voters. [28]

A decade later, this was no longer true. The constant racial innuendo against Barack Obama, from politicians as well as right-wing media outlets, made race an obvious and pervasive part of political conversations. Confirming this shift, in the midst of Obama's first term, a team of political scientists tested whether it mattered to respondents if a politician's racial message was implicit or instead overt.[29] Polling thousands of whites, they solicited responses to "news stories" they wrote themselves. The stories involved a fictional political candidate's opposition to the Affordable Care Act. One version talked about race in coded terms, featuring, among other things, a quote from the hypothetical politician asking, "Why is it that we suburbanites play by the rules, go to work, and have insurance, and then the city people want the rest of us to foot the bill for their health care?" An explicit version, in contrast, had the politician asking, "Why is it that the white Hartforders seem to play by the rules, go to work, and have insurance, but Black people want the rest of us to foot the bill for their health care?"

According to conventional thinking about the role of race in messaging, the racially explicit version should have performed far worse. But it did not. Test subjects recognized that the explicit version was more "racially insensitive," but this made no independent difference in their attitudes. What mattered more was their level of racial resentment. Persons who tested high in racial resentment on a standard psychological yardstick expressed the same favorable attitude toward the politician whether he talked about "city people" or "Black people."

In effect, the researchers found that during the Obama years, voters tolerated far more explicit racial rhetoric than in the past— and that many voters had few qualms about political messages that offended others. They didn't mind if other people found a politician's words "racially insensitive." This corresponded to another finding by these same researchers: in their survey of more than 3,000 whites, roughly five times as many thought "most people" were "too sensitive" in public conversations about racial issues, compared to those who said "not sensitive enough."[30]

When candidate Trump descended the gold-mirrored escalator into the marble lobby of Trump Tower to launch his campaign with a tirade against Mexican rapists and drug dealers, those mechanical stairs carried him downward through a fifty-year history of dog whistling to an audience primed for provocative messages that gave racial offense. In this political world where dog whistling was king, Trump had already donned the crown. He had substantial practice using racial innuendo to stir the GOP base, having built his political profile by floating lies about Obama's foreign birth and Muslim religion. He also lived in the same Fox News bubble that is home to most reactionary voters.

But in addition, Trump held another ace card over the career politicians he faced in the Republican primaries, one that would make it easier for him to beat them at the GOP's dog whistle game: Trump cared little about anything beyond himself.

The GOP has long understood that racial demagoguery is volatile. Its explosive force can propel a candidate forward, but the slightest miscalculation can spark fiery disaster. When Mitt Romney lost in 2012, the GOP produced an autopsy that blamed, among other factors, a lack of enthusiasm among African Americans as well as Latinxs offended by Romney's call for immigrants to "self-deport." The solution, the postmortem argued, was for the next candidate to tamp down on dog whistling and reach out to nonwhites, especially to Hispanics. Over the course of fifty years, the GOP has encouraged its base to respond to racial prods. But it has also urged some nominal limits on its candidates: don't trash the party's reputation; don't go so far as to make success in the general election impossible. The 2012 autopsy repeated this advice.

Trump felt no need to respect those constraints. Trump didn't care about damage to the Republican brand. He also didn't enter the race to win the general election, and perhaps never believed he could until he did. He entered the primaries to boost his name recognition and to force Washington insiders to take him more seriously.[31] The only constraint on his dog whistling was his own reputation, which he saw as burnished by attention and controversy. Trump understood dog whistling, and understood as well that the GOP's limits did not apply to him. Thus freed, he could and did take dog whistling to a whole new level.

Trump especially innovated by shifting racial appeals decisively into the audible range—but for his critics, not for his base.

Indeed, in one instance the Trump campaign bragged to its critics about race-baiting. The Republican National Committee ran an ad that went after the Democratic Party's vice-presidential candidate, Tim Kaine, saying that as a lawyer "he consistently protected the worst kinds of people." The video flashed mug shots of convicted felons while a voice-over described their crimes in lurid terms—"raped, sodomized, and murdered"; "sexually assaulted and murdered his elderly neighbor"; "brutally murdered three people."[32] The inside-the-beltway journal *Roll Call* immediately decried the ad as a "Willie Horton–style attack," likely intending a rebuke.[33] But Sean Spicer, then the RNC spokesperson and later Trump's press secretary, saw instead something to boast about. He promoted the story, tweeting out the headline, "Exclusive: Republicans Launch Willie Horton–Style Attack." The RNC's official Twitter account, @GOP, quickly did the same.[34] The Trump camp was not hiding their racial pandering, they were flaunting it—at least in terms that political insiders would recognize and react to.

Herein lies the most consequential way Trump changed dog whistle rhetoric. Trump made his racist narratives obvious to his critics and a constant focus of media storms. Rather than seeking to use dog whistles to keep race below the surface, Trump repeatedly stoked heated debates about his racial demagoguery. Trump was still dog whistling, using coded phrases that triggered racial stereotypes without directly communicating a message of raw racism *to his base*. But he no longer obscured his racial appeals from the engaged political center. Instead, Trump intentionally instigated accusations of racism, believing that such accusations helped him dominate the public's distracted attention.

How could Trump get away with courting repeated charges of racism without coming across to his base as a racist? Sure, he generated media storms, but those tempests frequently lashed him with lightning-bolt indictments of racist fearmongering. So how did he avoid being struck down, or at least badly singed?

Watch what happened when his Democratic presidential

opponent, Hillary Clinton, finally challenged the racial messages at the heart of Trump's campaign.

In late August 2016, just a few months before the election, Clinton criticized Trump's racial pandering. She released a commercial featuring Klan members speaking glowingly of Trump and also highlighting the close connections between Trump's campaign director, Steve Bannon, and white supremacists.[35] Coordinated with this, Clinton delivered a major address methodically presenting the lowlights of Trump's past, from his involvement in housing discrimination in the 1970s to his birther claims against Obama, before cataloging some of his most outrageous racial statements on the campaign trail. "This is not Republicanism as we have known it," Clinton warned. "These are race-baiting ideas, anti-Muslim and anti-immigrant ideas, anti-woman—all key tenets making up an emerging racist ideology known as the 'Alt-Right.'"[36]

"It's the oldest play in the Democratic playbook," Trump immediately fired back. "When Democratic policies fail, they are left with only this one tired argument: You're racist, you're racist, you're racist. They keep saying it. You're racist. It's a tired, disgusting argument. And it's so totally predictable. They're failing so badly."[37] Then Trump shifted Clinton's attack from himself to his followers. "She lies and she smears and she paints decent Americans—you—as racists," he said.

This claim that those who call out dog whistling are themselves the real bigots has a long dog whistle pedigree. When George Wallace took office as governor of Alabama in 1963, he infamously promised to protect "segregation now, segregation tomorrow, segregation forever!" But as the tides shifted against full-throated endorsements of white supremacy, he evolved too, moving toward dog whistles about "law and order" and "states' rights." Many accused him of coded racism. In turn, Wallace developed an effective rejoinder. By 1968, Wallace was saying to his crowds, "You know who the biggest bigots in the world are? They're the ones who call others bigots." He complained, "It's a sad day in the country when you can't talk about law and order unless they want to call you a racist."[38] The real racists, Wallace said, were the ones who thought conservative voters were racists, thus confirming the sense among many of his supporters that they, and not minorities, were the actual victims of racial discrimination.

Trump did something similar. He encouraged his supporters to see themselves as victims of reverse racism—the sort of bigotry that supposedly wrongly imputed bigotry to them. In September 2016, news broke that Clinton had said half of Trump's supporters belonged in "a basket of deplorables," people who were "racist, sexist, homophobic, xenophobic, Islamophobic—you name it." Trump released a statement saying Clinton's "true feelings came out, showing bigotry and hatred for millions of Americans."[39]

From its inception, dog whistling has always combined three moves. First, punch race into the conversation using coded language to stir voters' racial anxieties. Say things like "law and order" or "welfare queen," terms that trigger racial resentment but do not directly mention race.

Second, when accused of provoking racial resentment, issue an outraged denial, parrying the charges by pointing out that nothing you said directly references race. When DeSantis told voters in Florida not to "monkey up" the election and critics charged him with dog whistling, his spokesperson retorted that DeSantis was obviously talking about his opponent's "policies" and "to characterize it as anything else is absurd."[40]

Third, kick back, counterattacking by accusing your critics of being the real bigots. The day after the 2018 midterms, *PBS NewsHour* White House correspondent Yamiche Alcindor engaged in a back-and-forth with Trump about statements he'd made calling himself a proud nationalist.

"On the campaign trail you called yourself a nationalist," she said. "Some people saw that as emboldening white nationalists. Now people are also saying—"

Trump didn't even let her finish the sentence. "I don't know why you'd say that," he interrupted. "That's such a racist question."

The reporter persisted: "There are some people that say that now the Republican Party is seen as supporting white nationalism because of your rhetoric."

"Oh, I don't believe it. I don't believe it," Trump retorted. "I mean, why do I have my highest poll numbers—that's such a racist question. Honestly, I mean, I know you have it written down and you're going to tell me—let me tell you. It's a racist question."[41]

Until Trump, the second and third dog whistle moves—the claims of innocence and the counterattack—were last-ditch defenses, to be deployed if one strayed too close to audible racial instigations. Trump, in contrast, saw widespread criticism of his racial pandering as a gift of free media time and, even more importantly, as a basis for building a sense of shared victimization with this base.

The high decibels of Trump's scapegoating—audible by design to those in the political know but not to his supporters—helped convince mainstream critics that Trump had abandoned a dog whistle for a "clanging, blaring sound truck" of white nationalism. Trump seemed to count on this, calculating that he could parlay charges of racism against him into aggrieved outrage among his supporters. They're the real victims, falsely smeared by unfair charges of bigotry, he said. It was a nasty trap for the Left: Name Trump's racism and help him build support with his base, as shared victims of alleged liberal bigotry against them. Or stay silent on Trump's demagoguery, and let him whip up racial hysteria uncontested.[42] Versions of this conundrum have confounded Democrats for decades. As we'll see later, this is the knot the race-class narrative cuts through.

What Counts as "Dog Whistle Politics"?

Dog whistling fits within a larger pattern of right-wing culture war politics. Within this larger context, code is common. For instance, transphobia finds frequent political expression in arguments about protecting children from sexual predators in public bathrooms, rather than in outright denunciations of transgender identity. But the culture wars are not solely fought through ambiguous assaults. Especially surrounding appropriate gender relations, code often drops away, for instance in debates about whether feminism liberates women or instead betrays traditional norms. Wendy Davis, who rose to national prominence in 2013 by filibustering a highly restrictive anti-abortion law in the Texas state legislature, describes the gender analogue to racial dog whistling as "wolf whistle politics."[43] This metaphor helpfully captures how the political exploitation of patriarchy sometimes takes coded forms and at other times is direct and unvarnished. In any event, the first clarification regarding dog whistle politics is that not all right-wing culture-war assaults rely on the *coded* messaging that is a distinguishing feature of dog whistling.

The second clarification is that the mere use of code is not enough. Dog whistling involves two essential elements: (1) the use of code (2) to stoke social hostilities widely condemned by society.

It's common for critics to drop the second element, the effort to stoke group animosities, and to describe all sorts of political rhetoric as dog whistling simply because the language carries multiple meanings. Partly the fault lies with the metaphor itself. The dog whistle imagery seems to gesture toward rhetoric that communicates any sort of hidden message. But in a democracy filled with multiple heterogeneous audiences, politicians inevitably craft messages intended to speak differently to various populations. This is simply retail politics, not an ugly assault on society.

Understanding dog whistling as the use of code, without more, misses dog whistling's toxic heart: the intentional stoking of group hostilities. In the context of racial dog whistling, the fear and resentment being encouraged connect to racial hierarchy. It is the political exploitation of racial fear and resentment, not the use of language with multiple meanings nor even the effort to build rapport with a racially defined audience, that makes racial dog whistling democratically destructive.

Jack Kingston, a former Republican congressman from Georgia, accused Oprah Winfrey of engaging in racially tinged politics when she campaigned in 2018 for Stacey Abrams in the Georgia governor's race. Pointing out that Winfrey told a crowd of Black voters that failing to vote would amount to "dishonoring your family," Kingston said, "Oprah had a very deliberate racial message."[44] Likewise, Nia-Malika Henderson, writing in *Politico* in 2009, claimed that Barack Obama "benefits from what's known as 'dog-whistle politics.' His language, mannerisms and symbols resonate deeply with his black supporters, even as the references largely sail over the heads of white audiences."[45] Henderson cited Obama's use of phrases like "we as a people will get there," invoking Martin Luther King Jr., and "dreams that are being deferred," echoing Langston Hughes.

Surely these critics are correct that Winfrey and Obama sought to connect with Black audiences. But to label their actions "deliberate racial messages" and "dog-whistle politics" in a manner that implies an equivalence with racial demagoguery is jarring. By no conceivable stretch were Winfrey and Obama encouraging their Black listeners to band together out of anti-white racist fears—they were not, that is, dog whistling.

Similarly, it's common to hear an unexplained parallel between the racial polarization that leads whites to vote Republican and Blacks to vote Democratic. In one example, Nate Cohn in the *New York Times* casually observed in 2014, "In some states, the Republican advantage among white voters is nearly nine to one in presidential elections, a level of loyalty that rivals that of African-Americans for Democrats."[46] It's true that African Americans have recently voted Democrat at levels around 90 percent, higher for Obama, and slightly lower for Hillary Clinton. It's also true that voters focus on identity issues, and racial identity is key for many people of color. Nevertheless, there's a world of difference between voting in terms of race and voting because of racial anxiety.

Most of the white voters flocking to the GOP are doing so not because of anything so simple as skin color or descent, but because they're moved by the racial grievances the Right intentionally

pushes. Black voting patterns also reflect more than simple questions of racial descent, but in a very different way. Prior to 1948,
Blacks were about equal in identifying with either the Democratic
or Republican party. In that year, however, the Democratic Party
endorsed civil rights, and Blacks outside the South shifted solidly
toward that party. This shift consolidated in 1964, when president
Lyndon Johnson championed civil rights and the GOP aggressively wooed the segregationist South. More than 90 percent of
African Americans voted for Johnson—about the same proportion that voted for Obama—not out of racial affinity but in recognition that one party treated them as citizens and the other as
monsters.[47] Yes, Blacks vote Democratic in overwhelming numbers (joined by more than four out of ten whites). No, this is not
remotely like the white support for the GOP rooted in racial fear
and resentment.

What Do the Voters Rallying to Dog Whistles Hear?

Strategic racism by politicians is one thing. How does it come
across to the Right's base?

Because canines hear the shrill blast of a literal dog whistle, the
metaphor implies that the intended audience receives a plainly understood message. Sometimes political dog whistling does work
this way. A former Republican governor of Virginia remembered
the strategy like this: "The tactic was simple: lace your speeches
with coded appeals to racists in Southern states. . . . The intended
target of the message—the racist voter—understood completely,
while leaving the politician 'plausible deniability' with non-racist
voters."[48] In this version, dog whistling is, to switch metaphors,
like *a secret handshake*: a message designed to slip by the uniniti-
ated while being "understood completely" by insiders.

It's likely that dog whistling often worked like a secret racist handshake when it first arose. Many who cheered the arch-
segregationist George Wallace must have understood that when he

invoked "states' rights" in the summer of 1963, he was channeling his promise earlier that very same year to fight federal limits on segregation in the South now, tomorrow, and forever.

Likewise, even today dog whistling continues to work in this fashion for some audience members. After the white-power riots in Charlottesville in August 2017, Trump blamed "many sides" for the violence, and urged the country to respect our "history and heritage." Though he was superficially communicating a condemnation of the violence, white supremacists instead heard something very different: the clasped hand of a warm endorsement. "Trump comments were good. He didn't attack us. He just said the nation should come together. Nothing specific against us," the neo-Nazi website *Daily Stormer* chuffed. "Really, really good. God bless him."[49]

Nevertheless, major errors result from thinking of dog whistling as exclusively working this way. Relying solely on a secret-handshake conception of dog whistling pushes critics in one of two very different directions: Some critics assume almost all Republican voters understand the secret handshake of white supremacy, making that party seem a nest of racist vipers. Other critics start from the assumption that most Republican voters are not closet white supremacists, and therefore conclude that they must not receive the secret message, implying that racial dog whistling reaches few people and does little work.

On the contrary, the truth combines elements of both views. Most GOP voters (and many non-Republicans) are heavily swayed by the Right's racial innuendo, but they are not secret Klan members. Today, dog whistling overwhelmingly works by strongly resonating with voters who do not see themselves as racist but are jolted to action by warnings of racial threat. The success of this sort of dog whistling depends on hiding the racist nature of the messages from the intended audience itself. Rather than seeking to speak clearly to self-conscious racists, dog whistling in this vein aims to reassure those riled by racial appeals that they are *not* bigots.

For the most part, contemporary dog whistling is designed to muddy messages about racial threat. This is dog whistling as *a used-car fraud*. The dog whistle politician is peddling group resentment. But in its uglier forms—racism, xenophobia, bigotry—few would buy the merchandise. So the salesperson puffs it up, putting a new shine on it, and claims to be selling security, pride, patriotism, or dedication to a higher principle. It's still a racist clunker, the tires are retreads of worn racial stereotypes, and the engine can't pull a hill to actually get people to a better place. But the demagogue flogs it as a muscle car brimming with power, the envy of the neighborhood, the smooth ride good people deserve.

This fraud offers the base self-protecting fictions that mask a harder truth about what they're buying. They can believe themselves patriots or proud Americans and not have to confront the extent to which they subconsciously draw on racist myths and terrors to misperceive themselves and others. For these voters, the cloaked language hides—especially from themselves—the racial character of what the dog whistle politician is actually selling.

"Make America Great Again." Trump insisted it foremost expressed national pride. Yet just below the surface there roiled a call to return to a time of culturally sanctified white dominance. This kind of dog whistling both provoked and reassured the base. Trump riled his crowds by lobbing covert racial bombs. Sure, a few heard and celebrated the racism. But most were both racially anxious *and* opposed to stark racism.[50] Trump's racial dog whistling was surreptitiously manipulating people's deepest fears. His enthusiastic audiences seized on Trump's code, both because it spoke to their unnamed fears and also to protect themselves. The double meanings and ambiguity gave them cover to believe they were defending higher values, most often a sense they were protecting their families and the country, even as they tightly embraced a politics of racial resentment.

In 2017, the *Merriam-Webster* dictionary added the political meaning of "dog whistle" to its definition of the term, a fitting marker of the times. The dictionary defined dog whistle politics as "an expression or statement that has a secondary meaning intended to be understood only by a particular group of people."[51]

But *Merriam-Webster* defined dog whistling too broadly. Dog whistling should not be expanded to mean any coded language directed at select audiences. Seeking to communicate special meanings to particular populations is basic retail politics. The core of dog whistling involves code designed to stimulate widely condemned social hostilities.

And *Merriam-Webster* also characterized dog whistling too narrowly. Its definition picked up on dog whistling as a secret handshake, the sort of code that is clearly understood by its intended recipients. More often today, however, dog whistling seeks to hide the underlying racial appeal from the intended audience itself.

Finally, to retrieve a prior point, the intended audiences for today's dog whistling may include not just would-be supporters but hoped-for critics. Some dog whistles seemed designed to provoke liberal charges of bigotry. Dog whistling is a political strategy with a long, complicated pedigree that is undergoing rapid evolution. As a result, there's nothing uniform or simple about how dog whistling sounds to different audiences.

"Dog Whistle Politics" Defined for the Trump Era

"Dog whistle politics": The strategy of mobilizing electoral support by:

1. Stoking widely condemned social hostilities.
2. Through the use of code.
   (a) As in a secret handshake, sometimes the code hides the underlying message from the general audience but allows it to be clearly understood by intended supporters.

> (b) More often, like a used-car fraud, the code aims to stoke fear and resentment among intended supporters while hiding from that same group that the root appeal rests on socially unacceptable stereotypes.
>
> Note: The intended audience for the coded messages can also include potential critics, with the aim of provoking controversy and charges of bigotry.

Dog Whistle Politics Has Wrecked the Republican Party But They Can't Stop

Trump famously boasted he could stand in the middle of Fifth Avenue and shoot somebody and not lose any votes. Many took Trump at his word and quoted this to illustrate that normal political rules did not apply to him. But Trump and the politicians who imitate his antics nevertheless face two major constraints on what they can say, boundaries imposed by their reliance on racial dog whistling to motivate their base. They cannot say in plain, uncoded language that they represent white people against threatening minorities, let alone use racial epithets to make that point. They cannot, in other words, use a bullhorn to nakedly promote white supremacy. Doing so would reveal their racism to their supporters, the vast majority of whom strongly reject a view of themselves as racists.

On the other side, these dog whistle politicians cannot stop railing against the supposed racial dangers they invent. Once the specter of caravans of dangerous migrants has been invoked, it can't simply be ignored. Twice in his first two years in office, Trump moved to abandon his "big, beautiful wall," and both times he quickly retreated in the face of fire from Ann Coulter, Rush Limbaugh, and their (and his) racially provoked base. The second time, Trump shut down the federal government rather than risk their rage. Trump may have broken some of the rules, but he still played the dog whistle game and could not stop, not if he hoped to retain impassioned support from core Republican voters.

Today's dog whistling does not depend on Donald Trump, and will not cease to threaten the country the moment Trump exits the White House. As the *New York Times* editorialist Jamelle Bouie observed, "Beating Trump isn't the same as beating Trumpism. Unseating the president won't automatically undermine the white resentment and racial chauvinism that drives his movement."[52] The businessman's party is going to continue to be run by politicians talking about looming racial catastrophe and other culture war issues all day, every day. Partly this is their strategy to divide and distract.

But beyond strategy, the constant race talk reflects the fact that the GOP has trapped itself. Elected Republicans must each win their own elections. Every single one of them watched Trump prove that even a badly flawed figure can use racial hand grenades to defeat "serious" politicians. Today, GOP candidates understand that Republican primary voters will typically rally to the most racially reactionary candidate. In virtually every district, Republican politicians must racially pander to win their primaries, or they can retire and withdraw like Arizona senator Jeff Flake. Over and over, the GOP has seen one generation of politicians after another fall, as their voters swing to support someone even more extreme. Racial demagoguery has become a weapon not only against Democrats, but against any sort of moderation in the Republican Party itself.

Former Republican congressional leader John Boehner declared in 2018 that "there is no Republican Party. There's a Trump party."[53] He's wrong. That *is* the Republican Party—as it has been transmogrified by the strategy it adopted fifty years ago. They built their white man's party but cannot control it. The Silent Majority, Reagan Democrats, the Tea Party, Trump voters—these are all names for the Right's base voters, who decade by decade, through a dangerous call-and-response with their leaders and the right-wing media, have become ever more racially reactionary.

We should expect party elders, figures like George W. Bush and Karl Rove, to keep lecturing the party on the need to moderate its racism and broaden its appeal. But they don't have the power to force that change, and may find their reputations among Republicans going the way of the *Weekly Standard*, the recently shuttered conservative magazine. The most partisan Republican voters—the ones selecting GOP candidates in the primaries—have been moved for decades more by racial resentment than by dedication to core conservative principles.

If dog whistling convinced only those on the Right's margins, the Left could safely ignore it. But it doesn't. The messages of fear and resentment designed by GOP leaders and demanded by the Right's base also resonate far and wide. Dog whistling will continue, and the immediate question is how the Left can defeat it.

2

Testing Racial Fear

As the race-class narrative project was first getting going, a coalition called Our Minnesota Future saw promise in our approach. This group—led by Faith in Minnesota and SEIU Healthcare Minnesota—wanted to try a door-to-door canvassing experiment as soon as possible. Under time pressure as they evaluated whether to adopt the race-class approach in the looming 2018 election cycle, confirming that it actually worked in real conversations was key. Our research would not be done in time, so they decided to move forward independently, drawing on our as-of-then untested hypotheses.

For their experiment, they worked from an actual Republican mailer already circulating for the 2018 governor's race—a big postcard in red, white, and blue, with large font, a flag-draped photo, and typical dog whistle rhetoric about "sanctuary cities" and "criminal and illegal aliens." Our Minnesota Future would use this as the Right's message. Against this, they would test two possible Democratic responses: a standard progressive economic message that stayed silent on race, and also a race-class message.

Using these mailers, in January 2018 Our Minnesota Future canvassed eight hundred homes across Minnesota, divided evenly between white and nonwhite households. Demos Action, a race-class narrative project partner, helped with the door knocking and canvassing conversations. The idea of going house to snowy house in the middle of a Minnesota winter seemed foolhardy. As it turned out, though, the freezing conditions seemed to make residents more willing to open their doors to invite the canvassers in.

Standing in people's foyers or invited into their living rooms, the canvassers started by showing people the Republican mailer. After giving them time to look over its dog whistle message, they asked people to react to the flyer on a five-point scale: strongly agree, agree, neutral, disagree, or strongly disagree. Among white respondents, those saying they agreed outnumbered those disagreeing by almost two to one—45 percent initially agreed or strongly agreed, while only 24 percent disagreed or strongly disagreed, with the remainder indicating they were neutral or agreed with some parts but not others.[1]

The canvassers then tried one or the other of the hypothetical Democratic flyers, either the colorblind or the race-class version. After giving folks a chance to digest the new message, the canvassers cut to the chase to ask, "If the election were held tomorrow, which candidate would you vote for?" The point was to figure out which Democratic message, a colorblind one or the race-class narrative, would perform better against an actual Republican dog whistle message.

So how did the two Democratic flyers compare in their ability to compete against the Republican dog whistle message? Among those who initially disagreed with the GOP mailer, it did not much matter which Democratic flyer they saw. Almost all said they would vote for the Democratic candidate, whichever they were offered. No surprise there, since these were folks initially turned off by the Republican flyer. To them, supporting any Democrat—whether colorblind or race-forward—was preferable to voting Republican.

The important differences came in terms of the reactions among whites who initially *agreed* with the dog whistle message. Recall that people could either "strongly agree" or simply "agree." This mattered.

Just 7 percent among whites said they "strongly agreed" with the racial fear flyer. Within this group, more than a quarter said they would switch and vote for the colorblind populist Democrat. In contrast, only about one in ten said they would support the race-class Democrat. With this group, then, the colorblind version

Republican Dog Whistle Flyer

A GOVERNOR FOR MINNESOTA

WE NEED SAFER COMMUNITIES!

My opponents are demanding more sanctuary cities for criminal and illegal aliens.

My opponents want to increase taxes on gasoline, income and even support a death tax.

FAMILIES NEED MORE MONEY!

School should be focused on educating our children, so they are ready for success. My opponents want to use education dollars to fund Union Bosses, Political Cronies, and their own political campaigns.

CHILDREN NEED MORE OPPORTUNITY!

This is based on a Republican flyer that circulated in Minnesota in the fall of 2017. The dog whistling came through in the first sentence, "My opponents are demanding more sanctuary cities for criminal and illegal aliens." It also stated in big bold letters "We need safer communities!" Like most dog whistle campaigns, the flyer wove in other issues beyond race, for instance stating "Families need more money! Children need more opportunity." It also identified other enemies besides people of color, including "union bosses" and "political cronies." These additional enemies were not entirely independent of dog whistling, which often insinuates that unions and liberal politicians care more about undeserving people of color than hardworking whites. By juxtaposing the different messages about threat and a lack of opportunity, especially when expressed as shortchanging "our children," the flyer implied a link between threatening others and tough times for Minnesota voters. Finally, the flyer's image showed a man at a rally draped in an American flag, suggesting that the positions advocated by the flyer were patriotic and akin to a defense of the nation.

Colorblind Democratic Flyer

A GOVERNOR FOR MINNESOTA

FAIR WAGES!

INVEST IN SUCCESS FOR ALL STUDENTS!

TIME FOR A BETTER DEAL!

Minnesotans work hard and expect to earn enough to own a home, provide our kids a quality education, take occasional vacations and save for retirement.

Special interests are influencing elections to consolidate their wealth. Too many Minnesotans are unable to afford the basics.

We need a better deal: fair wages, fully funded public schools, and affordable healthcare for all. Protect our environment, invest in renewable energy and jobs, and maintain our roads, bridges, and transit across the state.

Our Minnesota Future used the Republican template to craft this hypothetical response. The message began in a colorblind form with no reference to race: "Minnesotans work hard and expect to earn enough to own a home, provide our kids a quality education, take occasional vacations and save for retirement." It then identified a culprit: "Special interests are influencing elections to consolidate their wealth. Too many Minnesotans are unable to afford the basics." Finally, it called for bold economic reforms: "We need a better deal: fair wages, fully funded public schools, and affordable healthcare for all. Protect our environment, invest in renewable energy and jobs, and maintain our roads, bridges, and transit across the state." In big letters, the flyer said "Fair wages! Invest in success for all students! Time for a better deal!" This language suggested an economic populism in line with Bernie Sander's 2016 campaign. The image showed a white family, presumably working class, walking together. No people of color featured in the image or the text.

Race-Class Democratic Flyer

A GOVERNOR FOR MINNESOTA

AFFORDABLE HEALTHCARE FOR ALL!

QUALITY EDUCATION FOR EVERY CHILD

CLEAN AIR AND WATER ACROSS OUR STATE

Minnesotans work hard to provide for our families. Whether white, black, or brown, 5th generation or newcomer, we all want to build a better future for our children.

My opponent says some families have value, while others don't count. He wants to pit us against each other in order to gain power for himself and kickbacks for his donors.

It's time for Minnesotans to join together and rewrite the rules so that all our families have the opportunity to pursue their dreams.

Our Minnesota Future crafted a second hypothetical Democratic response using the race-class formulation. It led with a shared value: "Minnesotans work hard to provide for our families." Then it highlighted that this value existed across racial communities: "Whether white, Black, or brown, 5th generation or newcomer, we all want to build a better future for our children." The culprit became the politician who seeks to divide people: "My opponent says some families have value, while others don't count. He wants to pit us against each other in order to gain power for himself and kickbacks for his donors." The flyer also included a positive ask: "It's time for Minnesotans to join together and rewrite the rules so that all our families have the opportunity to pursue their dreams." In bold letters, the race-class flyer insisted that everyone deserves to thrive: "Affordable healthcare for all! Quality education for every child Clean air and water across our state" The imagery showed people from different races standing shoulder to shoulder. It also mixed men and women together. An image of a white man wearing a small crucifix communicated that the positions in the flyer were consistent with the Christian faith.

substantially outperformed the race-class message. Their reactions suggest this cohort reacted to the racial content of the competing messages—and that among those most strongly in agreement with a Republican message of racial fear, a Democratic message of racial solidarity did not work well.

But that's not an argument against the race-class approach. Remember, just 7 percent of whites said they "strongly agree" with the racial fear message. The largest plurality of whites, almost four out of ten, instead took the more moderate position of saying they "agree" with the dog whistle mailer. One can imagine Matt and Tom in this group. So how did they react?

When shown the race-silent economic populist message, many switched from supporting the GOP candidate and said they would vote for the Democrat—but not a majority. The dog whistle candidate still received 55 percent of their support, compared to 44 percent who said they would vote colorblind blue. This was

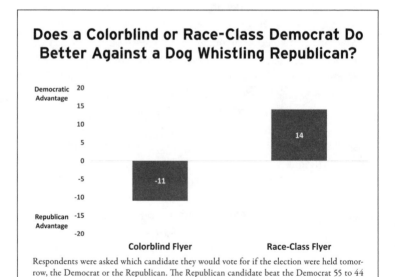

Does a Colorblind or Race-Class Democrat Do Better Against a Dog Whistling Republican?

Respondents were asked which candidate they would vote for if the election were held tomorrow, the Democrat or the Republican. The Republican candidate beat the Democrat 55 to 44 among those shown the colorblind flyer. The Democrat beat the Republican 57 to 43 among those shown the race-class flyer. These results are among whites who initially said they "agreed" with the Republican dog whistle flyer.

despite the fact that the economic populist message promised major reforms, for instance calling for fair wages and affordable healthcare for all.

In contrast, for those shown the race-class message, the numbers went positive. Now only 43 percent stayed with the Republican dog whistle candidate, compared to a winning 57 who favored the Democrat addressing both race and class.

Put differently, in a match-up with a Republican dog whistle message, a Democratic colorblind economic message lost, but a Democratic race-class message won. Moreover, there was a remarkable 25-point jump in net approval—from down by 11 to up by 14—when switching from the race-silent to the race-class script. Again, this was among white voters who initially said they agreed with the racially divisive message.

It's important that the race-class message outperformed the colorblind approach that constitutes standard Democratic fare. It is also critical that it successfully counteracted the Republican racial fear message, something the colorblind approach failed to do. True, the Minnesota Republican flyer did not offer the same full-blown racial hysteria portrayed by Richard Corcoran's "Kate Steinle" ad, but it used the same frame, warning about illegal aliens, criminals, and sanctuary cities. However demoralizing the success of such scaremongering messages in the Trump era, the Minnesota results—and the outcomes of the race-class project generally—show they can be beaten. Exploring how and why will occupy the bulk of this book.

At this stage of the book, however, the more important point is that progressives are up against *coded appeals* to racial fear, not clearly communicated and plainly heard endorsements of white solidarity. Look again at the visuals in the Minnesota flyers. The GOP mailer shows an American flag, whereas the race-class message features whites and Blacks shoulder to shoulder in camaraderie. If the white Minnesotans who initially agreed with the racial fear message were consciously committed to restoring white dominance, would they have switched their support to a candidate promising cross-racial solidarity? Would they turn and embrace a message that visually shows whites and Blacks with their arms around each other?

But they did switch, and not just a few, a majority of those who initially agreed with the dog whistle message. Yes, some whites are truly committed to restoring white dominance and, no, the race-class message will not sway them. But the Minnesota results strongly suggest—and research discussed later confirms—that the majority of whites who respond positively to stories of threatening nonwhites are not consciously committed to white superiority. On the contrary, though moved by narratives of racial threat, they also seem remarkably open to messages of economic populism tied to cross-racial solidarity.

Another aspect of the Minnesota research bears mention: the results among people of color. Strikingly, many respondents of color found merit in the dog whistle racial fear message. Compared to whites, fewer strongly agreed, but a roughly similar number said they "agreed" with the GOP flyer—35 percent among voters of color versus 38.5 percent among white voters.[2] These results confirm that for many people, including many minorities, attacks on "sanctuary cities for criminal and illegal aliens" and other racial fear messages work at a subliminal level. The core narrative involves a story about threatening nonwhites and innocent whites. But once translated into coded dog whistle terms, acceptance of this narrative transcends racial boundaries.

It's also important that, compared to whites, respondents of color were substantially more likely to switch to support the Democrat when given a chance. After being shown the race-silent Democratic message, people of color who initially agreed with the GOP message said they would vote for the Democrat by a positive margin of 15 points. They were even more enthusiastic when shown the race-class Democratic flyer. Given that choice, the positive Democratic margin increased to 34 points. It may run counter to the established wisdom that many people of color find dog whistle themes convincing. But even so, it remains true that voters of color respond very well to Democratic messages. The Minnesota results confirm the point made by many, for instance Democracy in Color founder Steve Phillips: there are big payoffs to reaching out to voters of color (including those who otherwise sympathize with some dog whistle messages).[3]

Testing the Right's Dog Whistle Racial Fear Message

The race-class narrative project aimed to show that race-class messages could compete against dog whistle rhetoric. The best way to test this was through direct comparison in the same survey instrument. This, in turn, required that the race-class project craft a version of the dog whistle narrative. We combed through campaign speeches and political ads in an effort to closely mimic the actual messages bombarding people daily.

Here is what we concocted. It combined veiled warnings about threatening nonwhites with reassurances that racial fear is just

Dog Whistle Racial Fear

Our leaders must prioritize keeping us safe and ensuring that hardworking Americans have the freedom to prosper. Taking a second look at people coming from terrorist countries who wish us harm or at people from places overrun with drugs and criminal gangs is just common sense. And so is curbing illegal immigration, so our communities are no longer flooded with people who refuse to follow our laws. We need to make sure we take care of our own people first, especially the people who politicians have cast aside for too long to cater to whatever special interest groups line their pockets, yell the loudest, or riot in the street.

common sense, echoing the way Trump implicitly assailed people of color but reassured his base.

How did the dog whistle message perform? Depressingly well. In national polling, we asked people to evaluate whether they found the statement convincing on a scale from 0 to 100, with 0 meaning not convincing at all and 100 meaning very convincing.* Republicans generally loved this statement. Almost three-quarters found it convincing, compared to roughly half of Democrats. There was also a sharp difference in the intensity of conviction. Almost one-quarter of Republicans rated this statement a perfect 100, for very convincing. In comparison, only 13 percent of Democrats gave it this highest possible score. It is good news that Democrats liked this statement less—but bad news that even among Democrats, it still received a generally positive rating. Indeed, less than one in three Democrats, 31 percent, rated it in the unconvincing range below 50.

What about the racial breakdown in how people reacted to the racial fear message? It stands to reason that people of color would overwhelmingly repudiate a message that describes them as threats to society. But as in the Minnesota canvassing experiment, that did not happen. Instead, there was a shared agreement across racial groups that this message was convincing. Among whites, roughly three in five found this message convincing—as did a similar number of Latinxs. African Americans were only slightly less convinced, with more than half rating it convincing. Indeed, there was more divergence in reactions to the racial fear message between Democrats and Republicans than between whites and Blacks.

---

* The March 2018 national survey reached 1,500 adults, plus oversamples of 100 African Americans, 100 Latinxs, 100 millennials, 100 persons who had voted in 2012 but not in 2016, and 100 persons eligible but unlikely to vote. We weighted the data slightly by age, region, race, gender, and education to reflect the attributes of the actual population. The margin of error for the total sample was +/− 2.5%.

Those Finding the Dog Whistle Racial Fear Narrative Convincing

By Partisan Identification

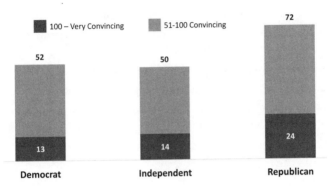

Respondents were asked to rate the racial fear message by how convincing they found it on a scale of 0 to 100, where 0 means not convincing at all and 100 means very convincing.

By Race

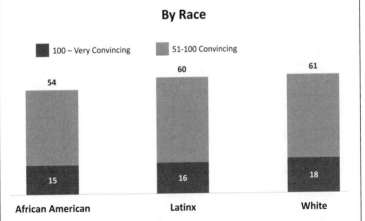

Respondents were asked to rate the racial fear message by how convincing they found it on a scale of 0 to 100, where 0 means not convincing at all and 100 means very convincing.

The racial fear message was widely popular. Here are two important implications. First, the Right's message has real traction with a broad swath of American voters. The term "common sense" in the message, and in Trump's mouth, captures how a dog whistle narrative of racial fear comes across as reasonable and convincing to very large numbers. Second, when majorities of Democrats, African Americans, and Latinxs find the racial fear message convincing, this is coded, not naked, racism.

Why does this message have broad traction across parties and racial groups? It's more than simple repetition, as powerful as that is. Rather, the racial fear message connects to a deeper story from the Right linking race, class, and government. Let's turn to examine that core narrative.

3

The Right Consistently Links Race, Class, and Government

Which traditionally Democratic group lost the day in the 2016 election? Was it whites in the upper Midwest, buffeted by economic decisions that shipped jobs overseas and frustrated that Hillary Clinton did not spend sufficient time talking with them? Was it African Americans, who stayed home after the high of voting for Barack Obama? What about Latinx voters, the perennial sleeping giant that did not awaken to its full power? After November 2016, various pundits laid out hypothetical scenarios in which each of these groups could have turned the election by contributing just a few more votes in key districts.

But each of these scenarios gained plausibility mainly because Donald Trump's victory depended on razor-thin margins against a backdrop of having lost the popular vote. In that situation, myriad groups could have swung the election. It makes little sense to single out any one of them for particular blame or to seek in their reactions a recipe for future success. The more fundamental question is why the election was so close in the first place. And the answer to that requires identifying the core base that voted red.

The standard consensus immediately after 2016 focused on the white working class. This was dubious from the outset. Almost one in three of all voters, 28 percent, had family incomes below $30,000. Among these financially strapped voters, nearly double the number supported Clinton (58 percent to 32 for Trump). When the poorest one-third of American voters preferred

Clinton by almost two-to-one, it was hard to take the class argument seriously.

Even among white voters, Trump's support did not come from those with the lowest incomes. Whites with family incomes below $30,000 effectively split their vote—44 percent for Clinton versus 43 percent for Trump. Among those in the middle-income bracket, enthusiasm for Trump sharply increased to 58 percent to 37 percent for Clinton. Maybe the class story was about a squeezed middle? But for whites making $75,000 or more, the numbers didn't vary much: 55 percent for Trump, 39 percent for Clinton.[1]

In other words, the main class effect was among poorer whites—where significant economic hardship made support for Trump *less* likely. Buttressing this, a large study of white working-class voters released in May 2017 found that financial pressure among whites generated support for Clinton, not Trump: "Those who reported being in fair or poor financial shape were 1.7 times more likely to support Clinton, compared to those who were in better financial shape."[2]

The initial intuition that class concerns drove the 2016 outcome only suffered further with more time and better research. By late 2018, a consensus had emerged among social scientists that instead racial attitudes were crucial. The most thorough analysis of the 2016 election concluded that support for Trump "was strongly linked to how Republican voters felt about Blacks, immigrants, and Muslims, and how much discrimination Republican voters believed that whites themselves faced."[3] Numerous other studies came to a similar conclusion that racial attitudes rather than economic hardship best explained support for Trump.[4]

But a pick-only-one choice between class or race won't do. In the run-up to the 2016 election, anger over surging wealth inequality and declining life chances propelled Bernie Sanders' political insurgency, and it stands to reason that this discontent also lifted Trump. The question is how economic hardship blended together with racial resentment.

Financial hardship, it turns out, can function as a relative term.

Compared to when? Compared to whom? In 2016, the Kaiser Family Foundation carefully looked at American working-class families. By 2021, people of color will be the majority of the working class in the 25-to-34 age bracket, and a majority across the entire category by 2032.[5] The Kaiser study found that among working-class families, almost half of Hispanics, 48 percent, expected their children to achieve a better standard of living than their own. More than a third of African Americans, 36 percent, agreed.[6]

Much less so their white working-class peers. "Whites without college degrees are less optimistic about their children's future than their black and Hispanic counterparts," the Kaiser study reported, noting that less than a quarter, 23 percent, expected better for their children. White working-class families were wealthier. For instance, among those without a college degree, roughly two-thirds of whites owned their own home in 2016, compared to about one-third of Blacks and Latinxs. Nevertheless, these relatively better-off white working families were more pessimistic about the future.

This pessimism proved politically powerful. In 2017, the Public Religion Research Institute (PRRI) conducted a major study of the white working class. PRRI found that direct measures of "economic hardship" predicted support for Clinton, not Trump. In contrast, PRRI reported that pessimism about future economic prospects correlated with voting for Trump.[7]

Scholars of social protest movements use the term "relative deprivation" to get at this dynamic. The question is not hardship in the abstract. Rather, it is the sense of losing ground compared to others, especially to groups perceived as undeserving.[8] In a related vein, a group of political scientists used the term "racialized economics" to explain enthusiasm for Trump. "The important sentiment underlying Trump's support was not 'I might lose my job,'" reported John Sides, Michael Tesler, and Lynn Vavreck in their 2018 book *Identity Crisis*, "but, in essence, 'People in my group are losing jobs to that other group.' Instead of pure economic anxiety, what mattered was racialized economics."[9]

The dynamic of relative deprivation or racialized economics gives white racial resentment a paradoxical relationship to class. On the one hand, from laborers to middle-class teachers to upper-middle-class lawyers, many whites have a sense of losing out to undeserving others. This helps explain the lack of a strong correlation in voting patterns between class position among whites and support for Trump. *New York Times* columnist Paul Krugman sees this phenomenon in the enraged demeanor of Justice Brett Kavanaugh during his Senate confirmation. Kavanaugh's "sneering, rage-filled scowl," Krugman wrote, drove home that "white male rage isn't restricted to blue-collar guys in diners. It's also present in people who have done very well in life's lottery . . . hatred can go along with high income, and all too often does." [10]

But on another level, racial views often find expression through narratives about class. In a 2016 book, the sociologist Justin Gest reported on conversations with members of the white working class in the decrepit ruins of Youngstown, Ohio, once the self-described "steel capital of the world" but now an economic wasteland. Mo Kerrigan, an unemployed sixty-five-year-old, told Gest:

> There's the NAACP, the Muslim Brotherhood—the white guy? All he has is his little church. White people don't have the strength or support to accomplish anything. All the wealthy people haven't done me any favors; I would have to do something for them first. And all the black folks look at me and literally say "What do you want, honkey?" I was born here, and they say, "Get out. This is our hood." I'm the cannon fodder.

Probing whether this mindset was widely shared, Gest gave people paper and pencil and asked them to sketch a simple model of class relations. One would expect drawings roughly placing the rich on top, above the middle class, the working class, and the poor. Instead, most people Gest interviewed offered this hierarchy: the rich, welfare recipients, the middle class, and themselves at the bottom.[11]

Gest found that working-class whites were prone to view themselves as doubly victimized: ignored by elites, sometimes Black but most often white, who care only about the welfare poor; and outstripped by welfare recipients, whom they saw as doing better than themselves. In the racialized class story Gest uncovered, class resentment punched up as well as down, faulting elites but also resenting people receiving welfare.

When Kerrigan talked about being reduced to "cannon fodder" in what had been his own neighborhood, he expressed a common sentiment among Trump voters. More than simply voicing economic pessimism, Kerrigan captured the sense of having been abandoned or betrayed. The 2017 PRRI study mentioned previously confirmed the political power of pessimism in pushing people rightward. It also found, though, that support for Trump was even more strongly predicted by the sense of being a stranger in one's own country.

PRRI asked working-class whites whether they agreed with the following statement: "Things have changed so much that I often feel like a stranger in my own country." Nearly half of whites without a college degree said they agreed with that statement—and those who felt like strangers in their own country were greater than three times more likely to vote for Trump. Indeed, other than identifying as a Republican, feeling "like a stranger in my own country" was the single strongest factor predicting Trump support.[12]

The phrase "stranger in my own country" echoes the title of Arlie Hochschild's 2016 book, *Strangers in Their Own Land: Anger and Mourning on the American Right*. A sociologist, Hochschild spent several years during the Obama era interviewing white Tea Party activists in Louisiana. Focusing on environmental issues, she wanted to understand why rural Louisianans so fiercely hated the government when they so desperately needed the government's help to restore and protect the lands and waters on which their families' livelihoods depended. Hochschild ultimately settled on a metaphor of people cutting in line:

> You are patiently standing in the middle of a long line stretching toward the horizon, where the American Dream awaits. But as you wait, you see people cutting in line ahead of you. Many of these line-cutters are black—beneficiaries of affirmative action or welfare. Some are career-driven women pushing into jobs they never had before. Then you see immigrants, Mexicans, Somalis, the Syrian refugees yet to come. As you wait in this unmoving line, you're being asked to feel sorry for them all. You have a good heart. But who is deciding who you should feel compassion for? Then you see President Barack Hussein Obama waving the line-cutters forward. He's on their side. In fact, isn't he a line-cutter too? How did this fatherless black guy pay for Harvard? As you wait your turn, Obama is using the money in your pocket to help the line-cutters. He and his liberal backers have removed the shame from taking. The government has become an instrument for redistributing your money to the undeserving. It's not your government anymore; it's theirs.[13]

Though Hochschild does not frame it this way, her narrative records the essential teachings of dog whistle politics. These teachings also inform the views that Gest uncovered.

Weaponizing Racism Against Government Efforts to Help Working Families

Underlying the Right's political strategy is a fundamental story about race, class, and government—a myth of dangerous and undeserving people of color, feckless liberal government, and market salvation. Where did this core dog whistle narrative come from and how does it work?

The Right's story profits from a genuine debate between

liberals and conservatives. At the most basic level, liberals and conservatives clash over the main reasons so many people struggle economically. Liberals mainly look to circumstances, like whether someone lives in a booming region or is trapped in a city without jobs. Conservatives primarily point to character, for instance the willingness to work hard. These are not exclusive alternatives. Few liberals assert that individual effort plays no role in shaping lives. Nor do many conservatives claim that accidents, for instance of health or birth, are irrelevant in shaping individual destiny. Instead, the difference lies in where people put the greatest emphasis for economic hardship, on circumstances or instead on character.

The primordial stories about circumstances or instead character in turn connect to views about government. If economic success largely depends on circumstances outside one's control, this implies a powerful role for government in protecting people from personal misfortune and creating the opportunities that allow people to thrive. In contrast, if financial security mainly stems from individual effort, then government assistance is less important and, conceivably, may induce laziness.

This is a real debate, and one can look to government policy during the long New Deal from the 1930s through the 1960s to see elements of liberalism (an emphasis on government intervention) combined with elements of conservatism (programs structured to promote work). But taken to an extreme, the conservative position can become reactionary—no longer an important consideration when helping people, but now an excuse to blame working families for their own suffering while absolving corporations and the very rich from having to pay taxes to support government for all. This is today's Right. And race has played a central role in the stories the Right has used to sell a reactionary distortion of conservatism to the American public.

We can hear these competing perspectives on circumstances versus character from two presidents who both won elections in just about equal landslides among white voters: Democrat

Lyndon Johnson in the 1960s and Republican Ronald Reagan in the 1980s.

Listen to one of Johnson's TV campaign commercials from 1964. As the screen flashes the faces of hungry children, the narrator's voice intones:

> Poverty is not a trait of character. It is created anew in each generation, but not by heredity, by circumstances. Today, millions of American families are caught in circumstances beyond their control. Their children will be compelled to live lives of poverty unless the cycle is broken. President Johnson's War on Poverty has this one goal: to provide everyone a chance to grow and make his own way, a chance at education, a chance at training, a chance at a fruitful life. For the first time in the history of America, this can be done.[14]

Johnson's ad rested firmly on the conviction that poverty typically stems from circumstances that require government intervention, warning that "children will be compelled to live lives of poverty unless the cycle is broken." Government, he urged, should provide "everyone a chance to grow and make his own way, a chance at education, a chance at training, a chance at a fruitful life." Johnson's smashing victory helped convince the pundits of the day that the United States was fundamentally a liberal nation that believed in the power and duty of activist government to improve the lives of working families.

Now listen to Ronald Reagan. In 1984 he won a second term in a landslide every bit as large as Johnson's victory twenty years before. Here is Reagan in 1986 delivering a major radio address urging cuts to welfare:

> We're in danger of creating a permanent culture of poverty as inescapable as any chain or bond; a second and separate America, an America of lost dreams and stunted lives. The irony is that misguided welfare programs instituted in the name of compassion

have actually helped turn a shrinking problem into a national tragedy. From the 1950s on, poverty in America was declining. American society, an opportunity society, was doing its wonders. Economic growth was providing a ladder for millions to climb up out of poverty and into prosperity. In 1964 the famous War on Poverty was declared and a funny thing happened. Poverty, as measured by dependency, stopped shrinking and then actually began to grow worse. I guess you could say, poverty won the war.[15]

In Reagan's story, the market was functioning well, hard work was paying off, and then government intervened to help—and made many people worse off, stunting their lives and creating a culture of poverty.

How might voters in 1964 have reacted to a tale painting government help as the cause of poverty? It likely would have made little sense to them. Sure, poverty was declining over the 1950s— because of important government programs, including the dramatic expansion of Social Security, as well as active government support for unions, infrastructure investment, and high corporate taxes that in combination helped spur a booming economy. The "economic growth" that provided a "ladder for millions" reflected, not the absence of government, but liberal government's aggressive efforts to make sure the economy provided for regular people, especially those who worked. Or so most believed in 1964, which is why by a landslide they were willing to support even more aggressive government efforts to help the millions of families still mired in poverty.

Moreover, these voters might have bristled at the claim that the War on Poverty they voted for was actually about to make poverty worse. Reagan asserted that after 1964, "poverty, *as measured by dependency*, stopped shrinking and then actually began to grow worse." This reflects a sleight of hand. On the Right, "dependency" is a tagline for welfare. Reagan's claim, then, is that the number of people receiving welfare went up after 1964—which is certainly true. The whole point of the War on Poverty, after all, was to reduce poverty, including by expanding access to government assistance. But Reagan then turned around and used the numbers receiving government help as a measure of poverty itself. These numbers are not completely unrelated, in the way that the number of people taking aspirin roughly corresponds to the number of people with headaches. But few would say that providing more aspirin increases the nation's headache level. Just the reverse, of course.

And so, too, with actual poverty. In the first five years after Johnson announced the War on Poverty, the number of poor people fell by more than 10 million individuals. This was more than a one-third reduction in the poverty rate, dropping it from roughly 19 percent of all Americans to around 12 percent. To continue the story, the numbers in poverty remained roughly steady through the 1970s. Poverty started to climb with a recession in 1979, however, and continued sharply upward under Reagan and then under his vice president and successor, George H. W. Bush. Their administrations' policies helped push 10 million people into poverty, erasing the successes of Johnson's efforts.[16] If someone deserves blame for driving millions of people into poverty, it is Reagan, not Johnson.

So why had the public shifted? What made Johnson's progressive story compelling in 1964, and Reagan's reactionary tale powerful in 1986? Any thorough answer must examine twenty-two years of tumultuous American history. The aim here is to examine how both of these narratives depended on a story about race.

Where was race in Johnson's story promoting the War on Poverty? The narrator never mentioned race, focusing instead on class and government. Meanwhile, visually, the ad featured photos of ten white children. For decades, New Deal and Great Society programs by design helped mainly whites.[17] The disheveled faces of poor white children in the ad amplified the message that whites were the poor the government should help. Many voters seemingly heard Johnson to be saying something like *poor whites need government help*, and they stood ready to support that effort.

Yet the War on Poverty was intimately linked to civil rights. In response to pressure from the civil rights movement and also reflecting evolving liberal commitments, including calculations about how to preserve the Democrats' electoral coalition, Johnson shaped the War on Poverty to also help the African American poor. Visually signifying this, his campaign ad included photos of three impoverished Black children along with the ten white children.

Thus, though the ad did not speak directly about racial issues, race played a role at the level of imagery and subtext. Present but not addressed, the racial elements of the ad raised but did not answer critical questions connected to the Left-Right debate about poverty: Were the Black poor like the white poor, beset by circumstances rather than character? Would government help make their lives better or instead encourage laziness? Also, would help to Blacks come at a high cost to the white poor or to white taxpayers?

Now fast-forward to Reagan. The Democrats largely had left those basic questions hanging for two decades. In this vacuum, Reagan provided some answers. Listen to a bit more of Reagan's radio address attacking the War on Poverty.

> Today I'd like to speak to you about a gathering crisis in our society: It's a family crisis. To some it's hidden, concealed behind tenement walls or lost in the forgotten streets of our inner cities. . . . I'm talking about the crisis of family breakdowns, especially among the welfare poor, both black and white. In inner cities today, families, as we've always thought of them, are not even being formed. Since 1960 the percentage of babies born out of wedlock has more than doubled. And too often their mothers are only teenagers. They're children—many of them 15, 16, and 17 years old with all the responsibilities of grown-ups thrust upon them. The fathers of these children are often nowhere to be found. In some instances you have to go back three generations before you can find an intact family. . . .

The family is the most basic support system there is. For two centuries now, it's been families pulling together that has provided the courage, willpower, and sense of security that have enabled millions of Americans to escape poverty and grab hold of the rungs on the ladder of opportunity. How often have we heard about the immigrant father laboring long into the night to give his children the advantages he never had? How many self-made men and women in America of all ethnic backgrounds owe their success to the strength of character given them by hardworking, loving parents? But for the children of child mothers and absentee fathers, there is often only a deepening cycle of futility, hopelessness, and despair.

Again one hears the Right's story that poverty reflects personal choices, especially decisions about family formation, teenage pregnancy, and irresponsible fatherhood. Reagan offered an antifeminist narrative, a parable of family values spun in terms of traditional gender roles, of stay-at-home mothers and responsible fathers supporting the family. This gender narrative meshed with the Right's larger politics supporting patriarchy.

In addition, though, a strong racial subplot comes through.

In the late 1960s, intellectuals like Patrick Moynihan and Nathan Glazer developed a thesis of Black pathology that centered on broken families in the ghettoes. Over the course of the 1970s the Right adopted those stories. In this saga, the supposedly damaged Black family, rather than racism in its multiple forms, explained Black poverty and marginalization. Reagan drew on that myth. The root cause of poverty lurked in the broken families living behind the "tenement walls" of public housing, along the "forgotten streets of our inner cities," and among the "welfare poor."

Further developing the racial tale, against this portrait of Black family dysfunction Reagan offered a contrasting image of white virtue. "Hardworking, loving parents" and "self-made men and women," with "the immigrant father laboring long into the night to give his children the advantages he never had"—these formed the ingredients of financial success. They also bore the stamp of whiteness. "Hardworking" and "self-made" were dog whistle terms that conjured white people, not African Americans or other nonwhites.

The reference to "immigrants" might seem to cut in the other direction, as talk of immigrants today typically invokes the phantasm of sinister nonwhite foreigners. But the United States has long embraced two immigrant stories—one of threatening others stealing jobs and consuming resources, the second of plucky migrants who come to the United States, work hard, and see their children become full Americans. This latter version especially celebrates European ethnic groups for supposedly overcoming discrimination and succeeding without government help. This story gained added prominence in the 1970s as a way to ridicule demands for racial integration and affirmative action.[18] It's this "good immigrant" that Reagan invoked.

It's true that Reagan carefully spoke of the "white and black" poor and of self-made individuals "of all ethnic backgrounds." He gave his tale a patina of racial neutrality. This was classic dog whistling: tell a racial story with just enough misdirection to allow for plausible deniability. At root, though, Reagan was peddling a racist mythology: bad Blacks versus good whites.

This basic story finds more familiar form in Reagan's repeated invocations of the welfare queen. Reagan first exploited this theme in 1976 when he warned the country about a "Chicago welfare queen" with a "tax-free cash income . . . over $150,000," though he neglected to mention she was white.[19] A couple of years later, another sensational welfare fraud case surfaced, involving an African American woman from Compton, California. Media accounts from the *New York Times* and the *Washington Post* repeatedly noted that she drove a Cadillac.[20]

Campaigning in 1980, Reagan conflated these individuals into a stock story of welfare queens tooling around in Caddies. Welfare scholar Kaaryn Gustafson observes that "politicians—and the media and public as well—adopted these cases as typifying poor,

African American women on welfare." According to Gustafson, "the welfare queen stereotype portrayed the welfare recipient as uneducated, lazy, and irrational," and also, as living off "taxpayer dollars, displaying neither gratitude nor remorse."[21] In a male version of the welfare queen story, Reagan also frequently criticized the food stamp program for helping "some young fellow ahead of you to buy a T-bone steak" while "you were waiting in line to buy hamburger."[22]

The welfare queen as well as the welfare recipient on a government-subsidized binge are now stock Black characters in this country's racial imagination. Recall Matt, one of the Ohio men we first met, offering a version of the T-bone steak narrative. What do these images communicate?

On the most obvious level, these are stories about race. For Reagan and his audience, the narratives about welfare queens and young fellows on food stamps, as well as about child mothers and absent fathers in urban America, conjured ugly stereotypes about African Americans. They were supposedly irresponsible and lazy. They could work if they wanted, but they lacked a work ethic and preferred food stamps over honest labor. More than shiftless, they were larcenous. They were not just receiving welfare, they were ripping off the system. Sometimes the theft was literal fraud; sometimes it was more metaphorical, with Black welfare recipients "displaying neither gratitude nor remorse." Either way, African Americans did not *deserve* welfare but instead abused it.

If Reagan told a story about Blacks, he simultaneously did so about whites. Alleged inferiority can only be measured against supposed superiority. This is the "you" that Reagan invoked when he said "you were waiting in line to buy hamburger." Reagan's audiences were overwhelmingly white. Indeed, in one awkward exchange, Reagan's wife, Nancy, looking out over a campaign crowd in a Chicago suburb, gushed to Ronnie about "all these beautiful white people."[23]

Reagan was talking to and also about his white base: unlike Blacks, they were not irresponsible but dutiful, not lazy but hardworking, not criminal but law-abiding. They were, to retrieve other dog whistle terms, the Silent Majority, the real Americans, America's heartland and its patriots, the makers rather than the takers.

Moreover, their hardworking, law-abiding, and decent character allegedly explained their having to make ends meet with hamburger instead of steak. In the same narrative in which Reagan presented the Black working class as lazy and larcenous, he painted the white working class as struggling precisely because they refused to cheat in a system rigged to help the undeserving. Reagan created a zero-sum frame in which government efforts to help Blacks came at the expense of whites. Government was not just misguided in its efforts to fight poverty. It became a threatening force in the lives of whites. Progressive government, Reagan insinuated, took crucial dollars in the form of unfair taxes from the pockets of hardworking, decent, financially struggling whites. Liberal government taxed "you," Reagan warned his white audiences, so that welfare queens could tool around in Cadillacs and young fellows could feast on T-bone steak.

To see these stories as only about race, however, misses the most important ideological work they perform. Even more than race, these stories were about character and government. Black poverty supposedly stemmed from Black pathology; white poverty supposedly resulted from white virtue. In both cases, poverty reflected character. And because poverty flowed from character, *government could not help*. Government could not assist Blacks, this narrative said, because their basic character ensured failure. And government programs to help the poor, this tale insisted, far from helping whites, instead stole tax dollars from them.

This is the point of Reagan's focus on welfare rather than on stereotypes disconnected from government. Attacking welfare allowed the Right to more broadly assail government help to working families. People were poor because of bad choices, and efforts to use government to help people actually made them lazy and dependent, Reagan warned. Government, not poverty, became the core threat that people faced. Whites would not have swallowed this story if it was told about themselves; indeed, they had rejected it in a landslide in 1964 by voting for the government's War on Poverty. It went down much easier in 1986, when told about Blacks.

The Right's Core Narrative

We're now in a position to describe the core narrative on the Right that solidified under Reagan and continues still.

A "core narrative" in politics is a skeletal story that can be told repeatedly, with different actors, facts, settings, and scripts. It's the hidden scaffolding that undergirds campaign speeches, political ads, and slanted media reporting. The constant drumming of a basic narrative is key in order to create a storyline that pervades people's consciousness. The aim is to color how people see themselves, who threatens them, and who protects them. The core narrative offers an *ideology*: a lens on the world. When the Right convinces people to view society through their lens, they move them decisively toward supporting the Right's agenda.

Core narratives differ from policy platforms. The core narrative is the way that policy—for instance tax cuts or reductions in social welfare spending—is packaged and sold to the public. This typically makes the narrative more powerful and certainly more enduring than particular policy proposals.

Core narratives are related to yet differ from the "frames" emphasized, for instance, by George Lakoff in his book *Don't Think of an Elephant*. Frames like the strict father or the nurturing parent offer metaphors that invoke unconscious sets of ideas.[24] When used in political messaging, these metaphors trigger ways of seeing the world. In this way, they offer implicit stories about who we are and how the world is. Paying attention to framing asks us to think about the metaphors we use and the multiple stories they invoke. In contrast, the focus on narrative directs our attention to the substance of the stories. For the political scientist Frederick Mayer, it's stories that move people to come together. "Stories are not merely the surface of politics; they are its heart. And they are particularly central for the core problem of politics: the problem of collective action." In turn, a core narrative is just that, a foundational story. It seeks, in Mayer's terms, to "define who *we* are, what *we* believe, and what *we* value." [25]

It's time to lay bare the Right's narrative bones. These bones are rarely the way the story is told in public. Frames, metaphors, policy proposals, anecdotes, all of these provide the sinew, muscles, and skin. Still, the narrative outline that lies beneath the Right's rhetoric and policies stays largely stable and plays a huge role in providing the basic structure to the Right's messaging. Over the last half century, these are the sturdy bones that have helped the Right march forward its agenda to help the very rich, not least by rolling back government efforts to help working families: 1. Fear and resent people of color; 2. Distrust government; 3. Trust the marketplace.

1. Fear and resent people of color. Fear people of color because their basic nature is violent. Resent them because they are lazy and undeserving and rip off government rather than do honest work.

The core narrative is highly racialized, a basic story about whites against people of color. But it is not told in those naked terms. Instead, the Right translates this core narrative into dog whistles that convey a more diffuse conflict between innocents and criminals, the lazy versus hard workers. This is key because it shrouds the racism from whites. It's also critical, though, because these less starkly racial terms help sell the Right's ideas to people of color. In its most naked form, few people of color and indeed few whites would accept a bald story about white virtue and minority venality. Dog whistling hides the essential racism and transforms this core narrative into a common sense accepted by many who repudiate racism, including many people of color.

2. Distrust government. Distrust government because it doesn't care about white people. Instead, it coddles undeserving minorities with welfare spending and it refuses to control violent minorities by leaving laws unenforced and borders open, while it taxes whites to pay for handouts and ineffective government programs.

There are numerous reasons beyond a racial tale for skepticism toward government. This includes government as a swamp of self-dealing by special interests and corrupt politicians, and also, repeated failures by government to help people with necessities like effective schools, good infrastructure, basic neighborhood services, and healthcare. For communities of color, government over-policing and mistreatment also fuel distrust. One key perversity here is that almost everything the Right does to frustrate the effective functioning of government helps support its ideological message that government cannot help working families.

Nevertheless, the Right relies especially heavily on racial resentment to fuel hostility toward government. The sense that liberal government favors undeserving people of color plays a large role. But perhaps the most visceral hatred of government comes from the sense that government puts people's families in immediate danger—a sense conveyed by the racial threat narratives told about people of color as criminals, terrorists, gang members, and invading aliens. The Right's story says that innocent people face danger from violent predators, and then blames government for refusing to restrain dangerous people or to secure the borders. Recall Richard Corcoran's "Kate Steinle" ad, with the hooded, dark-skinned man gunning down a carefree young white woman walking down a leafy sidewalk on a sun-dappled day. "This could have happened to any family anywhere," Corcoran tells the viewer. Remember that Bill O'Reilly laid the blame for Steinle's death at the feet of liberal government: "The mayor and city supervisors of San Francisco are directly responsible for the murder of Kate Steinle and the Obama administration is complicit," O'Reilly insisted.

In fact, the Right often suggests that government not only exposes decent people to marauders, it punishes people when they try to protect their loved ones. Among others, the National Rifle

Association has been instrumental in promoting this message. In a 2018 exposé on the NRA, the journalist Elliott Woods neatly summed up the tactic: "Since the 1990s, the NRA has been enormously successful at stoking white Americans' fears about their darker-skinned fellow citizens while simultaneously cultivating paranoia about left-wing politicians seeking to take away their guns."[26] *Government puts your family at risk because it won't imprison violent predators, but it will jail YOU for trying to protect your wife and kids.* That's a powerful story converting the abstraction of government into an immediate, threatening, and hateful actor.

3. Trust the marketplace. The market rewards hard work and whites work hard, so no government help is needed. People of color are poor because they make bad choices. Support the very wealthy and large corporations as the job creators.

This is the least convincing element to many voters. Right-leaning voters have high confidence that hard work is rewarded, but more mixed feelings toward the wealthy, with many seeing them as rigging the rules. Trust in the marketplace gains credibility often as a default position, the only alternative once one loses confidence in collective action and government. At its heart, the Right's message is that everyone is on their own and should fend for themselves and their families. On the level of physical safety, this might mean buying a gun. On the level of economic security, it means trusting the marketplace. For many, this is no more than an act of desperation because they believe government cares about others, not them.

The Right has been promoting this basic narrative for half a century. The next chapter measures its power in shaping the American political landscape on which the Left will have to build cross-racial solidarity.

Before that, though, one final question: How do core narratives collapse?

It might have seemed, during the first two years of Trump's

administration, that the Right would have to give up posturing against government. After all, not only did the GOP rule most state governments, on the federal level the Republican Party controlled the presidency and both houses of Congress, as well as the Supreme Court. But a core narrative offers an interpretive frame, not a statement of facts. The story can stand for a long while in the face of clear inconsistencies. This helps explain the constant right-wing carping against "the deep state," as well as Trump's feuds with the FBI and the Department of Justice. These broadsides breathed life into the lie essential to the Right's messaging that government is the greatest threat to the lives of Americans (even when Republicans controlled every branch).

Narratives do not collapse simply because they don't fit reality. The question is less the actual fit than the perception of whether they fit. Core narratives crumble when people *come to believe* that they are false. That, in turn, requires a counternarrative that offers a new way to see what's happening in society, giving some facts increased salience, downplaying others, and shredding falsehoods. Let's figure out the terrain for building that new story.

4

How the Right's Core Narrative Shapes the Political Landscape: Base, Persuadables, and Opposition

I deas about race, class, and government have been intertwined in the United States since the country's founding, and the Right continues to powerfully link them today. To gain a sense of the contemporary political landscape, the race-class project asked a series of survey questions designed to probe people's views on these three elements. Exploring the fundamental Left-Right divide regarding the root cause of economic hardship, we asked, for instance, if poverty stemmed from individual faults or instead resulted from structural factors. Exploring how this applied to people of color, we asked if minorities who cannot get ahead are mostly responsible for their own condition. We also asked whether government has a positive role to play in solving problems or instead should get out of the way.

Close to one in four respondents, 23 percent, gave consistently progressive answers, blaming structures more than personal dysfunction and endorsing government's power to help. These people were slightly more likely than the general population to be women, Democrats, African Americans, and/or Latinxs. Even so, white voters comprised more than half of this cohort. Together these voters form a solid progressive base. Energizing them is the first critical step to coalition building.

Standing opposite the progressive base were committed reactionary voters. They numbered almost one-in-five in the national sample, 18 percent, and adopted reactionary positions down the line, blaming individuals and disparaging government. Overwhelmingly comprised of whites and those who identified as Republican, this group is as terminally red as a stop sign. They will not join a progressive coalition, and shaping progressive messages and policies to win their support is a fool's errand.

Between the base of committed progressives and the opposition of fixed reactionaries live the vast majority of voters in this country. Almost three in five in our national survey, 59 percent, embraced both reactionary positions *and* progressive visions of society. For instance, when we asked whether "talking about race doesn't fix anything and may even make things worse," a supermajority of those in the middle agreed. But when we asked instead if "focusing on and talking about race is necessary to move forward toward greater equality," almost the same number said yes to that, too. Using a different method, the Pew Research Center came to roughly similar conclusions. They found that about seven out of ten voters hold beliefs that mix liberal and conservative commitments.[1] In contrast to the "base" and the "opposition," we called this cohort that could go one way or the other the "persuadables." Encompassing so many Americans, this group roughly tracks the demographics of the country generally; it includes people of color, white working-class voters, Democrats, Republicans, and some Trump supporters.

The next three boxes bring into view the conflicting perspectives held by the base and opposition regarding race, government, and the marketplace. They also illustrate how the persuadables typically hold both sets of beliefs, making this election-determining group susceptible to being pulled in either direction. A fourth box shows that the base-opposition split largely tracks an inclination to vote Democratic or Republican, while the persuadables straddle both parties.

Views Regarding Race

The base is worried about racism against people of color and thinks talking about race is necessary to move forward. The opposition is much more concerned with discrimination against whites, and believes focusing on race may make things worse. Persuadables are willing to agree with both perspectives.

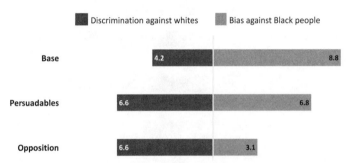

How concerned are you personally about:

■ Discrimination against whites   ■ Bias against Black people

Base   4.2   8.8
Persuadables 6.6   6.8
Opposition   6.6   3.1

Respondents were asked to indicate if they agreed or disagreed on a scale of 0 to 10, where 0 indicates strongly disagree and 10 indicates strongly agree. The numbers in the chart are the mean agreement rating for each statement.

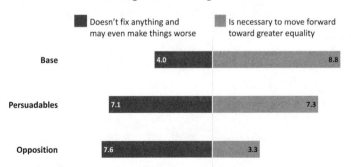

Focusing on and talking about race:

■ Doesn't fix anything and   ■ Is necessary to move forward
may even make things worse   toward greater equality

Base   4.0   8.8
Persuadables 7.1   7.3
Opposition   7.6   3.3

Respondents were asked to indicate if they agreed or disagreed on a scale of 0 to 10, where 0 indicates strongly disagree and 10 indicates strongly agree. The numbers in the chart are the mean agreement rating for each statement.

Views Regarding Government

The base and opposition also split on their views toward government, with the base strongly preferring that "government create opportunities for advancement" while the opposition preferred to see "government get out of your way." Persuadables fell between the base and opposition but closer to the base.

If you had to choose, would you prefer government to:

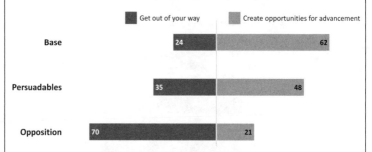

Respondents were asked to choose between the two, and the numbers represent the percentages choosing one response over the other. By cohort, those answering "unsure" were 14 percent among the base, 9 percent among the opposition, and 17 percent among the persuadables.

Views Regarding the Marketplace

The base and opposition also split in their views regarding the marketplace, again with persuadables agreeing with both sides. We asked: "In your opinion which of the following is the primary reason wealthy Americans have achieved financial success?" One choice highlighted circumstances ("Wealthy Americans achieved their success because they were given more opportunities than others"). The other emphasized character ("Wealthy Americans achieved their success because they worked harder than others"). In the progressive base, seven out of ten came down on the circumstances side. Virtually the same number in the opposition did the opposite, emphasizing character. Persuadables gave credence to both views.

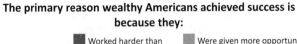

The primary reason wealthy Americans achieved success is because they:

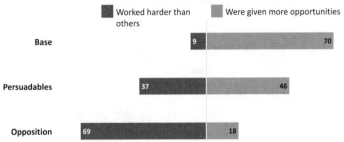

Respondents were asked to choose between the two, and the numbers represent the percentages choosing one response over the other. By cohort, those answering "unsure" were 15 percent among the base, 14 percent among the opposition, and 17 percent among the persuadables.

We also measured respondents' sense of whether the wealthy are greedy bosses or instead create jobs and prosperity for everyone. The base was much more inclined to see the wealthy as greedy bosses versus the opposition which viewed them as job creators. Persuadables largely accepted both propositions: the wealthy are greedy bosses and also job creators.

Do you agree that:

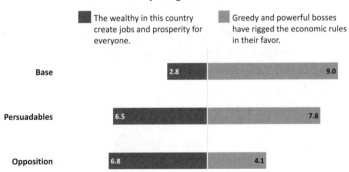

Respondents were asked to indicate if they agreed or disagreed on a scale of 0 to 10, where 0 indicates strongly disagree and 10 indicates strongly agree. The numbers in the chart are the mean agreement rating for each statement.

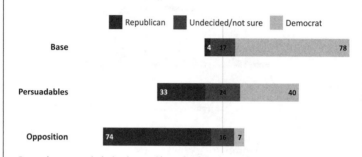

Base, Persuadable, and Opposition by Political Party

Party affiliation roughly tracks the base-opposition split, though in the broad persuadable camp the picture is much more mixed.

■ Republican ■ Undecided/not sure ▨ Democrat

Base 4 17 78

Persuadables 33 24 40

Opposition 74 16 7

Respondents were asked who they would vote for if the election for Congress were held today, the Democratic or Republican candidate in their district, or if they were undecided or unsure. The numbers reflect the percentages choosing the respective options.

Which Group Sits at the Heart of the Opposition?

Stephanie McCrummen is a Pulitzer Prize–winning journalist for the *Washington Post* who hails originally from Birmingham, Alabama. Like many other reporters after Trump's election, she sought to understand who elected him and why. To do so, McCrummen traveled back to her home state, to the small town of Luverne.

"I hate it," said Terry Drew, a congregant in the First Baptist Church. He was explaining to McCrummen the blatant moral compromise of voting for an immoral man like Trump. "My wife and I talk about it all the time. We rationalize the immoral things away. We don't like it, but we look at the alternative, and think it could be worse than this." What would be worse? High on the list was the possibility of a president who supported abortion rights.

Sheila Butler, another church member, also worried about "the annihilation of Christians." "Obama," Sheila said, "he carried a Koran and it was not for literary purposes. If you look at it, the number of Christians is decreasing, the number of Muslims has grown. We allowed them to come in."

"Obama woke a sleeping nation," her friend Linda added. Sheila corrected her: "He woke a sleeping *Christian* nation."

Sheila was certain the Bible's moral commands regarding how to treat others meant how to treat other Americans. Love thy neighbor, she said, meant "love thy American neighbor." Welcome the stranger? That meant the "legal immigrant stranger." "The Bible says, 'If you do this to the least of these, you do it to me,'" Sheila explained, "but the least of these are Americans, not the ones crossing the border." [2]

McCrummen had hit pay dirt.

In 2016, white evangelical Christians comprised one of every five voters in the country. They also came out for Trump by a margin of almost five to one. With their high numbers and impassioned fervor, white evangelicals alone accounted for one-third of all Trump's votes.[3] In other words, if there is a single group that put Trump into the White House, it's white evangelical Christians.

One reactionary evangelist put the point in more biblical terms. "If you back the evangelicals out of the white vote, Donald Trump loses whites," Ralph Reed told the crowd at the Values Voters Summit in 2018. "If the rapture had occurred, Donald Trump would have lost by the worst landslide since George McGovern." [4]

It's worth keeping in mind that 16 percent of white evangelicals voted for Hillary Clinton in 2016.[5] Also, in the first years of the Trump administration some anecdotal evidence emerged that a few white evangelical women might be turning away from the Republican Party.[6] In addition, long-term trends show that white evangelical Christians are declining in numbers and influence decade by decade—though this very decline may also lead to further radicalization.[7] Finally, on an interpersonal level, many are good people. They are not deplorables. Indeed, speaking personally, I'm fortunate to count some white evangelical Christians as wonderful neighbors and friends.

But these facts don't change the basic math. White evangelical Christian voters represent the perfect storm fueling the Right's electoral strategy.

Start with race and gender.

The roots of racial resentment among white evangelical Christians go down past the general racial grievances that trouble many whites. A strong taproot extends back to the fight against school integration. In the 1960s, initially in the South and then spreading across the country, many whites fled public schools to avoid racial integration. When they did, they often retreated to private academies associated with their churches. As these institutions came under criticism, defending segregation morphed into defending Christian schools and then more generally into defending Christianity.[8]

Likewise, the endorsement of patriarchy among white evangelical Christians also has especially deep political roots. In the early 1970s, evangelical churches as well as conservative Catholics led the countermobilization against feminism. To woo these groups, Republicans proclaimed a "pro-family" identity centered on supporting traditional gender roles for women, opposing abortion, and condemning homosexuality. As one critic observes, "For the Republican Party, long seen as the party of big business rather than labor, embracing the pro-family movement's positions enabled it to claim to be the champion of the family without championing programs designed to protect jobs or wages."[9]

In 2015, PRRI asked voters "whether American culture and way of life" had mostly changed for the better or worse since the 1950s. The highest rate of dissatisfaction from any large cohort came from white evangelical Christians. Nearly three out of four, 72 percent, felt that American culture and way of life had mostly changed for the worse.[10] Moreover, it was *white* evangelicals, not their religious brethren of color, who were so pessimistic.[11] Robert Jones, the head of PRRI, commented: "The leaders of the

Christian conservative movement won support by extolling the virtues of an orderly bygone era, where white Protestant Christian beliefs and institutions were unquestionably dominant and there were clearly defined roles for whites and nonwhites, men and women."[12]

To race and gender, add hostility to government regulation of the marketplace.

Princeton historian Kevin M. Kruse in his book, *One Nation Under God: How Corporate America Invented Christian America*, documents the role of big money in infusing Christian identity in the United States with a pro–free market ideology. Most historians trace the power of Christianity in American politics to the Cold War era and national hysteria about a supposed mortal threat from "godless" communism. But decades before the 1950s, Kruse writes, "corporate titans enlisted conservative clergymen in an effort to promote new political arguments embodied in the phrase 'freedom under God.' . . . This new ideology was designed to defeat the state power its architects feared most—not the Soviet regime in Moscow, but Franklin D. Roosevelt's New Deal administration in Washington."[13]

All of this combines to mean that white evangelical Christians are dream voters for the Right: staunch defenders of their right to remain racially segregated, committed to gender hierarchy, opposed to homosexuality, and often led by those Kruse terms "new evangelists for free enterprise."

Mike Podhorzer, the political director for the AFL-CIO, the nation's largest labor federation, has been waving his arms to get the Left to think through the implications of the white evangelical Christian voting bloc. Partly it's the numbers. As Podhorzer notes, "White Evangelicals made up 20 percent of the 2016 electorate, and voted 77 to 16 for Trump. How big is that? By themselves, White Evangelicals canceled the margin that African Americans and Latinx voters provided Clinton."[14]

The more important implications, though, extend to the Left's strategy for building an enduring coalition. Using bold to emphasize his point, Podhorzer asks, **"How much different would the current political debate be if 'White Evangelicals' replaced 'white non-college' to describe Trump's base?"** [15]

If Trump's base is "white non-college," often translated as the white working class, this suggests a sharp need to change course for Democrats. First, this group is huge: white non-college voters made up 44 percent of all voters in 2016. Second, the Democrats lost this group by a devastating margin, 28 percent for Clinton compared to 64 percent for Trump.[16] That sort of margin implies the Democrats are simply out to lunch in terms of the interests and values that matter most to this indispensable group of voters.

But what if Trump's base is white evangelical Christians? Correctly perceiving Trump's base as white evangelical Christians should give the Left more confidence that it understands the concerns of the white working class. The Left is competing far more effectively for this group than most recognize—when one subtracts out evangelical Christians. Podhorzer calculates that without these voters, 42 percent of whites without a college education voted for Clinton, compared to 51 percent for Trump. In other words, the gap among working-class whites goes down from losing by 36 points to losing by a more competitive 9 points.

The power of the white evangelical Christian bloc should also change the debate about the role of white women in supporting Trump and the Right. Many assumed that white women would help Clinton to shatter the ultimate glass ceiling, especially against the boorish Trump. Then the exit polls showed Trump winning among white women by 9 points, a crushing victory that stunned many. As it later turned out, these polls were wrong. More careful study showed the margin for Trump was 2 percent, a virtual tie. Still, all across the Left and especially among feminists, many wanted to know how so many white women could support a Neolithic man. That's the wrong question.

Writing in the *Cook Political Report* and drawing on Podhorzer, Amy Walter observes that here, too, it's evangelical Christians driving the voting pattern. "Among women, if you remove evangelicals, white women with and without a college degree have the same (very low) opinion of the president," Walter writes. Subtracting out evangelical women, Trump's approval among white women without a college degree was a punishingly low 35 percent, and among college-educated white women it was even lower, 30 percent.[17]

Putting white evangelical Christians at the center of the Right's base makes clear that the political advice for Democrats to tack rightward to win more support is highly questionable. In the short to medium term, the Left will not make more than marginal inroads into the white evangelical Christian voting bloc. In contrast, the Left can—and already does—compete effectively among white voters who are not evangelical, including among the white working class and especially with white women.

Understanding Persuadables: Most of Those in the Middle are Not Centrists

Three in five voters are in the convergence zone between the clashing Right and Left weather fronts. Does winning significant support from voters in the middle require that the Left compromise on its boldest aspirations? It's common to argue yes. Very often, politicians and pundits laud "the middle" as a center of moderation, a place where the extremes of the wings are thoughtfully and reasonably balanced. The imagery of Left, Right, and Center certainly feeds into this. There's a strong assumption that the middle is moderate, thoughtful, and, well, centrist.

A report issued in October 2018 by More in Common, a research group operating in Europe as well as the United States, illustrates this tendency. To be sure, their research findings paralleled those in the race-class narrative project. More in Common found that two-thirds of Americans, 67 percent, form a middle that is "considerably more ideologically flexible than members of the other groups." "For instance," the report said, "82 percent of

Americans agree that hate speech is a problem in America today, but 80 percent also view political correctness as an issue." They seemed to find what the race-class project found: conflicting views in a shifting middle that could go either way, in contrast to more consistent commitments among progressives and reactionaries. As the report stated, "members of the 'wing' groups (on both the left and the right) tend to hold strong and consistent views across a range of political issues."[18]

The problem comes in their interpretation of these findings. According to the report, wisdom lies with the middle. People in this range, the report said, share "a willingness to be flexible in their political viewpoints" and also "believe that compromise is necessary in politics, as in other parts of life." They stand in contrast to "partisan tribes" that are "fueled by a culture of outrage and taking offense. For the combatants, the other side can no longer be tolerated, and no price is too high to defeat them."[19]

Flexibility and compromise are desirable attributes. They imply thoughtful consideration of all sides and measured weighing of the issues. There's certainly an argument for deference to sober reflection, careful balancing, and reasoned judgment. But More in Common provides no evidence this is what's actually happening in the middle.

Against this unsupported assumption, a range of sources contradict the image of thoughtful centrism in the middle. Much of the field of social psychology revolves around studying the often minimal triggers that bring to the fore different ways of seeing the world.[20] There's also good evidence the middle is composed not by people who thoughtfully develop "centrist" views so much as by persons who pay relatively little attention to politics. The American National Election Survey routinely asks voters to identify themselves on a scale from liberal to conservative. Studying their responses, the political scientists David Kinder and Nathan Kalmoe show that little separates those who answer the question by selecting "moderate, middle of the road" versus selecting "haven't thought much about it."[21] Likewise, the Right does not appeal to nuanced centrist positions. Republican strategists like Frank Luntz build frames that spark and reinforce the reactionary views circulating in the middle. Or recall Matt on government spending: he invoked welfare recipients ripping off the system, yet also said government should fund education, food, and shelter for everyone. This is not thoughtful moderation. This is contradictory thinking that can be tugged in either direction.

More in Common also errs by dismissing the wings as "polarized," as if the fact of sharp disagreement is by itself disqualifying. But today's polarization is not primarily a defect in temperament among people inclined to take offense or energized by outrage. We *are* a deeply polarized society, precisely because the Left and Right advance profoundly different views on what a good society looks like. One side generally believes everyone deserves dignified treatment, with no distinctions based on race, gender, national origin, religion, or disability. The other generally promotes hierarchies of humans, where some belong in this country and others don't, some worship the correct god and others don't, some conform to the gender roles supposedly commanded by nature and others don't. Similar splits occur in views about whether government should help or get out of the way, whether the marketplace is rigged for the rich or rewards honest labor, whether the environment faces grave dangers or is just fine. At this moment, in this country, right now, we're choosing between very different visions for our future—and just about everything is at stake.

This is not to slight the concerns expressed about extreme partisanship. There are certainly dangerous trends of deepening division and conflict. Moderation, compromise, flexibility, and empathy are more important than ever. But these are qualities of thought and behavior to which all should aspire, not substantive positions exclusively held by those in the center.

The responses uncovered by the race-class project suggest that the Left need not trim its sails and set aside core beliefs to appeal to the "centrists" between the Left and Right. Instead, the results suggest those in the middle already hold progressive views though they hold reactionary ideas as well. This implies that the Left can build a broad, cross-racial movement for activist government by connecting to the genuinely progressive visions of society already circulating in the convergence zone.

People of Color are More Often Persuadable than Members of the Left's Base

It's tempting to view people of color as a natural progressive constituency. But as the race-class research demonstrates, progressive and reactionary ideas cut across racial lines. Recall that when we tested the racial fear message, similar numbers of Latinxs, African Americans, and whites found the Right's dog whistle message convincing.

Compared to whites, people of color more often want government to proactively create opportunities. They resemble the base in this respect. Also, people of color generally view activist racial justice groups positively, again closely resembling the base. In contrast, on economic individualism and the role of the wealthy in the economy, African American and Latinx views shift away from the base and toward a midway point between the base and opposition. In particular, Blacks and browns credit the notion that the wealthy create jobs and prosperity for everyone and that people of color who cannot get ahead are responsible for their own condition.[22]

Versions of this emerged in the race-class focus groups, where people of color often repeated stories quite close to the welfare queen narrative. In one instance, we asked two African American men in Virginia to respond to a remark made by former Republican Speaker of the House Paul Ryan when promoting cuts to social spending: "We don't want to turn the safety net into a hammock that lulls able-bodied people into lives of dependency and complacency, that drains them of their will and their incentive to make the most of their lives."[23]

We wanted to know whether they recognized it as a dog whistle. What do you think about this statement? the moderator asked.

"That is a lot of big words, but yeah, I just feel like it's a great way of saying we don't want people to have to depend on the government," one man said.

The moderator probed, "When you say people, what kind of people?"

"Lower-class people. People who would depend on my government funds and stuff like that, and different programs that the government will offer assistance rather than go out there and work hard for it and get it on your own."

Or listen to an African American woman and her Latinx friend in Cleveland. They've been discussing hard work and paying taxes when the conversation pivots to people abusing welfare.

"You've got people out here that have got five, six, and seven kids and they get Social Security and they get Section Eight and they get utility checks and they get food stamps."

"Well," asked the moderator, "do they fall under the welfare queen label then or no?"

"Yeah, I would say those people will," the woman responded. "When you sit there and you abuse the system, because you go and get your kid and say they are too hyper and they have ADHD and they need pills and now I can go collect Social Security and now I can get Section Eight and now . . ."

She let the sentence trail, but her companion summed up the complaint in a single word: "Welfare."

Despite such views, there's little risk that large numbers of African Americans or Latinxs will start voting Republican. Compared to whites, far fewer people of color stand in the opposition camp. But this does not mean that voters of color can be taken for granted. The GOP is doing virtually everything in its power to drive up the impediments that people of color confront before they can actually vote.[24] Partly because of this, though people of color overwhelmingly tend to vote Democrat, many who are eligible to vote ultimately stay home rather than face the voting gauntlet. As the Pew Research Center reported about the 2016 election, eligible nonvoters "were more likely to be younger, less educated, less affluent, and nonwhite. And nonvoters were much more Democratic."[25] In 2016, those not voting included a majority of Latinxs (52 percent) and a large minority of African Americans (40 percent).[26] Reaching persuadable people of color is key to political engagement and voter turnout.

There's a final reason not to take people of color for granted as part of the base. Dog whistling is a strategy of divide and conquer more than of whites over nonwhites. For politicians, the goal is to win elections, and many politicians are perfectly willing to pit nonwhite groups against one another. During the George W. Bush era, Republican Party leaders like Karl Rove thought that the party's future lay in convincing a large plurality of Latinxs that African Americans threatened them, too. For the moment, Trump has blown up the plans to recruit many more Hispanics into the Republican Party.[27] Those plans will certainly resurface. It's also quite possible for the Right to win votes from African Americans or to depress Black voter turnout by building divisions around national identity, pumping up the idea that the newest waves of immigrants threaten "Americans."[28] Simply being a person of color does not insulate one from strategically crafted dog whistle appeals.

A Caution About the Base: Liberal Whites Remain Susceptible to Racial Fear

In addition to being a majority in the persuadable group, whites comprise a majority of those making up the Left's base. There's genuine good news regarding the racial views among whites voting Democratic, but also sound reason not to count on an unshakable commitment to cross-racial solidarity among liberal whites.

Four in ten whites voted for Hillary Clinton in 2016, and among these voters there are encouraging trends in their racial attitudes, according to researcher Sean McElwee. For instance, in 1994, two years into the Clinton administration, two-thirds of white Democrats favored reducing immigration. By the end of Obama's presidency, less than one-third took that position.[29] And on the question of whether the country needs to continue making changes to give Blacks equal rights, among Democrats the spread between white and Black views shrunk by two-thirds during the Obama administration, closing to 10 points.[30] It's still true that Black Democrats overall are more racially progressive than their white counterparts. But as white liberals shift leftward in their racial views, these groups increasingly agree on racial issues.[31]

Nevertheless, the progressive racial commitments of many liberal whites remain shaky. In 2013, PRRI used telephone interviews to ask whites whether they agreed or disagreed with this statement: "The idea of an America where most people are not white bothers me." More white Republicans (18 percent) than white Democrats (11 percent) directly said they agreed.[32] But PRRI suspected that people might hesitate to plainly admit racial discomfort in a phone conversation with a stranger. To overcome this, PRRI employed a separate survey technique that allowed people to *indirectly* express their views. Measured this way, the proportion of white Democrats registering racial discomfort tripled to levels slightly higher than among Republicans (33 percent to 30 percent). White Democrats may have hesitated to admit being bothered by an America where most people are not white, but in fact seemed slightly more agitated about this than white Republicans.

PRRI's question about "an America where most people are not white" is hardly hypothetical. This is already a reality in many cities, regions, and states. Social psychologists Jennifer Richeson and Maureen Craig sought to measure the likely effect of this demographic shift by testing how whites react to census data.

Richeson and Craig found that when whites were presented with news stories about census projections, they expressed a greater preference for being with other whites, exhibited higher levels of pro-white bias, and demonstrated greater prejudice toward non-whites.[33] They also found that whites became more reactionary on racial policies, such as their views on immigration and affirmative action, as well as regarding nonracial issues, for instance military spending.[34] "Making the shifting U.S. racial demographics salient," they concluded, "leads whites to perceive greater threat to their racial group's status, which motivates them to increase their support for a variety of conservative positions."[35]

Craig and Richeson were careful to interview "self-identified politically independent white respondents." In other words, Richeson would later explain, "The point is that people who think of themselves as not prejudiced (and liberal) demonstrate these threat effects."[36]

Why did whites shift rightward when thinking about demographic change? In one of their experiments, Craig and Richeson showed whites a mock news article about changing racial demographics, but they also varied the test, with a second version reassuring whites that they would remain economically dominant. In this second version, they added a sentence indicating that "White Americans are expected to continue to have higher average incomes and wealth compared to other groups." When reassured of their continued economic preeminence, whites no longer shifted rightward. "And that's how you know it's status threat," Richeson explains. It's not the changing numbers that push whites rightward, but a fear they will lose their position at the top of the racial pile.[37]

Additionally worrisome, it took remarkably little to induce these negative effects. Even a slight prod could push liberal whites toward racially tinged political conservatism. Ryan Enos, a professor of government at Harvard, speculated that subtle intrusions on people's racial awareness could generate significant shifts in their views. To test this, he sent Spanish speakers to commuter rail stations in some of the predominantly white towns around Boston. The testers were instructed to merely ride the train like any other passengers. Separately, before and after sending the

Racial Groups by Base, Persuadables, and Opposition

African American

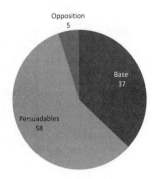

Latinx

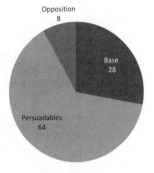

White

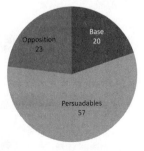

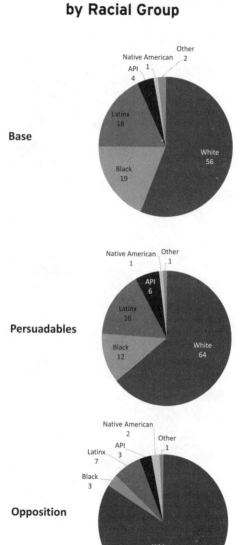

Base, Persuadables, and Opposition by Racial Group

testers, Enos surveyed passengers about their attitudes toward immigration. "After being exposed to the Spanish speakers on their metro lines for just three days," he found, "attitudes on these questions moved sharply rightward." Enos concluded, "The mostly liberal Democratic passengers had come to endorse immigration policies—including deportation of children of undocumented immigrants—similar to those endorsed by Trump in his campaign."[38]

These findings extend to younger whites as well. In the PRRI study on the number of whites who were "bothered" by the prospect of a minority-white country, whites aged 18–49 reported the lowest levels of concern when asked their views directly. But when they could express their discomfort indirectly, the difference between whites younger and older than fifty evaporated.[39] Likewise, Richeson and Craig also found similar effects without regard to the age of the respondents. "When it comes to our interpersonal biases," Richeson says, "it's simply not true that we just need to wait for the few old racist men left in the South to die off and then we'll be fine. The rhetoric for racism is still in place. The environment for racism is still there."[40]

The Left's task is to build a multiracial coalition to elect leaders who will promote racial justice and economic fairness. It's a mistake to translate this into a simple formula that calls for winning back the white working class, or appealing to supposed centrists in the middle, or depending on people of color as a natural base or on liberal whites as firm racial allies. The challenge instead is to encourage persuadables to align with an energized and unified progressive base. Broad popular support for rejecting racism and building solidarity will come from shared ideas and values.

So how can the Left build cross-racial solidarity? One strategy is to center racial justice.

5

Should the Left Lead with Racial Justice?

When Hillary Clinton ran for president in 2016, the dog whistling employed by her husband in the 1990s came back to bite her. On the campaign trail for his wife, Bill Clinton encountered a decidedly mixed reaction from the African American community. Older generations, particularly in the South, continued to feel warmly toward the white man whom some used to jokingly call the first Black president. But especially among younger African Americans in the country's cities and suburbs who came of age amid the fallout of Bill Clinton's tough-on-crime agenda, his contributions to mass incarceration damned him. He had expressed regret—for instance in 2015, when he admitted that the crime bills he promoted "overshot the mark." Nevertheless, Clinton still defended those policies, and his faint regrets mainly served to further antagonize his most vociferous critics.[1]

But it wasn't just transferred hostility that tarnished Hillary Clinton's progressive credentials. She had herself actively participated in 1990s dog whistling, and she paid a price.

Michelle Alexander, whose book *The New Jim Crow* helped generate waves of activism against mass incarceration, directly indicted Hillary Clinton. Alexander published a forceful essay in *The Nation* in February 2016, bluntly entitled "Why Hillary Clinton Doesn't Deserve the Black Vote." The short answer: "From the crime bill to welfare reform, policies Bill Clinton enacted—and Hillary Clinton supported—decimated black America."[2] Alexander was unsparing in her criticism, writing that "[Bill] Clinton was the standard-bearer for the New Democrats, a group that firmly believed the only way to win back the millions of white voters in the South who had defected to the Republican Party was to adopt the right-wing narrative that black communities ought to be disciplined with harsh punishment rather than coddled with welfare."

Hillary also deserved blame, Alexander argued, because "she not only campaigned for Bill; she also wielded power and significant influence once he was elected, lobbying for legislation and other measures." In particular, Alexander criticized Clinton for selling criminal measures by casting Black children as ferocious animals. "They are not just gangs of kids anymore," Alexander quoted Clinton as saying. "They are often the kinds of kids that are called 'super-predators.' No conscience, no empathy. We can talk about why they ended up that way, but first we have to bring them to heel."

This was a devastating quote, crystallizing in a manner no numbers or policy discussions could match precisely how the Clintons played to white racial fears by dehumanizing Blacks. It should not have been that much of a surprise, then, that two weeks after Alexander's essay appeared, a Black Lives Matter activist crashed a private Clinton fundraiser, unfurling a banner that read "We have to bring them to heel," and challenging Clinton to apologize for mass incarceration.

"You called people super-predators," said twenty-three-year-old Ashley Williams, resisting pressure to stay silent from the donors gathered at the intimate house party.

"Explain it to us," Williams persisted. "You owe Black people an apology."

In her response, Clinton conveyed more than anything else annoyance at the interruption. She tried to stick with her prepared remarks, though Williams would not relent. Clinton finally gave up and addressed Williams directly, with a response that was both empty and patronizing: "You know what? Nobody's ever asked me before. You're the first person to do that, and I'm happy to address it, but you are the first person to ask me, dear."

Then, as security removed Williams, Clinton said "Okay, back to the issues." Those issues seemingly did not include her role in 1990s dog whistling.[3]

If Hillary Clinton was evasive, at least she was relatively restrained. Not so Bill, when two months later Black Lives Matter activists held up signs at a Philadelphia rally to challenge him about Hillary's support for mass incarceration. Bill doubled down.

"I don't know how you would characterize the gang leaders who got thirteen-year-old kids hopped up on crack and sent them out on the street to *murder* other African-American children," Clinton said, wagging his finger at the protesters. "Maybe *you* thought they were good citizens. She didn't. She didn't. You are defending the people who killed the lives you say matter," he exclaimed. "Tell the truth. You are defending the people who caused young people to go out and take guns."[4]

Hillary Clinton seemed unprepared to answer for dog whistling's harms to Black communities. Apparently no one on her staff had communicated to her the core of Alexander's indictments, though she was one of the most well-known Black activist-intellectuals in the country, or at a minimum had reminded Clinton that she was on record equating Black children with vicious dogs.

Clinton was not the only presidential candidate confronted by racial justice activists. In addition to steady protests at Trump rallies, activists pushed virtually every Democratic candidate to speak to mass incarceration and other forms of systemic violence against Black and brown communities. Bernie Sanders faced these calls to account, and like Clinton stumbled. As Sanders rose to speak at the summer 2015 convening of Netroots Nation, a huge progressive conference, Black Lives Matter protesters seized the mic to talk about the jailhouse death of Sandra Bland, who was arrested after a minor traffic stop in Texas and later found hanged in her jail cell. The activists challenged Sanders to say concretely what he would do to address law enforcement violence. But Sanders "was defensive and cranky toward the protesters," reporters noted, answering back, "Black lives of course matter. But I've spent fifty years of my life fighting for civil rights. If you don't want me to be here, that's okay."[5]

Activists were also confronting Democratic leaders around immigration. In the fall of 2017, for example, protesters swarmed a press conference by then–House minority leader Nancy Pelosi, shouting her down with accusations that she was bargaining with Trump to increase deportations. Pelosi seemed stunned, since she was hoping to trade increased deportations for legislation protecting young people brought to the country without documents—the so-called Dreamers, a group that included some of the protesters. The activists, however, rejected the notion that their protection should be gained by sacrificing others, often family members. "You met with Trump and you call that resistance?" they chanted. "This is what resistance looks like!"[6]

The fire and fury on the anti-racist Left presents a direct challenge to politics as usual for liberals. Even strong racial reform proposals seem unlikely to assuage the demands of activists chanting "united we dream" and "Black lives matter." Clinton and Sanders offered some of the most progressive reform proposals of any Democrat in decades, and yet found themselves under fierce protest. More than policy ideas, the activists demanded a genuine commitment to racial change. Clinton struggled to convey steadfast concern, seeming not even to realize the human costs of her prior offenses, or perhaps not willing to acknowledge—in the midst of the most important political campaign of her life—the cynicism and social destructiveness of her past politicking. Sanders repeatedly rejected placing racial justice on par with economic justice, insisting that repairing the economy should be everyone's first priority. For however strong their policy prescriptions, many activists remained unconvinced of the Democratic leaders' actual dedication to racial justice.

It's hard to imagine Democrats on the national level returning to Bill Clinton's style of dog whistling without sparking a full revolt among racial justice activists. Moreover, this is not just a matter of a few activists; they shape the views of the much larger progressive base. "The progressivism of the base is being driven by the rise of mobilized racial justice groups like Black Lives Matter and the 'Dreamers,'" Sean McElwee reports. "Many young voters have warmer feelings toward movements like Black Lives Matter than towards established Democratic politicians."[7]

This emerging radicalism among young people likely contributed to voting dynamics in 2016. Among the Black voters who stayed home, it was overwhelmingly those aged 18–29, about half of registered Black voters in this age group, who ultimately decided not to vote.[8] Or if they didn't stay home, a pivotal chunk put the pox on Democrats by casting votes for third-party candidates. Cornell Belcher is a prominent Democratic pollster associated with Obama's campaigns, who also worked on our race-class research. As Belcher pointed out, "when you have between 6 to 9 percent of younger voters of color breaking 3rd Party in their 'protest vote,' that kills the Democrat's chance to reach Obama's margins, most notably in places like Florida, Michigan and Wisconsin."[9]

No Democratic resurgence is possible based on a game plan that expects racial justice movements to set aside their core concerns. Or, as Michelle Alexander put it, "If progressives think they can win in the long run without engaging with Black folks and taking history more seriously, they better get Elon Musk on speed dial and start planning their future home on Mars, because this planet will be going up in smoke."[10]

The question, then, is *how* the Left should engage Black folks and other people of color.

Activists currently put pressure on Democratic candidates to make helping communities of color a central commitment. There's a newly powerful demand that Democrats stop pretending their cell phone batteries have died when it comes to answering calls for racial justice.

But as an electoral strategy, leading with racial justice is clearly risky. The Right constantly warns that liberal government and the Democratic Party care more about people of color than about whites. Coming out strongly in favor of racial justice—endorsing reparations, or calling for sweeping reforms to policing, or for abolishing Immigration and Customs Enforcement—provides the Right handy ammunition. Should the Left do so anyway?

This chapter considers the "racial justice" approach advocated by many activists focused foremost on helping communities of color. To be clear, there's no argument here that the Left should abandon communities of color to win over whites. The next chapter examines the limits of colorblind economic populism. The point there is not to give up on progressive economic policies, but to explain why focusing on economic populism at the expense of talking about racial justice ensures that neither can be achieved. Likewise, here the argument is not that progressives should jettison efforts to promote racial justice. The argument is that the current way of explaining racial justice as a goal makes it harder to get there, at least in the context of electoral politics.

Talking to Whites About Racial Justice

It's conventional wisdom among many Democratic strategists that talking about racism against communities of color fails with white voters. Unfortunately, this is correct. The race-class narrative project explored in the focus groups how to talk to voters about racism. The reactions quickly confirmed that liberals rightly conclude that they should avoid talking about racial justice in ways that implicitly center white-against-nonwhite discrimination.

The most positive response the project elicited from a participant in a white focus group was indifference. In Atlanta, one woman seemed to speak for the other eight around the oval Formica table when she said: "We're all white. Race doesn't affect us day to day and so most of us don't have to worry about that." She knew racism mattered. She had been relaxed, reclining in her chair, but to broach this subject, she leaned forward earnestly: "I think it's important to remember that that's an issue that some people have to deal with every second of every day, they always have to keep race in mind," she said. But still, it did not matter much for people like them. "I think for white people, it's probably not going to be the thing that's keeping you up at night," she concluded.

Other reactions confirmed that whites tend to filter narratives about racism against people of color by asking what this means for them as white people. Another woman in the Atlanta group responded candidly that fixing racism isn't good for whites because that might limit their opportunities. "When we talk about diversity and race and how to minimize the difference between the whites and blacks . . . for example in college admissions . . . that case can hurt white people, because they will not be chosen to be admitted to college for the diversity reasons."

Other whites responded defensively to discussions of racism. In some focus groups, whites seemed to translate the conversation about how racism harms people of color into a perceived indictment of white people. Pushing back against this, a white man in an Ohio focus group—not the group with Matt and Tom—cast about for ways to spread the blame. He implied that many racial groups have participated in slavery and genocide. "Everybody equates all the slavery to the white man," he said. Then, apparently referring to practices of slavery in the history of African nations, he added: "Whereas when we go over there, yes, they were doing the exact same thing." He also extended allegations of barbarism to Native Americans, in the process recasting domination by whites as benevolence. "We try to give a lot of land back to the Native Americans," he said, "whereas the Native American tribes were warring tribes against each other and would enslave, rape, and pillage each other as well."

Visceral rejection was common when the topic of racism was on the table. "I hate the entire thing because it's fearmongering, is what it's doing," said another participant in the Ohio focus group of white men. Another, who might describe himself as colorblind, responded that the topic of racial discrimination "bothers me." He explained: "When you keep talking about racism . . . I don't really think that's it, it feels like one of those fake dividing lines they're throwing out for us to chew on. It's like 'it's all about skin color.' It's not, it's really not."

We varied our messages to explore different approaches. In one version, we encouraged whites to recognize that some of them belong to groups that were themselves prior victims of anti-immigrant racism. Immigration activists sometimes offer stories along these lines, hoping to show today's whites that their own ancestors faced discrimination decades ago when they were the unpopular immigrants of the time.

Again, however, many whites reacted negatively, repeating in particular the charge that naming racism was divisive and possibly racist itself. The race-class project asked people their thoughts on this statement: "Italians were once slurred as without papers, an insult familiar to Latinos today. The Irish were accused of gaming the system, a charge still made against black people. Asian Americans are seen as foreigners in their home."

"That just goes against my grain," said one participant in a focus group of white men and women in California's rural Central Valley. "In New York when they came off the ships, it was so divided and they were very racist against each other. I don't think everybody was but it was a very divided country back then . . . and I don't like that division." He seemed willing to concede there had been racism in the past. But making any comparison to the present seemed to strike him as offensive.

Speaking next, another man clarified what was bothering many of them: "I agree with a lot of what [he] said. It just reeks racism all throughout this statement."

The moderator followed up, "What do you mean it has racism?"

"Well, the racial references to various people here," he explained. "Italians without papers. Latinos. Derogatory terms. That's the way it was. I think it's just referring to how it was. That's the reality but that's what's frustrating. And it's trying to redirect it into current times. . . . I'm not saying racism isn't there but it's not as prevalent, at least publicly prevalent."

Lurking in their remarks was the sense that talking about racism, even racism in the distant past, is itself racist and divisive.

This resistance to history will likely come as a big surprise to many in the advocacy community. In laying the groundwork for messaging around race and class, Anat Shenker-Osorio interviewed several dozen union leaders, policy advocates, progressive storytellers, and racial justice organizers. Many favored educating the public about the past. "Our most compelling argument is that history unremediated has consequences," said one. Another added, "if we're really speaking about a society that deals with the historical and the current legacy of racism, you have to have an education program." (It's not possible to credit these speakers by name because they were promised anonymity, which was important so they could speak freely rather than feel pressure to repeat their organization's talking points.) I had started from this perspective, too. Recall that my initial approach with the unions involved day-long history lessons.

The focus groups revealed that people were uninterested in talking about past injustices. Celinda Lake was not surprised, as she had seen this resistance to history before. Based on her polling experience, Lake observed that Americans prefer to look forward rather than back. With racism in particular, though, yet another dynamic became apparent. The disinterest in history among whites when it came to racial issues seemed a form of self-defense.

In the various focus groups we conducted, we often asked about Jim Crow segregation—the separate and inferior schools, bans on interracial marriage, and other laws that for decades humiliated and oppressed African Americans. We hoped to gauge people's comfort in thinking about racism as structural, rather than simply in terms of individuals mistreating others. In a striking moment, one of the Ohio white men we interviewed in a large focus group claimed that "Jim Crow wasn't real." The flat denial seemed like a sudden flare of fringe internet propaganda, until it became clear no one in the group would contest this claim. Instead, one fellow responded: "I mean I have never researched it because I don't want to know about it to be honest." This admission says volumes about how numerous whites respond when confronted with injustices perceived as only affecting communities of color—"I don't want to know."

People of Color Are Not Happy to Talk About Racism, Either

We had anticipated that talking about racism would prove challenging for whites, and it was. More startling, even people of color did not want to hear about it.

In this, they differed dramatically from many in the advocacy community. Not only did activists want to talk about history, they were also comfortable and insightful when talking about "racism." Indeed—this will become important later—many advocates already understood racism could be a class weapon, as in this comment: "Race is a way of categorizing human beings that was invented a couple of centuries ago to create a hierarchy of human value for political and economic and social goals." Moreover, advocates readily singled out whites as the racially favored social group, with explanations like this: "Racism is the ways in which some groups of people, especially white folk—well, not especially, *specifically* folks who read as white—have set up systems of power vis-à-vis people who don't appear white, or are not coded as white."

This direct and sophisticated discussion of racism was almost entirely missing from the focus group conversations, even among people of color. In fact, people of color in our focus groups tended to resist all express discussions of white-over-nonwhite racism.

We presumed the statement comparing discrimination today to racism against European groups decades ago might resonate with Asian Americans and Latinxs. But a person in the Asian American focus group in Los Angeles said it felt like a way to build connections among "ethnic people" at the expense of white people, "almost like reverse racism." A member of the Latinx focus group in Los Angeles said the comparison was "very judgmental in regards to race. It's describing Asian Americans and then Italians and Latinos and Black people." The moderator pressed for clarification about what specifically bothered her. "I guess just like the Italians were once here without papers. That's kind of racial, like why would you say something like that. It's offensive. . . . As much as we don't want to point at certain classifications of people, that's all this thing is doing, whether it be past or present it's just a tag." She sounded a lot like the white guys in the Ohio focus group who felt that directly talking about racism was almost racist itself.

Among African Americans, we experimented with different approaches and encountered a range of responses. When we tried presenting racism as a structural issue, participants often balked. Asked if "certain power structures" limit African Americans, one woman in Columbus, Ohio, disagreed, putting the responsibility on Black people instead, "because I think that passivity has a lot to do with why we may not get ahead," she said. "I think that is what we tell ourselves, that it's not possible. Sometimes we don't always have the courage to push past certain things. . . . We've been shown that anything is possible, but I believe we tell ourselves that we can't."

Rather than accept racism as a structural impediment to advancement, this speaker seemed to invoke the personal responsibility frame promoted by the Right. This perspective rests on a view of racism as nothing more than rare instances of interpersonal bigotry, and therefore as an illegitimate excuse for economic hardship in communities of color. Such views are in wide circulation. Recall, for instance, Tom describing talk among African Americans of slavery and its legacy as "a horrible crutch to not trying, not working, not fixing yourself."

Unfortunately, similar stories downplaying structural racism and portraying poverty in African American communities as a matter of individual fault are also sometimes promoted by the Black leadership class.[11] In her deeply affecting memoir, Patrisse Khan-Cullors, one of the cofounders of Black Lives Matters, describes living this: "We lived a precarious life on the tightrope of poverty bordered at each end with the politics of personal responsibility that Black pastors and then the first Black president preached—they preached that more than they preached a commitment to collective responsibility. . . . They preached that more than they preached about America having 5 percent of the world's population but 25 percent of its prison population, a population which for a long time included my disabled brother and my gentle father."[12]

Here's another dynamic the race-class project encountered. We found that when we talked about racism as a problem for Black communities, many in the African American focus groups conveyed skepticism about whether anything would change. As someone in the Columbus session said: "You can have rallies and, you know, just do anything to try to make a change for the better, and whoever the powers may be, they're going to do what they want to do, what they're compelled to do anyway. We can demand, strike, boycott, whatever it is, but whatever the answer is at the end of the day that's what it's going to be. That's just my opinion. I think they just don't listen at all. We do a lot of walking and going down to the city council and all that but they don't hear nothing."

Others in the group nodded in agreement, with one adding, "Everybody that tries to stand up for something, for change, they die. Somebody gotta die. They go and stand up and—Martin Luther King, even presidents, John F. Kennedy—people who try to stand up for something they got killed, people scared."

If political change was not possible, that seemed to give greater weight to the personal responsibility frame. From the same Columbus group, another individual said: "We chose Obama, but guess what happened? More people started getting killed. More police started killing more Black people. . . . So it ain't about the leaders, it's about you yourself."

If people were skeptical of change, they were also cynical about our effort to talk to them about racism, suspecting that Black people had been singled out for a conversation that amounted to a form of pandering. At the end of one Black focus group in Atlanta, a participant expressed that very directly: "I feel like this is the Black script. I don't know how many groups you all have typically in here, but this feels like 'This is the Black group, so let's give them the Black script.' 'This is the Indian group.' And then the white group."

The Racial Justice Narrative

The pushback against a racial justice narrative was so strong in the focus groups that when we crafted and tested messages in a national survey, we omitted that frame. When we later ran surveys in California and Indiana, we returned to and tested a message built around fighting racism against people of color. As with the other messages, the race-class project built the racial justice narrative from language and arguments in common use by advocacy groups.

Why call this the "racial justice message"? It's the term that most activists use to describe their narrative, their policy proposals, and

Racial Justice

America is meant to be a nation founded on an ideal—that all are created equal. But from our founding, America has denied this promise to people of color and refuses to honor it still today. We see this in how police profile, imprison, and kill Black people. It's the reason why families of color struggle with lower wages and virtually no inherited wealth. And it's present in how we exploit immigrants' labor while denying immigrants' rights. To make good on our belief in liberty and justice for all, we must transform our criminal justice system, immigration policies, and economy to dismantle the barriers to well-being and opportunity for people of color in America.

their ultimate aim. To reiterate, the race-class project does not urge turning away from racial justice policies or racial justice as a foundational goal. The debate centers on the power of the different narratives to generate broad support for fundamental change.

Notice how the racial justice frame presents racism as something that harms people of color and implicitly something done by white society. This white-versus-nonwhite framing typifies how most progressives think about racism—understandably so, because white racial supremacy is a defining feature of racism's history in the United States. In short, this message says the route forward is to challenge white society's racism and to focus on helping communities of color. It centers structural racism as the problem and people of color as the solution's intended beneficiaries.

How did people we surveyed respond? The base was comfortable with this message, although they didn't love it. In both California and Indiana, the base thought more than half of the nine alternative race-class narratives we tested were more convincing. On the other hand, they did find the racial justice message more convincing than the narrative promoting colorblind economic populism. They were also much more positive toward it than to the dog whistle racial fear message. In short, if the goal is to win over the base, Democrats could go with either a race-class message or with a racial justice message. But this was among the base. What about among persuadables?

Even in a progressive state like California, the persuadable middle found the racial justice frame slightly *less* convincing than the opposition racial fear message, and significantly less convincing than colorblind economic populism and all nine of the race-class messages. In the more hard-fought swing state of Indiana, persuadables found the racial justice message the least convincing by a wide margin. Indeed, although persuadables tend to agree with most positions, in Indiana the rating for the racial justice frame stayed below the basic "convincing" threshold. In short, the research suggested that the racial justice message loses persuadables, potentially by a lot.

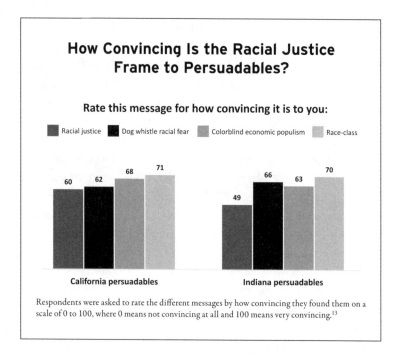

How Convincing Is the Racial Justice Frame to Persuadables?

Rate this message for how convincing it is to you:

■ Racial justice ■ Dog whistle racial fear ▨ Colorblind economic populism ▨ Race-class

California persuadables: 60, 62, 68, 71
Indiana persuadables: 49, 66, 63, 70

Respondents were asked to rate the different messages by how convincing they found them on a scale of 0 to 100, where 0 means not convincing at all and 100 means very convincing.[13]

Understanding Clinton's "Stronger Together" Campaign Through the Racial Justice Frame

It may seem surprising, given the protests against her by racial justice activists, but Hillary Clinton modeled her 2016 campaign around racial justice. In turn, the reactions to the racial justice frame encountered in the race-class research may shed some light on how voters responded.

To see that Clinton ran a racial justice campaign requires seeing how far Clinton traveled not just from the 1990s but from her campaign for the Democratic presidential nomination in 2008. In her match-up that year against Barack Obama, Clinton seemed to prioritize winning white voters. For instance, Clinton claimed during the 2008 primaries that support among whites made her a stronger presidential contender: "I have a much broader base to build a winning coalition on," she explained in an interview, citing a poll that she said "found how Sen. Obama's support among working, hard-working Americans, white Americans, is weakening again, and how whites in both [Indiana and North Carolina] who had not completed college were supporting me." [14] Clinton's equation of "hard-working Americans" with "white Americans" struck many as a form of dog whistling. [15] Perhaps it was. Or maybe this linkage was merely an unconscious slip, one that revealed the cultural power of the stereotypes contrasting supposedly hard-working whites and lazy Blacks. What was no mistake was Clinton's observation that race gave her an edge. Pushed by reporters on whether her remarks were racially divisive, Clinton insisted that "these are the people you have to win, if you're a Democrat, in sufficient numbers to actually win the election. Everybody knows that." [16]

Obama's triumph that year made it clear that "everybody" was wrong, and eight years later, Clinton embraced a different approach. Obama's election and reelection hardly offered a clear lesson. Obama's 2008 victory came against the backdrop of economic calamity, conditions under which voters routinely turn out the incumbent party. In a possible warning sign, Obama won his second term with fewer votes than his initial victory, a rarity, and white voters in particular shifted away from Democrats during Obama's presidency. Still, Clinton's view of how to assemble a winning electoral coalition evolved markedly.

In 2016, Hillary Clinton did *not* seek white voters at the expense of people of color. She apparently assumed she would get as many white votes as did Obama. Instead, anticipating some decline in support from African Americans after the excitement of voting for a Black president, Clinton formulated an electoral strategy predicated on energizing voters of color as well as women and millennials—the so-called New American Electorate.

Clinton kicked off her campaign with policy speeches proposing progressive reforms in the areas of mass incarceration, mass deportation, and voting rights. Many of her proposals went beyond positions taken by Obama, who feared creating the impression he especially cared about communities of color. In other words, Clinton proffered the most reformist racial justice policies a Democratic candidate for president had put on the table in decades. She might not have been the most credible messenger for racial justice, given her connections to Bill Clinton's racial pandering to white voters. Still, she used the racial justice frame to talk to the American electorate.

In her Democratic convention speech, for instance, Clinton promoted the campaign message that we were "stronger together." To be sure, she referenced groups that typically code as white, for instance the working class and law enforcement. But Clinton seemed to stress the need for more marginal groups to come together. "Let's put ourselves in the shoes of young Black and Latino men and women who face the effects of systemic racism, and are made to feel like their lives are disposable," she said. Point by point, to raucous cheers and applause from the activist base who made up the crowd, she listed additional groups needing protection: We must defend "civil rights . . . human rights and voting rights . . . women's rights and workers' rights . . . LGBT rights and the rights of people with disabilities!" The speech and the campaign covered much more ground than this; the passages highlighted here are far from the sum total of what Clinton promised at the convention or as a candidate on issues as varied as Wall Street, the environment, women's rights, and even the relevance of her own biography. Nevertheless, it seems fair to say Clinton sought to assemble a majority of minorities.

Moreover, within this coalition, Clinton gave pride of place to voters of color. It might seem she compiled an inclusive list of aggrieved groups, with no priority among them. But racial justice was foremost in the issues she stressed. Clinton did so because her campaign understood that the "New American Electorate" offered a coded way of talking about people of color as the cutting edge of Democratic politics. The phrase includes women and millennials, but those larger demographic groups are progressive primarily because of the number and influence of people of color within those broad cohorts. "Stronger together" may have called for people to protect a raft of marginalized social groups, but Clinton put a special emphasis on fighting systemic racism, mass incarceration, mass deportation, minority voter disenfranchisement, and, last but not least, the racism coming from the Trump camp.

Clinton won the popular vote but lost the race for the White House. Too many dynamics were at play to identify a predominant explanation for her loss. Still, without relitigating Clinton's campaign, the race-class research offers some insights into the impact her racial justice narrative might have had on voters.

If the progressive base responded to Clinton's racial justice frame as they did to the version we tested, they found Clinton's focus on remedying structural racism compelling. The cheers in the convention hall were real. The progressive base genuinely supports helping communities of color by redressing institutional racism.

But the response of the persuadables on the survey, and even more so the reactions in the focus groups, suggest that Clinton's racial frame ruffled many. The focus groups predict there would have been a range of negative responses among whites—from indifference to defensiveness to visceral anger at a perceived personal attack. In other words, in seeking to build a progressive movement by leading with racial justice, Clinton should have anticipated real challenges in generating enthusiasm among white voters. *Protecting the rights of everyone* was her intended theme. But to whites watching Facebook snippets of Clinton's convention speech, that may have been supplemented with *everyone but me*.

And regarding voters of color, the intensity of our focus group responses suggest Clinton should have anticipated skepticism and cynicism. Why should they believe structural racism was really going to ease? How could they be sure Clinton wasn't drawing on her own "Black script" just to win their votes? As it happened, many voters of color stayed home.[17] Clinton may have said we're stronger together, but large numbers of nonwhite voters seemed unmoved. No doubt many factors contributed. But it's likely that the racial justice frame designed to reach communities of color in fact fell flat with large segments of its intended audience.

Clinton's 2016 campaign seemingly confirms the conventional wisdom that telling a political story that implicitly condemns racism against people of color alienates many white voters. The race-class research suggests it also struggles to carry communities of color and loses the very valuable persuadable middle. But what follows from this? Two very different lessons are on the table:

1) Stop talking about racism entirely.

2) Talk about racism differently.

After 2016, most Democratic strategists defaulted back to lesson one, a race-silent approach that the party has been stuck on for decades. We turn to that option next.

6

Can Democrats Build a Supermajority While Staying Silent About Racism?

"Here's some free advice for all the liberals insisting that Trump was elected by racists," offered right-wing commentator Jonah Goldberg one week after the election: "The more you say that, the more you help Trump."[1]

Steve Bannon, the white nationalist provocateur who ran Trump's campaign and followed him into the White House, agreed. In August 2017, Trump provoked outrage for stating that the white-power riots in Charlottesville involved "very fine people" on both sides. Rather than urge retreat, Bannon cheered Trump's stance. Then Bannon egged on liberals, urging them "to talk about racism every day." Bannon boasted about the likely impact of that: "If the left is focused on race and identity, and we go with economic nationalism, we can crush the Democrats," he said.[2] "Our thing is to throw gasoline on the resistance," Bannon would later tell *Vanity Fair*. "I love it. When they talk about identity politics, they're playing into our hands."[3]

The evidence that Trump's primary strategy involved racial scapegoating was so overwhelming, it's unlikely that Democratic strategists listening to Bannon would have believed that Trump's secret sauce was economic populism rather than racial nationalism. Even Russia presumed that stirring racism was the key, launching their electronic troll armies to instigate racial anger that would seed division.

Still stinging from their electoral loss, however, the Democratic leadership seemed largely willing to agree with the thrust of Bannon's taunt—that talking about identity issues would be a disaster for them. This was the seeming trap that gave Bannon so much glee. He prodded Democrats to scream about identity issues, knowing that would push more whites toward Republicans. But he also realized that Democrats would suffer if they did *not* address the Right's racial attacks. Staying silent would communicate indifference to the concerns of many voters committed to racial justice. Plus, Democrats would then be letting Bannon and Trump command the fight for persuadable voters whose identity concerns could be triggered by racial scaremongering.

To the Democratic strategists, Bannon and Trump seemed to be playing chess, jumping all over the board, making identity appeals while also pretending to promote economic populism. Meanwhile, they saw themselves stuck playing checkers, able to make only one move at a time. What would it be: race-silent economic policies or addressing Trump's race-baiting?

Even before Bannon's Charlottesville taunting, the party's leadership had made their decision. Early in the summer of 2017, the Democrats rolled out a "strong, bold" agenda. Trump's campaign had promised more jobs and increased infrastructure spending, better and more affordable healthcare, a war against Wall Street's influence, and a commitment to "drain the swamp" in Washington, DC. But once in power, Trump treated these promises like tissue paper. The Democratic leadership maneuvered to commandeer his pocketbook themes. Self-consciously building on their New Deal glory years, their new catchphrase was "A Better Deal."[4]

Social media quickly and uncharitably pointed out that this slogan had already been claimed by the national fast-food pizza chain Papa John's. More damning, the Democrat's new worker-friendly policies seemed not strong and bold but merely stale and warmed over. They proposed job training programs, funded by tax credits paid to employers. That would certainly put money into business pockets; the benefits for workers were more speculative. Efforts to stop Big pharma from price gouging were also featured in the rollout, but no mention was made of the progressive holy grail: single-payer healthcare. And a rediscovered commitment to stop mergers and to roll back monopolies seemed promising, but there were questions about how seriously to treat these pledges from a party that was heavily indebted to corporate donors. Many immediately saw the new slogan as tired and irrelevant. Or, as a progressive wag put it, "much like a pizza from Papa John's, 'A Better Deal' mostly amounts to an uninspired, stale and cheesy agglomeration stuffed neatly into a box."[5]

Yet the most important objection to the whole better-deal rebranding was not its empty-calorie version of economic populism. The fatal flaw was that the Democrats' summer effort refused to lift the lid on Trump's exploitation of social acrimony.

As if to prove that the Democratic leadership had fundamentally misunderstood his political strategy, Trump responded to their "Better Deal" initiative in classic culture-war style. Two days after the rollout, he fired off an early morning tweet in bureaucratic-speak to announce he was banning transgender people from serving in the armed forces: "Please be advised that the United States Government will not accept or allow transgender individuals to serve in any capacity in the U.S. Military."[6]

The day after that, at a rally in Ohio, Trump ramped up his attacks on undocumented immigrants, describing them as "animals" who don't bother using guns to kill people "because it's too fast and it's not painful enough." He graphically described how these "animals" will "take a young, beautiful girl, 16, 15 and others and they slice them and dice them with a knife because they want them to go through excruciating pain before they die."[7]

Then, two days later, with a crowd of grinning police officers at his back, Trump urged law enforcement to rough up persons he again demeaned as "animals" and also as "thugs": "When you see these thugs being thrown into the back of a paddy wagon, you just see them thrown in, rough, I said, please don't be too nice. When you guys put somebody in the car and you're protecting their head, you know, the way you put their hand over . . . you can take the hand away, okay?"[8]

Within weeks, the Democrat's "Better Deal" reboot was litter blowing down the side of the road, one more discarded flyer from another forgotten campaign. It had simply failed to respond to the culture war politics exploited by the Right and of burning concern to the Left's activists and base. It's unlikely any Left effort to build a powerful political coalition can succeed without addressing racial division in some manner.

The consensus that liberals should run silent regarding race rests on the conviction that to do anything else risks alienating too many white voters. The race-class research suggests this is wrong and that it's possible to reframe racism as a weapon of the rich and thereby to directly and successfully contest dog whistling. But there's more going on here than simply flawed strategizing of the sort that can be corrected with anecdotes from focus groups and some polling data. Many on the Left have deep stories about why they should back away from racial justice. This chapter and the next surface these debilitating ideas that stand in the way of a movement for economic and racial justice founded on cross-racial solidarity.

Identity Politics All the Way Down

In the immediate aftermath of Trump's election, political scientist Mark Lilla wrote a *New York Times* op-ed calling for "the end of identity liberalism."[9] A few months later in the same paper, Democratic Party insiders Mark Penn and Andrew Stein said Democrats had lost support among "working-class voters" because their politics were "mired too often in political correctness, transgender bathroom issues and policies offering more help to undocumented immigrants than to the heartland."[10]

These complaints weren't limited to relative centrists. From the democratic socialist Left, Bernie Sanders cautioned days after Trump's election that "it is not good enough for somebody to say, 'Hey, I'm a Latina. Vote for me.' That is not good enough. I have to know whether that Latina is going to stand up with the working class of this country and is going to take on big-money interests." Sanders added to the chorus warning the party to reconsider its allegiance to race as a signature issue: "One of the struggles that you're going to be seeing in the Democratic Party," he said, "is whether we go beyond identity politics." [11]

"Identity politics" has been around as a bugaboo for a long time, dating back to faculty fights within universities in the 1990s.[12] The reference itself is typically dismissive, making "identity" seem a trivial matter of personality, like one's fashion sense or taste in music. When framed this way, the focus on identity seems self-indulgent, like a tween who thinks her father's criticism of her new nose ring is the gravest injustice in the world. Those criticizing identity politics like to portray themselves as the grown-ups, able to take a more mature view on what actually matters. In their telling, "identity" is something self-obsessed people focus on, whereas more objective adults recognize that just about every other issue carries greater importance.

But this willfully misreads the issues being dismissed as mere "identity politics." The term often functions as a condescending refusal to consider challenges to racism, patriarchy, class hierarchy, transphobia, religious bigotry, and ableism. In the academy, this offered an easy way to dismiss, rather than engage, challenges to the status quo. This was bad enough in university settings that, then and now, reflect and perpetuate social privilege.

It's far more consequential in the political realm for this simple reason: *all politics is identity politics, all the way down.* Just as no one stands outside of society, no one stands outside of pervasive social hierarchies. Everyone occupies identities relative to race, gender, class, sexual identity, and so on. To be sure, whether and to what extent people are privileged or disadvantaged is no simple matter. Nevertheless, we all draw on social identities in how we understand ourselves and relate to each other, especially in politics.

The political scientists Christopher Achen and Larry Bartels recently published a field-changing book, *Democracy for Realists*. Their central argument, demonstrated through an overview of centuries of democratic practice and theory, is this: "Voters, even the most informed voters, typically make choices not on the basis of policy preferences or ideology, but on the basis of who they are—their social identities. In turn, those social identities shape how they think, what they think, and where they belong in the party system." [13] The choice is not between identity politics and some other sort of politics, but about whose "identity" matters— that is, which group's concerns will be foregrounded and which shunted aside.

Put differently, "A Better Deal" purported to avoid "identity politics" but in the process simply offered a different sort of identity politics. Its chief virtue hardly lay in the weak tea of its economic proposals. Rather, its supposed strength rested on its silence about racism. For centrist Democratic strategists, the emphasis on class is often primarily a racial strategy—more precisely, a strategy for not alienating whites through frank talk about injustices to communities of color or the political exploitation of racial division. In today's political context, Democratic silence about race speaks loudly, though timidly, about race. It does not successfully sidestep the Right's white identity politics, but instead responds with its own insecure version of the same thing.

Is Racial Justice a Form of Liberal Charity?

"Did the Democrats doom themselves to lose much of the white middle class simply by demanding equal rights for black people?" Liberals have repeatedly asked themselves this question since dog whistling's inception, though this contemporary iteration comes from James Traub in the April 2018 issue of *The Atlantic*.[14] The question sets up another deep story told on the Left about why to avoid addressing racism. In this tale, racial justice is a form of liberal charity, and elites make a big mistake when, because of their moral concerns, they make commitments to racial justice that ultimately antagonize non-elite whites.

Traub answers his potted question by examining the Democratic Party's history going back to 1948, the first time in the twentieth century it adopted a major civil rights plank. He focuses on the impassioned case made by Hubert Humphrey, who is generally remembered as the Democratic presidential candidate who lost to Richard Nixon in 1968. But in 1948, Humphrey, then mayor of Minneapolis, was a rising liberal star convinced it was high time for the Democrats to push civil rights. Few thought he could succeed in securing sufficient votes for a civil rights plank, but his bold call to arms at the Democratic National Convention prevailed.

In turn, southern Democrats revolted. They were more committed to white supremacy than to party loyalty, temporarily organizing as the so-called Dixiecrats. This rebellion, Traub correctly notes, anticipated the eventual mass defection of southern whites to the Republican Party, something party leaders like Humphrey foresaw but accepted as the price of endorsing civil rights. What the party leaders had not counted on, says Traub, "was the mass defection of white voters *outside the South*, a process that would begin in 1968 and consolidate in 1980."[15] He continues: "Today, of course, the entrenched conservatism of much of the white middle class remains an obstacle in the path of Democratic majorities." Though he stops short of committing firmly to an answer to the question he raised, Traub's strongly implied conclusion is that, yes, Democrats' moral support for equality alienated the majority of whites, dooming their electoral prospects.

For support, Traub quotes from a 1991 book, *Chain Reaction* by Thomas Edsall and Mary Edsall. The Democratic Party's intelligentsia has long considered this volume a key resource for understanding the relationship between liberalism and white flight from the Democratic Party, and Thomas Edsall continued in 2019 to write a regular politics column for the *New York Times*. From *Chain Reaction*, Traub offers this: "As the civil-rights movement became national, as it became closely associated with the Democratic Party, as it began to impinge on local neighborhoods and schools, it served to crack the Democratic loyalties of key white voters."[16]

The nub lies in the supposed tension between civil rights as high ideals versus economic liberalism as concrete attention to the needs of working families. "Thanks to Humphrey," Traub argues, "the Democrats had done something even more dangerous than they understood: They had exchanged a politics of self-interest for a politics of moral commitment." Presumably Traub would recognize that people of color have a biting economic need for racial justice. But he's speaking relative to whites and white elites in particular, and for them, he argues, the civil rights laws prohibiting racial discrimination were simply an abstract matter of morality. From here, Traub, like *Chain Reaction* before, offers this central critique: insisting on doing what's right, when it is unpopular with a broad and indispensable constituency, is poor political strategy.

The notion that supporting civil rights costs the Democratic Party white voters implies that winning back white voters requires retreating from civil rights. With this argument, *Chain Reaction* helped set the terms for Bill Clinton's appeals to white anxiety in his 1992 presidential campaign. As Traub's 2018 resurfacing of this tale demonstrates, many liberal elites still hew to this conventional wisdom. But is the underlying history correct?

Traub's essay includes a telling historical footnote. Laying out how the Democratic Party in 1948 came to adopt a civil rights plank, Traub notes that Humphrey struggled to overcome racial prejudice at the convention, especially from southern Democrats. Then Humphrey found an unexpected ally from the Democratic political machine that controlled New York City politics. "Humphrey approached Ed Flynn, the fearsome boss of Tammany Hall; and Flynn, incredibly, said, 'We should have done this a long time ago. We've got to do it.'"

Had Flynn—an Irish Catholic known as "the Boss of the Bronx"—had a sudden anti-racist epiphany? No, Traub explains. "Flynn had not suddenly turned Lutheran moralist: He knew that the party couldn't afford to lose black and Jewish voters."

Traub gave insufficient weight to this incident. Moral demands may have been important to some Democratic leaders, but the party initially embraced civil rights in 1948 and more wholeheartedly in 1964 because of math. Its leaders could count, and they knew they needed votes from the people fighting for civil rights.

This applied to Humphrey as well. An idealist, he was also a pragmatist. "Humphrey saw demographic changes during World War II (Blacks coming North during the Great Migration, a rise in unionized households) and cultural shifts in attitudes toward race, and thought the party had to appeal to blacks and minorities," writes Yale historian and Humphrey biographer Michael Brenes.[17] Though it's a distant memory now, Republicans, the old party of Abraham Lincoln, were once champions of civil rights and Democrats had to compete for Black votes. Brenes distills Humphrey's simple calculation: "The [Democratic] party could not win national elections if it were tied to racist Southerners who made blacks flee to the Republican Party."

Traub may have begun his story in 1948, but typically the liberal charity tale starts with 1964, when Lyndon Johnson signed the most significant civil rights legislation since the end of the Civil War. After signing, Johnson said to an aide, "I think we just delivered the South to the Republican party for a long time to come."[18] This phrase, for many, encapsulates the notion that Democratic leaders took the high road even though they knew it would be costly. It also fosters the notion that liberalism and racial justice were largely disconnected until that point.

In *Racial Realignment: The Transformation of American Liberalism, 1932–1965*, the political scientist Eric Schickler meticulously demolishes the charity story's false history. That narrative generally claims, says Schickler, that "it was only in the 1960s that the cause of social democracy became linked to racial justice in the

United States—and this linkage is what ultimately brought down the liberal project. But this gets the history wrong." [19] For Schickler, the turning point in the relationship between liberalism and anti-racism comes as early as 1932.

In the three decades prior to the 1930s, racial politics barely divided the parties: both supported white supremacy—with casual violence in the North, through systematic terror in the South. If undifferentiated in terms of race, though, these decades saw the Democratic and Republican parties move further apart in their class politics.

The Democratic Party increasingly took up progressive efforts to restrain large monopolies, prevent fraud and unfair business practices, improve workplace conditions, and support the rights of workers to bargain collectively. The Republican Party increasingly spoke in the language of laissez-faire economics and rugged individualism, insisting that the marketplace should be unfettered by government efforts to protect consumers and workers, or to tax great wealth for the general benefit of society.

These positions grew further polarized after the market collapse of 1929 and the sweeping devastation of the Great Depression. Against the do-nothingism of the Republican Party, the Democrats under Franklin Roosevelt launched the New Deal in the early 1930s, and this in turn developed into decades of progressive governance.

At the very outset of the New Deal, Democrats in the North barely supported racial equality, while their colleagues in the South fervently defended white supremacy. This guaranteed that the New Deal would neglect the interests of African Americans. Roosevelt needed southern Democrats to support a raft of new legislation, and was willing to pay their price of a New Deal for whites and the same raw deal for Blacks. The Democrats designed government programs around social insurance, wage protections, and other benefits that either directly excluded African Americans or allowed local implementation that would achieve the same thing. [20]

Even so, progressive activism around jobs and government programs changed northern racial dynamics. African Americans saw the Democratic Party as offering important help, even though the benefits to them were limited by racism. As Blacks moved out of the South seeking opportunity, their votes became an essential resource for the Democratic Party. After 1948, in all but one election—Lyndon Johnson's 1964 landslide—the party has required significant and more often overwhelming support from African American voters to land a Democrat in the White House.

This is not simply a story about party politics. It also centrally concerns labor. Proceeding on a track parallel to the Democratic Party, the more radical elements of the labor movement, especially the Congress of Industrial Organizations (CIO), recognized the critical necessity of building common cause with African Americans. If Blacks in the North and also the South were not unionized, the CIO understood, they would continue as underpaid and exploited labor that could undercut union workers.[21]

In short, says Schickler, "by the time of World War II, the liberal coalition identified civil rights as a critical front in the battle for economic and social progress, and its members understood that defeating southern defenders of Jim Crow was essential for liberalism's future."[22]

This warrants repeating: By the late 1930s, liberalism's future depended on fighting for racial justice. The Democratic Party needed Black voters. Labor needed Black workers. That combination made racial justice a practical necessity if activist government for anyone was to endure and advance—from the late 1930s forward. As Schickler would write directly in response to Traub's *Atlantic* essay: "By the late 1930s, without racial justice, there would be no program of economic equality. It is New Deal liberalism itself that upended the supposed distinction between identity politics and class politics."[23]

It is true that liberalism in the United States has historically struggled to build and maintain a cross-racial coalition for economic and racial justice. It is false that this reflects a naïve politics in which Democratic elites ask working-class whites to sacrifice for others in the name of morality and charity.

From party leaders to union workers and from whites to Blacks, the main reason people fought together for liberalism and racial justice was self-interest. This is not to slight the spiritual leadership of churches and synagogues in the fight for racial equality. That, too, was important. But the main driver for cross-racial solidarity was self-interest all around. This self-interest included winning elections and it included achieving economic security. For Blacks, freedom and equality were also on the line, while for whites, in contrast, their supposed superior racial status was at risk. There is nothing simple about managing the competing interests of different groups with divergent race and class concerns, especially because neither "whites" nor "people of color" are monoliths. But make no mistake: the main impetus for linking economic fairness and racial justice was interest convergence, not liberal charity.

White Self-Regard and the Refusal to Engage with the Privileges of White Identity

Why do liberals so often get this history wrong? It's not just because Americans are lousy historians. Rather, look again at the story Traub was telling, and consider in particular what that story said about him, other elite whites, and the whites who fled the liberal coalition.

In Traub's narrative, who are these liberal elites? Are they cold mathematicians willing to throw African Americans aside if that's the way to win elections? No, they come across as well-meaning people who want to help others, including people of color, though their laudable commitments sometimes lead them astray. Traub describes Hubert Humphrey as "the Joe Biden of his day— irrepressible, unscripted, prolix," and also with "the unquenchable zeal of a reformer."[24] White elites, it seems, are bumbling saints.

And what about the racially resentful white voters who broke from liberalism? According to Traub, especially outside the South, the whites abandoning the Democratic Party were racially innocent. "Beyond the Jim Crow South," he writes, whites "had no consciousness of having kept blacks down" and were "unconscious beneficiaries of entrenched white privilege." They didn't know they were white, didn't recognize racial hierarchy, and didn't fight to preserve white dominance, Traub's characterization suggests.

Indeed, Traub invites *The Atlantic*'s readers to emulate him as he puts himself in the shoes of innocent, beset northern whites. When he writes about busing children to promote school integration, Traub imagines how his own childhood would have been disrupted had he not been, well, a member of the white elite. "But how would I have felt, and how would my parents have felt, if the bus had come for me?" That formulation—"if the bus had come for me"—makes integration sound like the Grim Reaper. Shifting to contemporary white angst, Traub suggests that "Trump voters also may have reason to feel that something precious is being taken from them." Then he advises, "Maybe it behooves today's Democrats to take those grievances more seriously than they're inclined to."

Traub is indirectly explaining the interests of whites, himself included, in preserving the advantages of being white. Yet he does not investigate the actual contours of these "precious" things, and he certainly does not examine the reality of how whites fiercely defended their racial privileges.

Nor does he have much to say about communities of color. Regarding nonwhites, Traub mainly offers silence. He does not urge his readers to imagine how they would have felt as children if trapped in a school dilapidated by racism. He does not speculate about those denied a fair shot at making it in a competitive economy or making it out of an impoverished community because they did not receive a quality education. He does not reflect on the family-twisting stresses of high unemployment on the next generation of students themselves doomed to still-segregated and neglected schools.

At work is a form of white identity politics that expresses itself through an unconsidered sympathy and indifference—sympathy for the racial in-group, indifference for the out-group. White suffering is real; white anger is reasonable; white people deserve sympathy, whether they're liberal elites trying to do the right thing or working-class whites walking away from liberalism rather than endure integration. In contrast, people of color are absent, objects of indifference, unimagined except as beneficiaries of optional moral concern.

The decisions by Democratic leaders both to endorse and then to abandon the core concerns of African Americans reflected electoral math. But beyond the strategizing, selective sympathy and indifference has also contributed to the Democratic Party's tendency over the last fifty years to prioritize the interests of whites and to default to a position of silence on racial justice. Like a compounding error in a spreadsheet formula, Democratic leaders often run their calculations in ways skewed by racial loyalty to other whites combined with indifference to communities of color.

Is this conscious bias? On the contrary, the dynamic is more innocent than that—and thereby more pervasive and insidious.

Legal scholar and critical race theory pioneer Angela Harris offers a helpful framework. Harris developed the term "essentialism" to explain how feminism in the 1970s and '80s easily defaulted to the idea that "women" meant white women, or even more narrowly, financially well-off, straight, cis-gendered white women. For many white feminists, other social hierarchies such as race, class, and sexual orientation seemed like distractions in the feminist movement—they wanted to keep the focus on "gender alone."[25]

This typically did not flow from a malicious supremacism. Rather, it reflected an unconsidered tendency to center one's own experiences of harm—while normalizing various forms of privilege. Some feminists argued that there was an "essential" experience of gender that involved being disadvantaged exclusively by gender. In practice, this typically involved ignoring being otherwise *advantaged* by family connections, education, class, sexual orientation, race, and so forth. Latinx women or queer women became, somehow, different from "just women," a term implicitly reserved for the white women burdened by no other social hierarchy but gender. In this way, gender essentialism made white identity central yet invisible. "Women" were assumed to be white, though this assumption operated subliminally so that whiteness was taken for granted rather than carefully examined.

For many white Democratic decision makers, a similar dynamic seems to blinker their vision. They simply fail to appreciate that being white matters to their views, experiences, assumptions, and priorities. As a form of privilege, white identity becomes normalized and colorless, invisible and unnoticed.

The solution to essentialism is "intersectionality," another term that comes out of critical race theory, this time from Kimberlé Crenshaw.[26] Crenshaw proposed the metaphor of an intersection to highlight how various forms of identity interact—for instance, race and gender. This insight has been picked up by many groups fighting for racial justice, as a reminder that communities of color contain people advantaged or disadvantaged by many different sorts of hierarchies. For example, Black Lives Matter activists proclaim, "We are guided by the fact that all Black lives matter, regardless of actual or perceived sexual identity, gender identity, gender expression, economic status, ability, disability, religious beliefs or disbeliefs, immigration status, or location."[27]

Often, intersectionality is taken to refer to multiple forms of disadvantage, for example as experienced by Black women imperiled by both racism and sexism. But the insight is rather that 1) *everyone* moves at the intersection of various hierarchies and 2) coalitions require that people pay attention to any source(s) of oppression *and also any source(s) of privilege*. Thus, Crenshaw first proposed the intersectionality analysis to urge white feminists to see that they too had identities composed by race and gender, and that feminism could not include all women if it rested implicitly on an unwillingness to recognize or challenge white privilege.

By extension, white men, too, have intersectional identities— positions shaped by both race and gender, though they are advantaged along both dimensions. Just as all politics is identity politics, everyone's identities are intersectional.

Coalitions risk fragmentation when they rest on an essentialism that demands some movement members endure continued oppression rather than discomfort others by asking them to think about their privilege. Likewise, movements and political parties are more likely to thrive when members and decision makers carefully consider how they might be blinded by previously unexplored forms of advantage.

The White Working Class Through the Lens of Stereotypes About Blacks

It's no surprise that when liberal elites fail to take racial dynamics seriously, they disserve communities of color. But it will be news to many that doing so also betrays working-class whites. Many of the Right's most debilitating stories about working people—including white working families—are recycled stereotypes about African Americans. Ignoring this racial element contributes to liberal elites all too often accepting racially tainted narratives of dysfunctional working people.

In the immediate wake of the 2016 election, the premier translator of white working class angst was J. D. Vance, the author of *Hillbilly Elegy.* Vance grew up white and poor in Appalachia, yet made it to Yale Law School. His memoir—self-deprecating, carefully crafted, brutal about his family's faults—promised a tour of the world of the working-class whites who flocked to Trump. Vance's travelogue flew to the top of the *New York Times* bestseller list and then seemed pinned there. He became one of the liberal media's favorite explainers of the confounding Trump voter.

Vance's popularity partly came because he downplayed any role for "racism." His people, he claimed, resented Obama "for reasons that have nothing to do with skin color." Instead, Vance insisted that white working class resentment rested on class and cultural foundations: Obama attended Ivy League schools; Obama had a stable marriage and was a model father; "Obama wears a suit to his job while we wear overalls."[28] To explain why Appalachia and the South more generally flipped from staunchly Democratic to staunchly Republican in a generation, Vance especially singled out a rising hatred of welfare. "As far back as the 1970s," Vance wrote, "the white working class began to turn to Richard Nixon because of a perception that, as one man put it, government was 'payin' people who are on welfare today doin' nothin'! They're laughin' at our society! And we're all hardworkin' people and we're gettin' laughed at for workin' every day!'" Vance experienced this resentment himself, recalling one of his first jobs at a grocery store, where "every two weeks I'd get a small pay-check and notice the line where federal and state income taxes were deducted from my wages. At least as often, our drug-addict neighbor would buy T-bone steaks, which I was too poor to buy for myself but was forced by Uncle Sam to buy for someone else."[29]

When Vance attributed white working class anger to a hatred of undeserving people on welfare, including welfare abusers buying T-bone steaks with money taken by the government from hard-working whites, he seemed to parrot Ronald Reagan. What was next, broadsides against welfare queens? Well, yes. Vance used that disparaging term to describe his neighbors, calling one "a welfare queen if one ever existed."[30]

Vance understood full well the racial connotations of "welfare queen." Yet he sought to use the term to *remove* race as a possible factor in his analysis. "I do hope that readers of this book will be able to take from it an appreciation of how class and family affect the poor without filtering their views through a racial prism," Vance wrote. "To many analysts, terms like 'welfare queen' conjure unfair images of the lazy black mom living on the dole. Readers of this book will realize quickly that there is little relationship between that specter and my argument: I have known many welfare queens; some were my neighbors, and all were white."[31] Vance's logic seemed to proceed like this: *I'm not invoking race because I'm applying black stereotypes to white people.* But as *The New Republic* staff writer Sarah Jones observed, "*Elegy* is little more than a list of myths about welfare queens repackaged as a primer on the white working class."[32] Applying black stereotypes to whites provided Vance's narrative throughline.

How do we know that Vance's narrative was at its core a racial one? Like the nervous tick that betrays an unsettled conscience, Vance invoked Charles Murray as an intellectual inspiration. His nod to Murray is telling, because a closer look at Murray reveals the anti-black racism lurking beneath Vance's attack on white culture. In his 1984 bestseller *Losing Ground*, Murray used stereotypes of black cultural pathology to explain the fate of America's inner cities. Murray not only faulted African Americans for their supposedly defective cultures, he blamed liberalism for exacerbating the problem, contending that government programs encouraged welfare dependency and promoted the breakdown of marriage.[33] "Charles Murray's seminal *Losing Ground*," Vance wrote, "described my home perfectly"—it was a "book about black folks that could have been written about hillbillies."[34]

In *Losing Ground*, Murray was still insisting the story was cultural. But a decade later, he dropped the pretense and expressly promoted biological racism. Murray in 1994 co-authored *The Bell Curve*, a bestseller that generated a firestorm of controversy because it argued that genetic differences between the races explained black inferiority both intellectually and in terms of social outcomes.[35] Then Murray published yet another best seller, and this one precisely anticipated Vance's thesis. In *Coming Apart: The State of White America, 1960–2010*, published in 2012, Murray transferred his attacks against blacks to the white working class, condemning them for adopting self-defeating cultural patterns around marriage, children, work, civic engagement, and religion. Murray blamed culture and character—much more than structural dynamics like the Great Recession—for the growing income inequality in America. He also again cast government assistance as part of the problem, blaming it for driving many of the destructive changes evident in white culture.[36]

And as in the *Bell Curve*, so too in *Coming Apart*: fixed and natural inferiority also resurfaced. When it came to the white working class and other groups, Murray pointed to genetic differences as drivers of social inequality: "people grouped by gender, ethnicity, age, *social class*, and sexual preference, left free to live their lives as they see fit, will produce group differences in outcomes, *because they differ genetically in their cognitive, psychological, and physiological profiles*."[37]

Among its other functions, racism offers a story to society's well off that excuses poverty, marginalization, and social disregard. Yes, this primarily paints communities of color in despairing shades. But today the current plausibility of stories that blame the white poor for their own poverty are also at root racist tales. As Murray and Vance show, it's tales of black inferiority, tied to genetic differences, that in the contemporary United States undergird narratives of cultural pathology in the poor, including poor whites. This is not the first time that myths of racial inferiority have been told by elite whites about poor whites. In her book *White Trash*, Nancy Isenberg focuses on how biological rationalizations of poverty have long applied to whites, too. In the colonial era, she writes, "The poor were not only described as waste, but as inferior animal stocks." Today, she argues, "white trash remains fraught with the older baggage of stereotypes of the hopelessly ill bred."[38]

The enthusiastic reception accorded Vance's book should serve as a wake-up call. Neither Vance nor the liberals relying on him as a guide for understanding the white working class managed to steer clear of a racial story. Instead, they accepted a racially tainted narrative of Black pathology, though this time transferred to working-class whites. Defamations about pathological culture don't stop being wrong and racist when applied to whites. They remain vilifying lies, now with more casualties.

7

When Economic Populists Talk About Racial Justice

The economic populist Bernie Sanders sees racism as a major problem. During his 2016 campaign, for example, Sanders endorsed important racial justice measures regarding mass incarceration, and was justifiably proud of his five decades of civil rights activism. Nevertheless, like other members of what might be termed the class Left, Sanders believes that progressives must put the bulk of their energy into building economic justice first. Why do some economic populists promote a class-first approach that displaces racial issues to the back burner? They do so because of particular ways of conceptualizing race that carry significant limitations. These blindspots put at risk racial justice, support from people of color, and economic populism itself.

The Scapegoat Theory and Its Limits

Let's call one argument for prioritizing class the scapegoat theory. Here's Bernie Sanders advancing this way of thinking during the 2016 Democratic primary campaign: "The average guy, he is asking why he has to work longer hours for lower wages. He's really worried, or she is really worried," Sanders told CNN in March 2016. "People are angry," he explained. "What Trump is doing is taking that anger and saying, 'It's the fault of the Mexicans,' or, 'It's the fault of the Muslims. We've got to scapegoat people!' Well, beating up on Mexicans who make eight bucks an hour is not going to deal with the real issue."[1]

The scapegoat theory makes intuitive sense to many people as the basic explanation for how race and class connect in politics. In the Atlanta focus group with white men and women, one participant had this to say: "Growing up in the Midwest with a lot of working-class, blue-collar family, there's a lot of fear of losing [one's] job to someone from Mexico or some unnamed foreign country." That fear, he explained, creates "a dry patch of kindling and it doesn't take much of a spark for someone to feel really strongly about job insecurity, or income insecurity." Then he summed up: "It's always easier to scapegoat somebody you don't know from some foreign place, 'it's them, they're the problem . . .'" As he trailed off, the moderator asked whether the scapegoating came from his family members themselves. The participant conceded they have their "prejudices, conscious and unconscious." But he added, "they're being corralled into buying something that they don't need to buy, for the sake of agendas that don't represent their interests."

The scapegoat story is an accessible frame to explain racism as a weapon of the rich and can form an important element of a race-class message. Useful as it is, though, the scapegoat story gives an incomplete view of the relationship between race and class in American politics, a limitation that has implications for the sorts of solutions scapegoat theory proposes.

A short piece written by former labor secretary Robert Reich in 2018 illustrates these shortcomings.[2] To be clear, I esteem Reich, a colleague of mine at UC Berkeley. I've lectured in his class and cowritten an op-ed with him. Far from objecting to the sorts of fundamental populist reforms he proposes, I wholeheartedly endorse them.[3] And that's why it's so important to critique scapegoat theory. It not only slights racial justice, it gets in the way of the ambitious economic revolution that Reich and Sanders propose.

Reich started his short essay with this question: "Why did so many working class voters choose a selfish, thin-skinned,

petulant, lying, narcissistic, boastful megalomaniac for president?" The answer, Reich contends, "lies in the interplay between
deep-seated racism and stagnant and declining wages. Both must
be addressed."

Reich noted that many whites rallied to Trump in response to
his bigotry: "Some white working-class men and women were—
and still are—receptive to Trump's bigotry." But this was not the
surprise. Reich explained that racism has always been endemic to
America. "Racism and xenophobia aren't exactly new to American
life. Fears of blacks and immigrants have been with us since the
founding of the Republic."

For Reich, the mystery was why race factored so prominently
in 2016. He wondered what made the white working class receptive to racial appeals then and not at other times, when racism was
always present in American life.

"What changed was the economy," Reich concluded. Reich is
one of the country's foremost experts on how the last few decades
have destroyed the economic security of working families. He
reprised this analysis: "Since the 1980s, the wages and economic
prospects of the typical American worker have stagnated. . . . The
near meltdown of Wall Street in 2008 caused a recession that cost
millions their jobs, homes, and savings."

And the connection to racism? "Trump's racism and xenophobia focused the cumulative economic rage on scapegoats that had
nothing to do with its causes. It was hardly the first time in history
a demagogue has used this playbook," Reich wrote.

In truncated form, Reich argued that racism has always permeated American society but for the most part has not been politically relevant; that the recession impelled people to look for
someone to blame; and that racism disposed whites toward arguments faulting people of color, making racism politically explosive
after 2008. In this story, racism is like a sleeping dog, largely irrelevant to politics until kicked awake in times of economic stress.

Does this match the historical record? No. The tectonic shift of
whites into the Republican Party started in the South in 1948 and

accelerated after 1964, spreading nationally in 1972. It initiated at the pinnacle of New Deal and Great Society efforts to lift up the white working class, not in the midst of recession. The waves of plant closings that would generate terms like "deindustrialization" and "the rust belt" really hit after Nixon's 1972 landslide. For most whites, the economy had not yet suffered sharp setbacks when dog whistling began resetting the American electoral landscape. Whites started abandoning the Democratic Party in droves at a time of relative prosperity for them.

No sharp decline in living standards or sustained economic hardship pushed whites to look for "scapegoats." It was not primarily economic hardship driving a search for someone to blame, not at the outset of dog whistling—and not in 2016. As we've seen, the most financially pressed whites were less, not more, likely to support Trump. Relying on a scapegoat theory cannot explain the inception or continuing power of dog whistling.

The limited analysis then generates inadequate solutions. A singular reliance on scapegoat theory implies that the "real" problem is economic hardship. In turn, this suggests that the appropriate solutions are pocketbook ones. Create economic prosperity, the reasoning goes, and not only is everyone better off, but social animosities fade as well, or at least they cease being major factors in American political life.

Within that frame, Reich concluded his essay with a series of what he termed "ambitious ideas": a jobs guarantee, single payer healthcare, industry-wide collective bargaining, universal basic income, taxes on carbon and Wall Street trading, progressive taxes on wealth, and innovative suggestions for limiting money in politics. All great. Utterly missing? Anything to do directly with racial justice.

It's easy to see that by focusing on only half the story, racial justice simply drops off the table. But the larger point is that this analysis makes it difficult to achieve major change, whether racial justice or sweeping economic reforms.

Scapegoat theory sees racial resentment in politics as flowing from economic hardship, and this secondary role implies that race plays a relatively marginal and infrequent part in politics. But racial fear and resentment pervade politics and are so powerful they have been the major weapon used to divide working people for the last five decades, if not from the beginning of the country.

Reich and Sanders assume that economic anxiety leads to racial scapegoating. That is, they draw a one-way arrow from economic stress to people supporting a racist demagogue. In fact, racial resentment and economic hardship exist in a mutually reinforcing relationship. Racial resentment among voters encouraged many in the 1960s and 1970s to walk away from Democrats and New Deal liberalism, and to instead support the party of big business, a pattern that accelerated with white working-class support for Ronald Reagan in the 1980s. As Reagan's policies made times tougher for working families, people looked for someone to blame, and the Right was quick to point the finger at Black and brown communities. The result was mutually reinforcing dynamics of racial resentment and rule by the rich. Racial resentment helped build enthusiasm for dog whistle politicians, who then did favors for the economic royalty, which caused economic misery, which set the conditions for more racial scapegoating, which built more support for dog whistle politicians serving the interests of plutocracy, more wealth being siphoned skyward, more scapegoating, and down the country slumped.

Racial resentment is made worse by economic hardship and scapegoating, but it does not depend on those dynamics to play a decisive role in American politics. Indeed, it's precisely the colossal political power of racial fear and division that shattered the New Deal coalition of Blacks and working-class whites and that prevents building the progressive supermajorities needed to enact bold economic policies. It's racism as a divide-and-distract weapon that keeps so many in the persuadable middle voting for rule by the rich. Here's what this means: *Economic populism cannot be achieved by focusing on economics alone.* The only way to build the durable and robust progressive majorities needed for genuine economic justice is to defeat dog whistle politics.

Economic Justice *as* Racial Justice

"For young people who have graduated high school or dropped out of high school, who are between the ages of 17 and 20, if they happen to be white, the unemployment rate is 33 percent," Bernie Sanders said at a 2015 campaign rally in Maine. "If they are Hispanic, the unemployment rate is 36 percent. If they are African-American, the real unemployment rate for young people is 51 percent."[4]

This sort of setup is common in progressive circles. Often, communities of color appear in formulations like this: *Z afflicts everyone, and it's especially bad for African Americans and Latinxs.* "Z" can be unemployment, inadequate healthcare, environmental dangers, underfunded public schools, or a range of other social harms. Typically, this narrative then segues to a follow-on claim: *Let's fix Z, and by remedying the general harm we will promote racial justice by disproportionately helping people of color.* Sanders often uses this logic, arguing that a focus on economic justice does more for people of color and women than for white men. In a more snippy version, sometimes the message from the class Left to racial justice advocates comes across as this: *Stop the complaints about racial injustice because by ignoring race and focusing on class the Left actually does more for people of color.*

This line of thinking relies on what we might call the *class-intensifier theory of race.* Race is, in this formulation, a more intense experience of class harms.

Early in 2016, a reporter asked Sanders whether he would support reparations to African American communities for slavery. "No, I don't think so," he responded. "I think what we should be talking about is making massive investments in rebuilding our cities, in creating millions of decent paying jobs, in making public colleges and universities tuition-free, on working on child care, basically targeting our federal resources to the areas where it is needed the most." And "where it is needed the most is in impoverished communities, often African American and Latino," he said.[5]

The real issue, Sanders seemed to say, was not racism's historic injustices and current manifestations, but the poverty that especially afflicts brown and Black communities. His response to reparations was to restate the general case for massive investments in cities, jobs, higher education, and childcare. These are crucial and necessary reforms, and Sanders was correct that they would disproportionately help African Americans and Latinxs.[6]

Yet Ta-Nehisi Coates wasn't having it. A leading public thinker on racism, Coates had written a compelling piece making the case for reparations two years earlier.[7] He quickly zeroed in on the underlying logic of the "class first" approach, chastising Sanders for adopting policy responses that "address black people not so much as a class specifically injured by white supremacy, but rather, as a group which magically suffers from disproportionate poverty."

To flesh out Coates' critique, here's what seeing Blacks as "a group which magically suffers from disproportionate poverty" misses. This view misses the way in which centuries of racism have hammered inequality so deep into American society that general solutions will not suffice. It's unwarranted to suppose that a rising tide lifts all boats. Without special repairs being done alongside universal efforts, the tide cannot help those boats that are holed and wedged among rocks. As economist William Darity forcefully argues, economic justice for African Americans requires direct efforts to build wealth in those communities.[8]

It misses the fact that, in addition to widely felt class harms, economic disparities afflicting communities of color stem from multiple forms of contemporary racism, for instance structural racism and unconscious biases. The Harvard sociologist Devah Pager documented that many employers prefer whites with criminal records to African Americans with unblemished credentials.[9]

"This suggests that being black in America today is essentially like having a felony conviction in terms of one's chances of finding employment," she observed. It was far worse, Pager found, for African Americans who themselves had criminal records, a reality for many given the racialized war on crime. Employers often used this information as a proxy for racial discrimination, refusing to consider Black job applicants without bothering to evaluate their individual achievements or circumstances.[10] This is the structural racism of over-policing combined with unconscious bias, not just class hardship.

The class-intensifier theory of race also sidesteps the widespread violence done especially to communities of color through dog whistle attacks and policies. These politically motivated assaults on basic human rights drive police aggression and mass incarceration, xenophobic deportation campaigns and the taking of children from their parents, invasive surveillance campaigns and the taint of one's religion being branded as un-American. Focusing foremost on economic issues does not resolve these harms. Indeed, too often it avoids even naming and acknowledging them.[11]

Precisely because the class-intensifier theory of race misses so much about the many forms taken by racism, relying on this theory can communicate to racial justice activists a damaging, even disqualifying, disregard for communities of color. This is where Coates was headed.

When Sanders declined to endorse reparations, he was running 50 percent or more behind Hillary Clinton among Latinxs and African Americans.[12] The gap partly reflected Clinton's higher name recognition and long-standing political connections to these communities. But as Coates pointed out, Sanders was also failing to convey a compelling understanding of the challenges facing Blacks. "Jim Crow and its legacy were not merely problems of disproportionate poverty," Coates wrote. "Why should black voters support a candidate who does not recognize this?"[13]

Sanders's class-intensifier approach to race carries real costs, creating blind spots regarding how racism works today as well as alienating racial justice activists who form an influential part of the Democratic base. So why maintain this particular stance? The answer seems to point beyond simply a truncated understanding of race and toward a political calculation regarding how to win elections.

Consider how the reparations debate played out when it re-surfaced in the spring of 2019 among candidates vying for the Democratic presidential nomination. In a remarkable political evolution, virtually everyone supported reparations—except for Sanders, who once again declined to endorse reparations, saying "I think there are better ways to do that than just writing out a check." [14]

In reality, at the time no candidates were saying they would support programs exclusively designed to help African Americans. Senator Cory Booker, for instance, invoked "baby bonds," that is, government putting money into savings accounts for each child born in the United States, with more money placed into accounts for children born into poverty. Senator Kamala Harris pointed to a tax plan that was geared toward helping people in poverty rather than directly addressing racism's legacy. By this yardstick, Sanders too could have proclaimed himself all in for reparations—while extolling precisely the universal economic reforms he had been ad-vancing for decades.[15]

The reparations debate, at least as it initially evolved in 2019, was more about messaging than substance. The candidates' policy positions were similar: efforts to help the poor though not African Americans especially. Rather, the dividing line was this: whether candidates would foreground the responsibility of American soci-ety to make amends to African Americans as a reason to support broad programs to help the poor.

Presumably, the campaigns had looked at the polling numbers. A Marist poll from May 2016 asked whether the United States should pay reparations for slavery and other forms of racial discrimination to all African Americans. A very large group of whites, 85 percent, said no. Coming out for reparations seemed likely to lose white voters. But the same poll showed African Americans supporting reparations by almost two to one, 63 percent to 32 percent. That was a strong majority. Was it strong enough to risk losing support from the much larger white voting bloc? After all, when aggregated, more than seven in ten adults, 72 percent, said they opposed reparations.[16]

Here's another way to understand the 2019 split in the Democratic field regarding reparations: where most candidates apparently concluded they needed to lead with racial justice and speak to the progressive base, especially people of color, Sanders seemed to be sticking with the conclusion that running silent on race offered the wiser course. As Sanders had said back in early 2016 when he first explained why he would not support reparations, "I think it would be very divisive."[17] On that, Sanders had a point. As we've already seen, the sorts of racial justice messages favored by activists may move the base but they risk losing those in the middle.

But does it follow that avoiding race in favor of colorblind economic populism is an effective strategy for building a new progressive majority? This seemed to be Sanders's thinking. It is also the conclusion reached by a large number of centrist Democrats. Let's see how race-silent economic populism fared in the race-class research.

Can Colorblind Economic Populism Compete Against Racial Fear?

As with the dog whistle racial fear message, the race-class project crafted a sample colorblind economic message by drawing upon phrases and frames already in use. Here's the colorblind economic message the project tested:

Colorblind Economic Populism

We live in the richest country in the history of the world, but that means little because much of that wealth is controlled by a tiny handful of individuals. Despite advancements in technology and productivity, millions of Americans are working longer hours for lower wages. Wall Street and the billionaire class have rigged the rules to redistribute wealth and income to the wealthiest and most powerful people of this country. We must send the message to these greedy billionaires that you cannot take advantage of all the benefits of America, if you refuse to accept your responsibilities as Americans.

First, the good news. If Americans were voting their economic policy preferences alone, disconnected from racial resentment and stories of government helping undeserving people, progressives would dominate. We found that voters generally take progressive positions on economic policy.[18] Multiple surveys find the same.[19] Is it any wonder Republicans do not campaign on economics stripped of racial warnings? Which is why colorblind economic populism must win not just against right-wing economic messages but against the Right's racial fear message.

Against a dog whistle message, the race-silent economic message performed in a manner that roughly modeled the actual political world. Given a choice between a racial fear narrative and a progressive economic message, the wings rallied to their respective sides and the middle divided. Notice in particular how persuadables gave roughly equal support to colorblind economic populism as well as racial fear. This suggests they could go either way depending on various factors.

To dig a little deeper into respondents' reactions, we also added a "dial test," which plays an audio recording of the message and

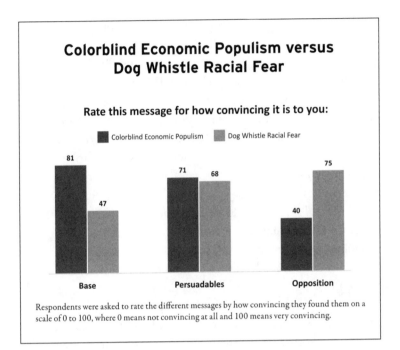

Colorblind Economic Populism versus Dog Whistle Racial Fear

Rate this message for how convincing it is to you:

■ Colorblind Economic Populism   ■ Dog Whistle Racial Fear

Respondents were asked to rate the different messages by how convincing they found them on a scale of 0 to 100, where 0 means not convincing at all and 100 means very convincing.

asks people to move a slider to indicate their reaction moment by moment. The instructions say: "As you listen to the audio, use the slider to show how you feel about what you're hearing, where 0 is very cool, negative feelings and you strongly disagree with what you are hearing and 100 is very warm, positive feelings and you strongly agree with what you are hearing. 50 is neutral." The dial test is designed to measure immediate and thus more unconscious reactions.

Using the dial test, economic populism failed to carry persuadables, who slightly favored the opposition racial fear message (they gave it an average dial rating of 64, compared to 66 for the racial fear message). These numbers are very close, and don't change the basic takeaway that persuadables found both messages roughly equally compelling. But they do hint that the racial fear message taps into unconscious ideas and so remains a potent weapon against the Left.

Here's the reality of colorblind economic populism. With a strong candidate, the colorblind economic message is probably compelling enough for Democrats to continue winning the popular vote nationally. It's also likely sufficient in jurisdictions where the progressive base significantly outnumbers the opposition. In other words, colorblind economic populism should be adequate to maintain the status quo of the last several decades, with the presidency going back and forth, a divided Congress, many states in dog whistle lockdown, and the racial resentment of whites continuing to build.

But that also means colorblind economic populism is unlikely to generate the substantial political power necessary to enact economic populism at the federal level. The class Left argues for avoiding divisive racial issues in favor of colorblind economic populism, insisting that this will be good for everyone but especially for disproportionately poor communities of color. Implicit in this argument is the promise that their route forward can lead to bold economic reforms. That's the trade-off they offer to the race Left: delay your demands for attention to racism's specific harms in exchange for a genuine chance at fundamental economic reform. But this is a bargain the class Left seems unlikely to be able to honor. At best, colorblind economic populism seems to hold out the possibility of narrow victories and bitter political gridlock.

Or maybe the outlook is bleaker than that. Perhaps some sort of political rupture is upon the United States, one way or another. The power of dog whistle politics looks likely to keep growing, in which case, there's no standing still. Things are going to change, for the better or for the worse. The next chapter sketches trends among whites suggesting a dire future if dog whistling is not actively contested and defeated.

8

The "Merge Right" Chapter, or How Trumpism Mines and Fuels Dangerous Trends Among Whites

For the last half century, wealthy elites and the dog whistle politicians they bankroll have been pursuing a "merge right" strategy, seeking to convince as many people as possible to vote their racial fears and in the process to entrust their fates to the plutocrats. Through dog whistling's exploitation of coded language, this strategy has found traction across racial lines, and in fashioning a response it's helpful to focus on political views rather than skin hues.

But the main driver behind Donald Trump's election, as well as the prior fifty years of American politics, is nevertheless color-coded. Van Jones memorably described it as "whitelash"—the political reaction of a majority of whites to a society struggling to transcend white dominance.

It's time to look directly at troubling new trends among whites. The place to start is with Trump. He personally espouses many of the racist views that the Right seeks to activate and promote, he understands better than perhaps anyone how to exploit racial division for ulterior ends, and his campaign and presidency added propellant to the danger.

Trump's Racist Inheritance

Donald Trump's father, Fred C. Trump, was among those arrested at a Ku Klux Klan rally in Queens, New York, in 1927. "1,000 Klansmen and 100 policemen staged a free-for-all" in the streets, one newspaper reported then. Newspaper articles covering the fracas do not explicitly label Trump's father a Klan member, leaving open the possibility that he was simply a bystander caught up in what newspapers described as a "near riot." But the articles do make clear that this was Trump's father who was arrested for "refusing to disperse," though the charge was later dismissed. One newspaper also mentioned that all those arrested were "berobed marchers," suggesting the elder Trump was there in Klan regalia. At the time, Fred Trump would have been twenty-one.[1]

Donald was born nine years later, and reared as an heir to the real estate empire Fred was building in the boroughs surrounding Manhattan—an empire erected on a bedrock of racial discrimination. In the 1950s, this reflected ambient racism as well as federal housing policy, which encouraged the creation of segregated suburbs.[2] It also reflected Fred Trump's personal antipathies. The legendary folksinger Woody Guthrie lived in Trump's first housing development, a six-building, 1,800-unit apartment complex called Beach Haven, near Coney Island. Guthrie is most famous for "This Land Is Your Land," a ballad inspired by the Depression that lifts up the ideal of a country by and for all of us. Beach Haven was far from that. Seeing segregation at work there, Guthrie wrote a song titled "Old Man Trump" that included the lyrics: "Beach Haven ain't my home! No, I just can't pay this rent! My money's down the drain, and my soul is badly bent! Beach Haven is Trump's Tower where no black folks come to roam. No, no, Old Man Trump! Old Beach Haven ain't my home!"[3]

Did Donald internalize his father's racism? In a 2016 interview for the PBS documentary series *Frontline*, Trump biographer Michael D'Antonio identified eugenicist beliefs as "a very deep part of the Trump story." A racial theory that arose early in the twentieth century, eugenics drew on the then-new study of genes to postulate that biology drives almost every major difference between groups, connecting race to character, culture, religion, and ultimately national destiny. Such beliefs were foundational among white supremacists in the United States at the time Trump's father was arrested at the Klan rally.[4]

"The family subscribes to a race horse theory of human development, that they believe that there are superior people, and that if you put together the genes of a superior woman and a superior man, you get superior offspring," D'Antonio explained.[5] Trump had expressed such views in a 2010 interview with CNN, in which he attributed his business success to his genes. "I'm a gene believer . . . hey when you connect two race horses you usually end up with a fast horse," he said, adding, "I had a good gene pool from the standpoint of that."[6] Trump has also been recorded saying, "You know, I'm proud to have that German blood. There's no question about it. Great stuff."[7]

By the 1960s, eugenics as a philosophy had been debunked and racial attitudes among whites had begun to evolve. Many, prodded by civil rights activism, moved toward support for racial equality. Federal and state laws followed and encouraged this shift. In the area of housing, this meant that laws soliciting segregation gave way to laws prohibiting racial discrimination.

The Trumps did not evolve. In fact, so many complaints of discrimination were lodged against Trump Management that in 1973 the federal Department of Justice sued both Trumps—Fred as company chairman and Donald as president—for racial discrimination against African Americans and Puerto Ricans.

In one among many incidents cited by the federal government, a young Black couple, Haywood and Rennell Cash, were told no apartments were available in a Trump housing complex. They knew this was a lie because they were working with a civil rights organization that had arranged for a white "tester" to apply for that same space. While Haywood waited in a car, having just been told there were no apartments available, Maggie Durham, the tester, went in. She was quickly offered a unit. Durham stepped out to get Haywood, then together they returned to the leasing office.

The rental agent exploded, calling Durham a "nigger-lover" and a "traitor to the race," according to the complaint. This was "one of the first [Trump real estate] projects in which Donald Trump, fresh out of college, played an active role," according to the *New York Times*. Trump would later praise that same rental agent as a "fabulous man" and "an amazing manager."[8]

The federal allegations, Donald Trump told reporters at the time, were "absolutely ridiculous. We never have discriminated," he insisted, "and we never would."[9] Then he counterpunched. As summarized by the *New York Times*, "He turned the lawsuit into a protracted battle, complete with angry denials, character assassination, charges that the government was trying to force him to rent to 'welfare recipients' and a $100 million countersuit accusing the Justice Department of defamation."[10] Two years later, in 1975, the Trumps declared they had been vindicated, though in reality they had signed a consent decree promising reforms. In the opinion of the Justice Department, though, they flouted that commitment. "We believe that an underlying pattern of discrimination continues to exist in the Trump Management organization," the Justice Department wrote to Donald Trump's lawyer in 1978.[11] It seems clear that even forty years ago, appearance mattered more than reality to Trump. He'd learned that vigorously denying racism was more important to his public persona than actually ending discriminatory practices.

Another infamous incident from Trump's past involves the Central Park jogger case. New York City in the 1970s and 1980s was in fiscal crisis, prompting severe cuts to public services and layoffs of public servants, including police. A crime rate that had been climbing through the 1960s continued upward over the next two decades, peaking in 1990. Near the highpoint, in 1989, the police coerced five teenage boys of color into confessing to the brutal rape of a young white woman in Central Park. Though horrific, the Central Park jogger case was one of more than 3,200 rapes that year in New York City. This case, though, particularly seized the city's fevered imagination because it featured Black and brown teens supposedly running wild and beating and raping an innocent white woman.[12]

Mayor Ed Koch pled for calm and warned against unfocused hate. Donald Trump instead took out full-page ads in the New York papers, including the *Times*, extolling hate and calling for executions. "Mayor Koch has stated that hate and rancor should be removed from our hearts," he wrote. "I do not think so. I want to hate these muggers and murderers. They should be forced to suffer and, when they kill, they should be executed for their crimes."

Trump's full-page ad followed the dog whistle script the Right had been promoting since Nixon's 1968 campaign. Trump painted people of color as savage and dangerous: "roving bands of wild criminals [who] roam our neighborhoods," "crazed misfits" who "terrorize New York." In contrast, whites were decent people: no longer "safe from those who would prey on innocent lives," they were vulnerable to "criminals of every age [who] beat and rape a helpless woman." And government was to blame: it fostered a "reckless and dangerously permissive atmosphere" by its "continuous pandering to the criminal population," who if they are ever arrested "laugh because they know that soon, very soon, they will be returned to the streets to rape and maim and kill once again."[13]

In that atmosphere, the five teenagers were coerced to confess and on that basis were convicted. In 2002, they were exonerated after the actual perpetrator confessed and was tied to the crime by DNA evidence. The teenagers—by then young men—fought for more than a decade to be compensated for their stolen years, and settled their lawsuit against the city in 2014 for $41 million.

That prompted Trump to weigh in again, with an opinion piece in the New York *Daily News* that trashed the settlement as a "disgrace." He insisted that "settling doesn't mean innocence," even though their innocence had been conclusively established. He warned that "these young men do not exactly have the pasts of angels," though they were imprisoned as teenagers and so hardly had any pasts at all. He jeered that the men "must be laughing out loud at the stupidity of the city," though the city was hardly the victim.[14] In sowing racist lies, Trump was unrepentant as well as resistant to facts, traits the country has come to know well.

Trump's first significant run for office came in 2000. He briefly sought the presidential nomination from the Reform Party. To woo this small progressive party, Trump positioned himself as a liberal supporter of abortion and gay rights. His competition included the hard-right commentator Patrick Buchanan, who hoped to hijack the Reform Party. Trump took aim, claiming the liberal high ground. Speaking to *The Advocate*, the national LGBTQ magazine, Trump fired at Buchanan: "I read the things he had written about Hitler, Jews, Blacks, gays, and Mexicans. I mean, I think it's disgusting. . . . He wants to divide Americans."[15]

Trump saw clearly Buchanan's tactic "to divide Americans," and positioned himself to campaign against that strategy. The irony of that isn't lost on Buchanan. In the aftermath of the 2016 election, Buchanan returned the favor, saying "Donald Trump stole my playbook." And what did Buchanan identify as the main play stolen by Trump? The decision to attack non-European immigration to the United States, capitalizing on the realization that "people want to be with their own and want to be separated from others," Buchanan explained.[16]

A decade after campaigning to be the Reform Party candidate, Trump was ready to try politics again. This time, he sought the GOP presidential nomination. He began his campaign with a speech before the Conservative Political Action Conference in February 2011, testing themes of American economic decline and the incompetence of Washington's political insiders.[17] It fell flat, and his chances of climbing through the presidential primaries seemed nil.

The next month, Trump altered tack. He called Joseph Farah, a conspiracy theorist from the fringe of American politics, whose contentions included, among other things, that soybeans caused homosexuality and that Barack Obama was foreign born. Claims of Obama's foreign birth had been so thoroughly debunked by then that continued insinuations to that effect seemed as outlandish as the soybean claim.

But Trump made the rounds of news and talk programs, refloating the rumors about Obama's birth and religion while envisioning TV ratings gold.[18] The gambit worked. Quickly Obama's birth certificate moved to the eye of a media storm that kept offering Trump an ever-expanding platform and rising standing with Republican voters.[19] In mid-April 2011, Trump was tied for first place among Republicans and GOP-leaning independents, well ahead of the establishment figure and eventual GOP nominee that year, Mitt Romney.[20] By mid-May 2011, his publicity stunt having paid out handsomely, Trump announced he was no longer running for president.

Trump's birtherism taught him a critical lesson. In promoting that lie, he lost what little credibility he had with most serious Republican politicians and came across as a pathetic carnival barker to Democrats. But he'd absorbed a fundamental truth about the Republican base. With little more to his campaign than unsubstantiated insinuations about Obama's foreign birth, Trump had surged among reactionary voters. Trump grasped that he could generate impassioned support from the Republican base through coded racist campaigning. For 2016, he prepared to do just that, updating his arsenal by having aides listen to thousands of hours of Fox and talk radio, mining it for talking points about migrant invasions, Muslim terrorists, and Obamacare.[21]

During the 2016 campaign, Trump boasted to the *New York Times* of his ability to read his crowds. "If my speeches ever get a little off," he said, "I just go: 'We will build a wall!' You know, if it gets a little boring, if I see people starting to sort of maybe thinking about leaving—I can sort of tell the audience—I just say, 'We will build the wall,' and they go nuts."[22] It's possible this reflects merely Trump's extraordinary showmanship. Far more likely, this emerges from Trump's previous experience exploiting racial provocations, along with dog whistle advice from his closest political mentors—among them Roger Ailes, Roger Stone, and Paul Manafort, who cumulatively had more than a century of experience as practitioners of political race-baiting.[23]

Even Democrats had to admit that Trump had tapped into a virulent power. "I think Donald J. Trump is plenty bright," said Paul Begala, a political insider close to both Bill and Hillary Clinton. "He has a cynical, innate intelligence for what his base wants to hear. It's like a divining rod for division, prejudice, and stereotyping."

Trump deserves a bit more credit than that. It is not just an "innate" sense of how to divide people. It is one that Trump has studied and perfected. For Trump, racial dog whistling is a practiced strategy. In this sense, Begala's conclusion from 2018 is sound: "So don't call him 'moron' or 'idiot'; call him what he is: a conniving, corrupt con man, a dangerous, divisive demagogue—and, most sobering of all, the man who carried 30 states in the last election, and may well do it again."[24]

Hating and Helping African Americans

Drawing on lessons learned, in 2016 Trump made some key innovations to dog whistling. We discussed one at the outset of the book: Trump's strategy of instigating charges of racism from political elites. Trump also altered dog whistling about African Americans.

During campaign rallies, Trump frequently encouraged violence against Black demonstrators. At various times he said, "Knock the crap out of them," and "I'd like to punch him in the face," and "Maybe he should have been roughed up because it was absolutely disgusting what he was doing."[25] This seemed to function as a new form of dog whistling. Trump's exhortations to violence could be defended as directed only toward individual protesters, though the larger message seemed to invite violence and anger toward Blacks generally.

This new whistle drew on but also vivified the stock depiction of African Americans as threatening criminals. Trump repeated the usual dog whistles invoking Black criminality. He described himself as the "law and order" candidate, denounced "thugs," and called for a return to racially discriminatory "stop and frisk" policing. The state violence typically attendant to dog whistle politics would follow during Trump's administration. For instance, Jeff Sessions, Trump's first attorney general, would reboot the war on crime that fuels racialized mass incarceration and rampant police violence in communities of color. But during the campaign, by focusing his crowds' attention on individual protesters, Trump made his rallies performance pieces in which the rumored Black criminal appeared in the flesh.

The "thug" was no longer an abstraction. Now he was supposedly standing right there, jeering Trump and by extension his fans. When Trump exhorted his crowd to rough up these people, he invited them to participate in dehumanizing violence—the protesters were no longer fellow members of society but objects of scorn who deserved a punch in the face. Trump's crowds could do much more than vote their racial fear and resentment. They could give it direct voice, through boos and sometimes spit and fists.

Trump didn't stop with dog whistles that portrayed Blacks as dangerous predators. During his 2016 campaign, Trump frequently regaled crowds with stereotypes about the abysmal conditions of African American neighborhoods. "Poverty. Rejection. Horrible education. No housing, no homes, no ownership. Crime at levels that nobody has seen," Trump bellowed at an Ohio rally. "You can go to war zones in countries that we are fighting and it's safer than living in some of our inner cities."

This language encouraged his base to see African Americans through ugly stereotypes. Yet in a contradictory twist that worked to assuage any concern that this was bigotry, Trump framed his remarks as arising out of concern. Trump instigated hate against African Americans in some of his remarks. And in others, he proclaimed his heartfelt commitment to help the Black community.

To the Ohio crowd he said, "Give me a chance. I'll straighten it out. I'll straighten it out. What do you have to lose?" And again, this time in Florida: "Our inner cities are almost at an all-time low, run by the Democrats for sometimes more than a hundred years, chain unbroken. So they have no jobs. They have horrible education. They have no safety or security. And I say to the African American community, what the hell do you have to lose? I will fix it. I will fix it."

Trump made these remarks before overwhelmingly white audiences who cheered lustily. It didn't much matter that crime rates were at fifty-year lows and that cities had largely rebounded from Trump's implicit reference point of the crime-plagued 1970s, or that most African Americans these days reside in suburbs.[26] Trump was spinning racist stereotypes, not stating socioeconomic facts. Yet even as he confirmed the worst myths about Black people and cities, he wrapped them in promises to help. In this refresh of dog whistling, Trump encouraged his base's tendency to believe in Black pathology, but reassured them of his (and their) noble intentions.

Indeed, Trump assured his supporters that Democrats were the real bigots. "We reject the bigotry of Hillary Clinton, which panders to and talks down to communities of color and sees them only as votes," Trump told a predominantly white crowd in Wisconsin in August 2016. Voters should "reject the bigotry of Hillary Clinton, who sees people of color only as votes and not as human beings worthy of a better future," he said a week later in Ohio. In Mississippi, Trump repeated the claim, stating bluntly, "Hillary Clinton is a bigot."[27] CNN's Anderson Cooper challenged Trump to explain, and he offered this: "Well, she is a bigot because you look at what's happening to the inner cities, you look at what's happening to African Americans and Hispanics in this country . . . she's selling them down the tubes."[28]

Trump was repeating and amplifying Ronald Reagan's attacks on welfare families. Reagan had claimed that liberal efforts to help the poor created an entitlement mentality that further trapped them in poverty. Trump expanded the welfare frame into a general description of Black life, and made Democratic betrayal of African Americans a major campaign theme. "Democratic politicians have run nearly every inner city in America for the last 50, 60, 70, 80, 90, 100 years," said Trump, speaking to a white crowd in Manchester, New Hampshire. "Every policy Hillary Clinton supports is a policy that has failed and betrayed communities of color in this country. But she doesn't care. She's too busy raking in cash from people and rigging the system and taking the African American vote." And the Republican position? "Donald Trump will fix it," he said. "We're going to make it better."[29] Because Republicans, Trump boasted, are the ones who genuinely care about Black people.

Creating New Racial Threats

Contrast Trump's occasional expressions of concern for African Americans with how he presented Latinxs and Muslims. Trump launched his campaign with claims about Mexican rapists, led his crowds in chants of "Build the Wall," dwelled on gory crimes committed here by Central Americans, and invited the families of people killed by undocumented immigrants to join him on campaign stages. Trump lied about Muslim Americans cheering the 9/11 attacks, called for waterboarding and worse forms of torture for Muslims, speculated that Muslim Americans knew about but refused to alert authorities to dangerous members of their mosques, and demanded "a total and complete shutdown of Muslims entering the United States."[30]

What explains the venomous tone regarding Latinxs and Muslims? Partly it reflects the increasing social salience of these groups over the last couple of decades. Latinxs recently became the country's largest minority group, with numbers that will continue to rise. Muslims are newly visible as the country has locked itself into endless wars across the Middle East.

But there's an additional, important dimension to the vilification of Muslims and Latinxs. Confusion about whether Latinxs and Muslims should be considered races, or instead ethnic or religious groups, provided added leeway for savaging them while pretending not to be intentionally stirring racial hysteria.

Even liberal pundits were befuddled. Witness the summer 2016 exchange between MSNBC political commentators John Heilemann and Mark Halperin, who had cowritten the bestselling book *Game Change* about the 2008 presidential race and were working on a book about 2016. When Heilemann claimed that Trump's attacks on Mexicans were "pure racial politics," Halperin shot back, "No, it's not racial." Heilemann insisted, "It's racial politics. It is." But Halperin retorted that "Mexico isn't a race."[31]

Halperin's argument that Mexicans cannot constitute a race is consistent with a continental theory of races—that "whites" hail from Europe, "Blacks" from Africa, "yellows" from Asia, and "reds" from the Americas. Under this thinking, Mexicans can't be a race because Mexico is a country, not a continent. More generally, this continental theory implies Latinxs can't be a race because they're a mixture of peoples from different continents, and Muslims can't be a race because they're members of a religion present throughout the world.

Halperin's mistake lay in crediting as factual the cultural belief in the continental origins of races. This sort of myth is important to how race works. The tale of continental origins seeks to attribute racial groups to nature. This hides from view the more inconvenient fact—inconvenient to those claiming to be naturally superior—that societies create races. Societies create races by how they treat groups and through what the general culture believes. The key to whether a group is a "race," therefore, has nothing to do directly with continents or nature. No races exist in nature. Rather, what matters are *the social practices and beliefs*—including about nature and continents, superiority and inferiority—that foster notions of fixed difference and inherent hierarchy.[32]

Today, the Right broadens the targets of dog whistle politics by making Muslims and undocumented immigrants into races that supposedly threaten whites. Trump, *Fox & Friends*, Breitbart, talk radio, and the whole right-wing echo chamber are busy promoting a public belief that "Muslims" and "Mexicans" are in their natural essence inferior and threatening groups, and that "whites" must band together to protect themselves.

To be sure, Trump and his friends are not inventing new races out of whole cloth, but instead weaving a new tapestry from durable pieces of racist fabric. After the attacks on the World Trade Center, muddy beliefs linking religious, cultural, and racial differences provided fertile ground as right-wing politicians and media organs built the "Muslim terrorist" into a racial beast.[33] Soon after 9/11, to say "Muslim terrorist" or "radical Islamic extremist" in the United States was to conjure for many the face of Osama bin Laden. It was to invoke burkas and hijabs; a deep, hostile, and strange foreignness; unfamiliar languages and a singular fanaticism. Most Arabs in the United States are Christian, which itself reflects decades of discrimination in immigration practices, but no matter.[34] The majority of Muslims in the United States—and the world—are not Arab, but so what. The particular history of 9/11 and the ensuing politics of endless war warped the American racial imagination.

If criticism of religious differences provides a thin veneer of legitimacy to dog whistle attacks on Muslims, then stories of inherent illegality play that same role with respect to Latinxs. Those stirring dread around Latinxs frequently assail "illegal aliens." The term offers a ready means to tether Latinxs to myths of criminal depravity. The propaganda deviates from the reality, of course, as a survey of research by the American Immigration Council found: "For more than a century, innumerable studies have confirmed two simple yet powerful truths about the relationship between immigration and crime: immigrants are less likely to commit serious crimes or be behind bars than the native-born, and high rates of immigration are associated with lower rates of violent crime and property crime."[35]

But anecdotes carry more power than statistics, especially among audiences primed to perceive racial threats. The "beautiful Kate" story out of San Francisco and the many other bloody shirts waved by the Right give "illegal" a frightening weight. Indeed, the term is not limited to immigrants at all, but rather expresses an alarm that applies to almost all persons of Latinx descent, most of whom are U.S. citizens.[36] Cumulatively, the invective transforms "illegal" into an emotional knife to the throat, implying that the essential identity of Latinxs is criminal, lawless, and bloodthirsty.[37]

"Mexican" in this discourse is a race that covers almost all Latinxs. As a factual matter, Mexican Americans account for just more than six out of ten in the Latinx population. Among Latinxs, two-thirds are citizens by birth and only a third are foreign born—the majority of whom have naturalized as citizens or are lawfully present in the country.[38] But the fearful gaze on the border with Mexico helps transform every group from south of there into a single menacing racial bogeyman. In March 2019, Trump cut aid to El Salvador, Honduras, and Guatemala. Frankly, the move seemed designed to deepen the humanitarian crises in those countries in a manner likely to generate more people fleeing north, in time for the 2020 elections and a new wave of anti-migrant fearmongering. More telling here, though, is how a *Fox & Friends* chyron distilled the news: "TRUMP CUTS AID TO 3 MEXICAN COUNTRIES."[39]

The Right actively constructs Muslims and Latinxs as races marked by inferior cultures and threatening agendas. Moreover, though the dog whistles themselves rarely invoke biology, the public is quick to fill in that last detail. Dark skin, black hair, brown eyes—people "know" how to recognize a Muslim Arab (even if some turn out to be Latinx or South Asian, Christian or Sikh). The public also knows an "illegal" when it sees one (but doesn't look at Europeans or Canadians that way, whatever their immigration status).

There's no sharp line between racism versus xenophobia against Latinxs. Or between racism, xenophobia, and religious chauvinism against Muslims. They bleed together in a dog whistle technique that conjures these groups as racial threats, but then defends itself by denying that they are races at all. It's precisely the confusion about whether these groups are races that allows extreme language to be used against them.

White Pride Rising

Trump's stoking of racial fear toward brown and Black contributed to a rising sense among many whites that being white forms a key part of their identity. This played into a larger shift already under way among whites about how to understand who they are and how they relate to others in society. Even before Trump's campaign, many whites were already moving toward a conscious embrace of their white identity.

This racial backsliding must be viewed against decades of progress. In the 1950s, large numbers of whites saw being white as important to their identity. Back then, being white was an obvious source of pride as well as a get-in-free pass to jobs, neighborhoods, social and civic clubs, churches, retail establishments, and so on. Knowing yourself to be white was like knowing the sky is blue on a sunny day, the sort of self-evident fact that allows you to breathe a sigh of relief: no matter what else might be happening, at least you weren't Black.

But the civil rights movement convinced most Americans that beliefs in white superiority were morally repugnant. In the years that followed, many whites adopted the "colorblind" norm of trying not to see others or themselves in racial terms. Colorblindness has admirable liberal roots, resting on the ideal of not seeing others through racial stereotypes. That said, racial reactionaries quickly hijacked the ideal, turning it into something very differ-ent.[40] Colorblindness became less an injunction to avoid stereo-types, and more a command to never directly mention race or racism. This enforced silence about race and racism has greatly impeded efforts to foster racial integration, in much the way that refusing to acknowledge a problem ensures it won't be solved. On the Left, this version of colorblindness still limits progress.

In contrast, for the middle and on the Right, colorblindness is fading, and society may rue its demise. Whatever its perversities, even the reactionary version of colorblindness condemned con-sciously foregrounding racial identity as a source of pride. Dur-ing the Obama years, however, many whites started shifting back toward taking pride in being white.

In three studies in 2012 and 2013, political scientist Ashley Jardina asked nationally representative samples of whites this question: "How important is being white to your identity?" Re-spondents could answer on a spectrum from "not at all" to "ex-tremely." Across all three studies, she found a consistent pattern. About a fifth said being white was not important. In contrast, three times as many, about 60 percent, said being white was at least moderately important to them, with about one-third say-ing being white was very or extremely important.[41] She asked this question again three years later, in October and November 2016, in the heat of the election. The numbers saying being white was "very" or "extremely" important had crossed above 40 percent. More than half, 54 percent, said that "whites have a lot or a great deal to be proud of."[42]

People taking polls often give different answers on socially controversial matters depending on how exposed they feel to judgment. Few people want to risk a reproving stare. Jardina had been asking her questions in face-to-face interviews. Was it pos-sible that Jardina's respondents were actually underreporting their commitment to white identity, worried about violating the color-blind social norm against expressing racial pride? In addition to the in-person interviews, Jardina also surveyed respondents over the internet. The results came back the same.

On one hand, the redundancy in her methods generates greater confidence in the results. On the other, the similar results are themselves an important finding: Respondents did not seem embarrassed about saying being white was very or extremely important to them. "It seems quite unlikely," Jardina concluded, "that reporting a strong white identification feels widely inappropriate or in violation of a norm in recent years." [43] If that's true, then what happened to colorblindness? Under the old norm, whites should have hesitated to claim that being white was important to them.

Jardina's work has since been replicated and other social scientists are noticing significant changes in how whites think about themselves. "Trump's success reflects the rise of 'white identity politics,'" the social psychologists Eric Knowles and Linda Tropp report. "Our research shows that the era of 'white invisibility' is coming to a close." [44] Another group of social psychologists studying white identity added this prediction: "As White Americans' numerical majority shrinks and they increasingly feel that their group's status is threatened, White identity will become increasingly salient and central to White Americans." [45]

Jardina cautions against interpreting this development as an increase in white bigotry. She explains that even though most whites say that "whites have a lot or a great deal to be proud of," they are not expressing "a marginalized, extremist identity that is often associated with white supremacist groups like the Ku Klux Klan, neo-Nazis, skinheads, and militia movements." [46] Certainly, compared to the number of whites that Jardina finds now embrace white identity, far fewer whites endorse white supremacy. "White identity politics," Jardina concluded in 2017, is "clearly part of mainstream opinion." [47]

But there remains cause for concern. Derek Black is a former white nationalist whose father founded *Stormfront*, one of the most popular white supremacist websites. In a conversation with

NPR's Terry Gross in 2018, he offered an insider's view on how white supremacists see Trump. Black said they think of him as akin to George Wallace, the segregationist Alabama governor from the 1960s. When Wallace ran for governor the first time, he did so as a racial moderate, and lost. Then he publicly postured as a racial firebrand and won. White supremacists at the time, Black observed, viewed Wallace "as an opportunist who was using white grievance and who was speaking things that the media didn't want him to speak." Today, Black explained, they view "Donald Trump as a very similar person who was tapping into latent social racial opinion and using it to win campaigns"—in other words, not a true believer so much as an opportunist seizing rhetoric that works.

But, Black hastened to add, even if they see Trump as a carpet-bagger, white supremacists nevertheless celebrate the mainstreaming of their ideas from the pinnacle of American power. Whatever Trump's motive, they believe his adopting white nationalist language "could only help" their cause.[48] White supremacists seek "to recruit normal people," said Black. "The people who start a sentence by saying, 'I'm not racist, but . . . ' And if they've said that, they're almost there. All we have to do is get them to come a little bit further."

They seem already on their way. Several polls asked about white supremacy in the wake of the Charlottesville white-power marches. In one poll, just 1 percent of whites said that they mostly agreed with Klan beliefs.[49] That number jumped to 4 percent among those who approved of Trump. In another survey, 4 percent of whites said they held a favorable opinion of neo-Nazis. Among people who voted for Trump, the number was 7 percent. Yet another poll asked again about neo-Nazis, and found that 6 percent of Republicans viewed them favorably. Among those who strongly approved of Trump, that number doubled to 12 percent. After the Charlottesville white riot, Trump said some of the marchers were "very fine people." His comment inspired this poll question: "Do you think it is possible for white supremacists and neo-Nazis to be 'very fine people,' or not?" Among whites in general, 13 percent answered yes. Among Trump voters, the number rose to 22 percent, more than one in five.[50]

Trump's Connection to White Supremacy

Trump's campaign was in free fall in August 2016. He had done little to build a campaign machine, relying instead on the Republican National Committee. "The Trump campaign," the reporter Bob Woodward wrote, was at the time "a few people in a room—a speechwriter, and an advance team of about six people that scheduled rallies in the cheapest venues, often old, washed-out sports or hockey arenas around the country."[51] This was classic Trump, running for president on the cheap as a publicity stunt. But he had clinched the GOP nomination, and the party's leaders and their dark money backers were in despair.

Rebekah Mercer saw a possible solution. Mercer's father had amassed billions as the head of a hedge fund, and she and her father were major funders of the far right.[52] Among their projects was Breitbart and its director, Steve Bannon. Mercer demanded a meeting with Trump. "Your campaign is in chaos," she told him. "What do you recommend?" Trump asked. "Steve Bannon will come in," she responded.[53] This may mark the moment Trump went from encouraging white supremacists through his rhetoric to bringing them into his inner campaign and administration.

What were Bannon's racial views? Bannon saw immigration as a major threat to the continued dominance of whites. "It's not a migration," Bannon said in January 2015. "It's really an invasion. I call it the Camp of the Saints." This obscure reference is telling. *Camp of the Saints* is an apocalyptic novel from 1975 that describes the onslaught in Europe of sexually perverted brown and Black hordes, and that vigorously denounces white Europeans for their refusal to wage a race war for survival.[54]

After his conversation with Mercer, Trump welcomed Bannon

on board to run his campaign.[55] Bannon didn't shrink from taking charge. "I realized," he would say later about helming the Trump campaign, "I'm the director, he's the actor."[56] On the day he came aboard, Bannon told Trump, "Number one, we're going to stop mass illegal immigration and start to limit legal immigration to get our sovereignty back."[57]

At Breitbart, Bannon had used his position to promote the ideas of the self-styled "alt-right." "We're the platform for the alt-right," he boasted at the 2016 Republican National Convention.[58] Understanding that term clarifies the connection between white supremacy and dog whistle politics. As a term and a movement, "alt-right" seeks to exploit code to build mainstream support for racial hatred. The use of code makes it a ready companion to dog whistling.

Richard Spencer coined the "alt-right" term the summer before Obama's 2008 election in order to sanitize hard-core white supremacy.[59] Outlining the phrase's etymology, Southern Poverty Law Center researcher Heidi Beirich reported that among those attempting to mainstream racial hatred, "it went from white supremacy to white nationalism and now from white nationalism to the alt-right or the alternative right." By ditching "white" for "right," Beirich explained, the term effectively wrapped white nationalism in the mantle of the larger conservative coalition.[60]

In his public appearances, Spencer favored clothes that were the sartorial equivalent of the alt-right's linguistic camouflage. He often donned khakis and button-down oxford shirts, exploiting a clean-cut image to smile into the camera as the bright face of reasonable-sounding white pride.[61] In reality, Spencer's convictions were supremely racist.

Graeme Wood, a correspondent for *The Atlantic*, grew up with Spencer in Dallas and knew him distantly. In 2017, Wood traced Spencer's racial thinking to time spent in Germany early in the new millennium, where Spencer encountered the notion of *Volksgeist*. Roughly meaning "spirit of the people," this nineteenth-century term contends that races are marked by physical variations and, much more important, that race determines group destiny. Facial features and skin colors carry little independent importance. Rather, *Volksgeist* argues, visage and hue only matter because they provide a surface marker of fundamental differences in character, temperament, intellectual ability, the capacity to reason and to produce high culture—in short, all of the traits that racists believe separate civilized from savage races.

Spencer stuffed these ideas into his luggage when he returned from Germany to Texas. Back in Dallas, he was distraught by what he perceived as whites squandering their greatness. Dallas, Spencer thought, was "a class- and money-conscious place— whoever has the biggest car or the biggest house or the biggest fake boobs. . . . There's no actual community or high culture or sense of greatness, outside of having a McMansion." [62]

Frustrated, Spencer found a personal mission in rekindling the flame of racial glory among whites. His core proposal became what he termed "peaceful ethnic cleansing." [63] That is, Spencer advocated making the United States or major portions of it for whites only. Left unexplained was how the roughly four in ten Americans who are not white might be convinced to "peacefully" decamp.

Immediately after Trump launched his campaign in June 2015, Spencer stood up as a fan. "I don't think Trump is a white nationalist," he told *The New Yorker*'s Evan Osnos. But he did believe that Trump reflected "an unconscious vision that white people have—that their grandchildren might be a hated minority in their own country. I think that scares us. They probably aren't able to articulate it. I think it's there," he said. "I think *that*, to a great degree, explains the Trump phenomenon. I think he is the one person who can tap into it." [64]

This was the coded white supremacy of Spencer's alt-right that Breitbart propagated. In spreading these views, the key piece was an article from spring 2016, "An Establishment Conservative's Guide to the Alt-Right," by Allum Bokhari and Milo Yiannopoulos. [65] Leaked emails subsequently showed that Yiannopoulos solicited early advice on arguments and sources from writers at the white supremacist sites *Daily Stormer* and *American Renaissance*; circulated drafts to them and other avowed white nationalists; and received back detailed comments and line-by-line annotations.[66] Nevertheless, the guide sought to present the alt-right as disconnected from white supremacy. The guide strongly contrasted the alt-right with "old-school racist skinheads," dissing them as "low-information, low-IQ thugs driven by the thrill of violence and tribal hatred."[67] The alt-right was something different, the guide insisted.

Breitbart's guide located the main impetus for the alt-right in people it termed "natural conservatives." Their conservatism was "natural" insofar as it supposedly reflected instinct: "They instinctively prefer familiar societies, familiar norms, and familiar institutions," it said. "For natural conservatives, culture, not economic efficiency, is the paramount value. More specifically, they value the greatest cultural expressions of their tribe."

The guide particularly stressed the alt-right's opposition to nonwhite immigration. "While eschewing bigotry on a personal level," the guide insisted, "the movement is frightened by the prospect of demographic displacement represented by immigration." Every group, the guide claimed, rightfully seeks to promote its culture. The inevitable result, the guide warned, was conflict. "You'll often encounter doomsday rhetoric in alt-right online communities: that's because many of them instinctively feel that once large enough and ethnically distinct enough groups are brought together, they will inevitably come to blows."

The alt-right, according to Breitbart, is not racist. Instead, it merely recognizes that all groups are marked by inherent cultures and destinies, that groups inevitably cross swords, and that each group must defend itself. The talk of "tribes" does much of the work here.

+ "Tribe" shifts attention from social practices and instead invokes nature. It repositions racism as basic instinct.

Every person belongs to a tribe, tribal members instinctively prefer their own, and tribes inherently war against each other.

♦ "Tribe" also flattens racial hierarchy. It erases centuries of white-over-nonwhite domination. Now whites are just one more racial-cultural group in a melee of many.

♦ "Tribe" also excuses white supremacist violence as self-defense. Because the term is associated with Native Americans and because "tribes" are responsible for inevitable conflict, the term subtly implies that racist violence begins with nonwhites and that whites merely defend themselves.

Breitbart's guide to the alt-right said "tribe." But "tribe" functioned as a disinfected version of *Volksgeist*.[68]

Breitbart broadcast these refurbished racist beliefs, greasing Trump's path to the White House and marching with him into those halls. Yochai Benkler, a law professor at Harvard, studies the spread of ideas on the internet, tracing the links, Facebook posts, and retweets that push some ideas viral. Parsing the 2016 campaign, Benkler found that on the liberal side, the two primary sources for news stories were CNN and the *New York Times*. On the Right, it was Breitbart. Benkler's data showed that Breitbart had three times the reach of the right-wing behemoth Fox News. Citing Benkler's data, the investigative journalist Wil S. Hylton wrote in the *New York Times*, "If you wanted to know who was driving the Republican agenda in 2016, you didn't need to look much farther" than Breitbart.[69]

A few weeks after the 2016 election, the National Policy Institute hosted its annual gathering. Its plain name was another cloak. In fact, Richard Spencer led the outfit. At the convention, Spencer took to the podium in a gray three-piece suit, sporting a haircut called the "fashy," as in "fascist"—with buzzed sides, long on top and gelled back, it's often a coiffured homage to Nazi style. The veils were dropping.[70]

"Hail Trump, hail our people, hail victory!" yelled Spencer, leading the crowd in a rousing cheer. Some in the audience responded with stiff-armed Nazi salutes. "For us, it is conquer or die. This is a unique burden for the white man," Spencer inveighed. "We were not meant to beg for moral validation from some of the most despicable creatures to ever populate the planet. We were meant to overcome—overcome all of it. Because that is natural and normal for us. Because for us, as Europeans, it is only normal again when we are great again."[71]

Spencer was welding *Volksgeist* to Trump's campaign slogan. His listeners cheered and saluted. And Trump embraced that philosophy in notable ways, from bringing Bannon into the White House to giving over much of his immigration policy to people with white nationalist views, like Stephen Miller.[72]

Indeed, riling his base in the final days leading up to the 2018 midterm elections, Trump adopted the "nationalist" label. "Really, we're not supposed to use that word," he told a crowd in Houston, but then proceeded to do it anyway. "You know what I am? I'm a nationalist, okay? I'm a nationalist," he crowed. "Nationalist!" As the crowd roared its approval, Trump chanted back to them, "Use that word! Use that word!" The next day in the Oval Office, reporters challenged Trump over its racist connotations. He professed ignorance. "No, I never heard that theory about being a nationalist," he said. Then he reiterated his stance. "I am a nationalist. It's a word that hasn't been used too much. Some people use it, but I'm very proud. I think it should be brought back."[73]

Here is one of the most important questions for the future of American democracy: What does it mean to be white in the United States today? The majority of whites already believe that being white is important. They want to know what it means for them and their children in a society that's increasingly nonwhite. This question matters greatly to people of color as well. It helps answer which way whites are moving and how communities of color should respond.

This is the question dog whistle politics constantly puts into the minds of the majority of whites, and then answers with tales of peril and instigations of resentment.

How can the Left answer this critical question? The next chapter turns to the race-class approach toward building political power. In the context of responding to dog whistling, it offers a potential answer rooted in racial equality and cross-racial solidarity. Thus the race-class approach intentionally speaks to people of all hues, not alone nor especially to whites. Nevertheless, the race-class response does offer an answer to what it means to be white in the United States today:

> To be white means to be an equal member of this society, like people of every other color, and therefore to be better off practically and morally by coming together across racial lines to demand that government and the marketplace truly work for all working families.

Let's turn to more fully explore the race-class approach.

9

The Race-Class Approach

The Right's core narrative urges voters to fear and resent people of color, to distrust government, and to trust the marketplace. The Left can respond by urging people to join together across racial lines, to distrust greedy elites sowing division, and to demand that government work for everyone. This is, to repeat, a core narrative, not a recommendation regarding precise language. This is the foundational scaffolding the Left can use to build a multiracial movement for racial and economic justice. The first box puts the

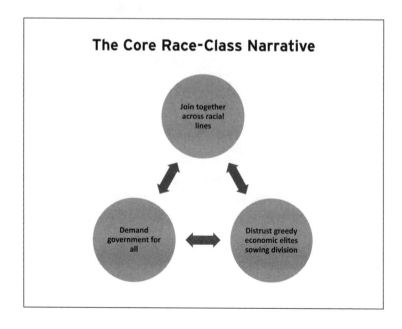

core narrative into visual form. The next puts flesh on the bones, offering three versions of the race-class message.

How did the race-class messages perform compared to dog whistle racial fear? We tested nine versions of the race-class message. *Persuadables found all nine race-class messages more convincing than the dog whistle racial fear message.* It's an impressive result for a first run. Recall that familiar messages typically do better simply because they're familiar. Those in the middle hear racial fear messages every day, and yet even when first exposed to the race-class messages, this group found all of them more convincing.

From an electoral perspective, the most important question is which progressive narrative performs better against the opposition message among persuadable voters, the almost six in ten in the swing middle. Here, too, the race-class approach did well. *Among persuadables, the race-class messages were more convincing than colorblind economic populism, which in turn struggled to win against the opposition message.*[1] And just to be clear: approval for the race-class messages does not merely reflect support from people of color obscured behind the persuadable label. Broken down by racial group, whites, African Americans, and Latinxs all found the race-class messages more convincing than colorblind economic populism, and by similar margins.[2]

While much more research remains to be done and the race-class messages will certainly evolve, we're confident the early positive results were not a fluke. Other groups subsequently tested versions of the race-class message and also report strong findings. Rural Organizing, a progressive group focused on rebuilding rural America, surveyed their constituents in 2018. Unsurprisingly, they found rural-specific messages to be very popular. For instance, this message garnered approval from 94 percent of respondents: "The rural and small-town way of life is worth fighting for." Now compare how the novel race-class arguments did. Rural Organizing also tested this message: "In small towns and rural communities we believe in looking out for each other, whether we're white, Black or brown, tenth generation or newcomer." Almost nine out

Three Race-Class Narratives

Working People

No matter where we come from or what our color, most of us work hard for our families. But today, certain politicians and their greedy lobbyists hurt everyone by handing kickbacks to the rich, defunding our schools, and threatening seniors with cuts to Medicare and Social Security. Then they turn around and point the finger for hard times at poor families, Black people, and new immigrants. We need to join together with people from all walks of life to fight for our future, just like we won better wages, safer workplaces, and civil rights in our past. By joining together, we can elect new leaders who work for all of us, not just the wealthy few.

America's Strength

America's strength comes from our ability to work together—to knit together a landscape of people from different places and of different races into one nation. For this to be a place of freedom for all, we cannot let the greedy few and the politicians they pay for divide us against each other based on what someone looks like, where they come from, or how much money they have. It's time to stand up for each other and come together. It is time for us to pick leaders who reflect the very best of every kind of American. Together, we can make this a place where freedom is for everyone, no exceptions.

Divide/Come Together

"United we stand, divided we fall." This doesn't mean we always agree. It means that when we come together, we have the power to make things better. Certain politicians and the greedy lobbyists funding them pit our communities against each other based on what we look like or where we come from, making us believe we can't all have what we need while they help themselves to even more. When we're divided, the people demanding seconds before everyone has firsts gain power to take away things like money for good schools, support for seniors, and affordable healthcare. When we come together, we have the power to make government work for all of us, not just the greedy few.

of ten, 89 percent, agreed. And this message: "Instead of delivering for working people, politicians hand kickbacks to their donors who send jobs overseas. Then they turn around and blame new immigrants or people of color, to divide and distract us from the real source of our problems." Three-quarters of all respondents, 76 percent, agreed.[3]

In the summer of 2018, Latino Decisions polled more than 2,000 registered voters in the 61 most competitive House districts. They tested this statement: "Today, certain politicians and their greedy lobbyists hurt everyone by handing kickbacks to the rich, defunding our schools, and threatening our seniors with cuts to Medicare and Social Security. Then they turn around and point the finger for our hard times at poor families, Black people, and new immigrants. We need to join together with people from all walks of life to fight for our future."[4] More than 85 percent of respondents agreed.

These high levels of agreement are heartening, especially coming from rural areas and competitive districts where one might expect a more lukewarm reception.

We've also seen the race-class approach picked up in campaigns and by politicians across the country. In Minnesota, for instance, the early success of the race-class canvassing experiment—discussed in chapter 2—led a coalition of progressive groups to build a 2018 race-class campaign under the tagline "Greater than Fear." Anat Shenker-Osorio was heavily involved in developing this effort, which the state Democrats soon integrated into their own messaging. Indeed, Tim Walz, running for governor, closed his campaign by invoking taking care of "every child, black, white, brown or indigenous," and by asking Minnesotans to stand "in this time of division" and say, "We are greater than fear."[5] Progressive candidates won across the state, including Walz for governor and the races for attorney general and secretary of state, while also flipping the Minnesota State House blue. On the federal level, Democrats won both Senate seats and five of eight House races.

Senator Elizabeth Warren also moved race-class to the heart of her messaging. She had already hit some of its notes in her 2016 Democratic convention speech.[6] Two summers later, giving a keynote at Netroots Nation 2018, she put "the politics of division" at the core of her story about the challenges progressives face and how to win.

Elizabeth Warren on "the Politics of Division"

The rich and powerful profit when government doesn't work for working people.

And they have learned that the best way to stop us from changing the system is to set working people against each other.

So they have become the experts at the politics of division. Frankly it might be the one thing that Donald Trump is really good at. . . .

Trump and his pals tell working people a story about what's gone wrong with their lives.

This story is not about big banks cheating customers, or insurance companies discriminating against people with pre-existing conditions. Nope, that is not the story. . . .

It isn't even about billionaires who get out of paying their fair share while we hold back on rebuilding our roads, subways, and power grid. Or about lobbyists who write tax bills so that the corporations that they work for get special breaks, while the average family in America gets nothing.

Nope, those aren't the stories that Trump tells.

In Trump's story, the reason working families keep getting the short end of the stick isn't because of the decisions that he and his pals are making in Washington every day.

No, according to Trump, the problem is other working people—people who are Black or brown, people who were born somewhere else, people who don't worship the same, dress the same, or talk the same as Trump and his buddies.

And it comes in all sorts of flavors: racism, sexism, homophobia, xenophobia. It comes in all sorts of forms: nasty personal attacks, trolling on Twitter, winking at white supremacists.

It all adds up to the same thing: The politics of division.

Politics that tries to pit Black working people against white working people so they won't band together.

Politics of division that tells Americans to distrust each other, to fear each other, to hate each other.

Because while we're busy doing that, Mitch McConnell gets to raid the Treasury and give a trillion bucks to their rich friends, destroy healthcare for millions of families, and wipe out Social Security and Medicare.

They want us pointing fingers at each other so we won't notice their hand is in our pockets.

Well, it stops here. It stops here. It stops now. It stops with this movement and this moment and this election.

It is time for us say no! to the politics of division, to say no! to the ugly use of bigotry and fear.

We say, No, you will not divide us!

We are here to bring working families together, to demand a government that works for all of us. That's why we're here.

Netroots Nation, August 3, 2018.[7]

The Critical Role Played by Advocates: Repetition and Passion

The heartening results provide a solid starting place, but because persuadables often default to what they heard last, to move them requires a compelling story told over and over. The Right understands this and daily bombards the middle with messages of racial threat. The Left must be similarly relentless, inundating persuadables with messages of cross-racial solidarity, energized by hope for practical improvements as well as by moral conviction. Our initial message testing shows that the race-class message has an advantage over the negative opposition message. But this means very little unless the broad Left picks up the message and repeats it at every turn.

To craft the race-class message, the project extensively consulted with activists from unions, racial justice organizations, workers' movements, and progressive political groups. We did so cognizant that any new message would have to be something that advocates—the ones who engage in politics and organizing as professionals, who live and breathe mobilizing people—would enthusiastically repeat. The project found that the race-class message immediately resonated with advocates, as many had already developed a similar political analysis. For instance, in response to a question about racism, one activist offered: "Going back to the '60s and certainly even earlier, the political right in the United States has sought to construct ideas about hard work in racialized terms that suggest that they value white working people . . . where in fact what they intend to do is make sure that their pay goes down." These sorts of comments helped shape the development of specific race-class messages. In addition, they boosted confidence that advocates would embrace and promote the core race-class story.

Further confidence comes from recognizing that while the race-class story may be novel in mainstream electoral politics, it strongly echoes a major element of Black radical thought.

From W. E. B. DuBois to Martin Luther King Jr., Black radical thinkers have long wrestled with how to respond to the deep connections between capitalism and racial oppression. One recurrent strain of thought posits that Black salvation requires cross-racial solidarity and likewise that white salvation requires precisely the same. In her insightful book *From #BlackLivesMatter to Black Liberation*, Princeton professor Keeanga-Yamahtta Taylor makes this argument.

> Racism in the United States has never been just about abusing Black and Brown people just for the sake of doing so. It has always been a means by which the most powerful white men in the country have justified their rule, made their money, and kept the rest of us at bay. To that end, racism, capitalism, and class rule have always been tangled together. . . .
>
> In this context, solidarity is not just an option; it is crucial to workers' ability to resist the constant degradation of their living standards. Solidarity is only possible through relentless struggle to win white workers to antiracism . . . to win the white working class to the understanding that, unless they struggle, they too will continue to live lives of poverty and frustration, even if those lives are somewhat better than the lives led by Black workers. Success or failure are contingent on whether or not working people see themselves as brothers and sisters whose liberation is inextricably bound together.[8]

The race-class approach adopts this call for class-based cross-racial solidarity, connecting it to insights about the destructive power of dog whistle politics. It points to dog whistling to demonstrate how the economic royalty maneuver to racially divide us, and it points to the actual policies pursued by the party of corporate America to show precisely how every racial community loses when too many people vote their racial anxieties.

The race-class project also directly probed the willingness of advocates to share the various messages the project tested.

Understanding that people's willingness to share a message is important to its spread, the national survey asked: "How likely are you to share this message with your friends and family on social media on a scale of 0 to 100, where 100 means you are very likely to share this and a 0 means you are very unlikely to share this?" The race-class messages strongly resonated with the advocacy community. Advocates expressed greater enthusiasm for sharing seven of the nine race-class messages, compared to colorblind economic populism. Not surprisingly, the advocates indicated virtually no likelihood of sharing the dog whistle fear message.

We also paid close attention to the reactions of the opposition—the roughly one in five voters convinced that the poor and people of color bear individual responsibility for their condition, that government should get out of the way, and that the marketplace will provide jobs and prosperity for all. Typically, message testing looks at overall favorability across the greatest range of people. While that might work for laundry detergent, it is a mistake in politics. Trying to please everyone requires saying nothing of substance. Or worse, seeking to appeal to everyone can lead progressives to adopt and reinforce reactionary messaging. "Security" might test well across a broad audience when mouthed by a Democrat, but it does so partly because it resonates with and further entrenches a Republican frame.

Predictably, the opposition embraced the dog whistle message, giving it a convincing rate of 75. In contrast, the opposition rated the race-class messages between 41 and 52, with only two messages receiving scores above 50. The convincing rating scale sets 50 as neutral. In other words, with the opposition, the race-class messages did far worse than the racial fear message and were mainly unconvincing. That's the result we were looking for.

Joining Together

How do you convince people beset by daily struggles to march, recruit friends, organize with strangers, summon the energy to vote, or take myriad other forms of political action? This challenge is often described as the problem of moving people to collective action. Whether in social movements or election campaigns, the principal task is to move people off the sidelines and into action with others.

In this regard, though, messages about economic hardship face a steep hill. Getting people to collective action requires showing them that the economic problems in their lives reflect structural dynamics, and then convincing them that they should work with others to fix these large-scale problems they cannot solve on their own. The challenge comes from the fact that people typically understand their financial position in personal, individual terms, and struggle to comprehend a structural analysis.

The race-class focus groups tested messages stressing structural accounts of poverty, using the more accessible language of a lack of opportunity. For instance, in a conversation with African American female friends in Richmond, Virginia, the moderator offered this: "Some people say that the primary reason that people struggle financially is that they did not have as many opportunities as others from the get-go. What do you think about this?"

The response seemed to reject that sentiment as whining: "I don't think so. It's all researched," said one friend. "Everybody has the same opportunity. Whether they take advantage of it or not, that's on them. That's a personal thing."

Compare the reaction when the moderator offered this alternative message: "Some people say the reason that individuals struggle financially is that they haven't worked as hard as others, or they just made bad choices. What do you think about that?"

The notion resonated: "I think they make bad choices, too," the other woman insisted. "Because you would rather go out and buy something designer than pay your mortgage or your rent or your car note or put food on your table. 'I have to get the next bag' or 'I have to get the next pair of Jordans.'"

Individual conduct is familiar from their own lives; structures are distant abstractions. It's no accident unions develop extensive training and education programs to move members toward an understanding of how the economy and government function. The personal fault frame is simply more accessible, obvious, and understandable than a story about large impersonal forces—and it's the story the Right broadcasts 24/7 on every wavelength it can reach.

In contrast, the race-class conversation often generated intuitive agreement with the need to move toward collective responses.

In the Columbus, Ohio, focus group with white men, we asked an icebreaker question about whether they saw themselves as urban or rural. This was early in the conversation and well before we introduced our race-class narratives. Yet simply by raising the urban-rural split, we got an earful about intentional division as a strategy of economic elites.

"They want us to be divided," one man said. "They want us to be squabbling amongst ourselves, while they take the bags and walk away. If we're fighting, we can't see what they're doing. It's a distraction. It's a major distraction I would say."

"Yeah, exactly," another responded. "They don't want us to be in community, because they understand the power in our numbers, if we are unified."

The moderator followed up with a question about other sources of division, and the top two answers were skin color and wealth. Moreover, again with no direct prompting, the men connected those two elements.

"I think that racial division is something that is pushed by those in power. It's a way to keep us arguing. It's a way to oppress people, keep them uneducated. It's a big issue," one participant said.

Another added that most people aren't racist and don't consider race when choosing their friends. "Not everybody is the term 'racist.' Most people probably have friends and don't even consider what color skin they have." This participant seemed generally resistant to imputing racist motives to his peers. Notably, though, he was willing to see racism as being pushed by elites: "But the people that are above everybody just kind of push that as a thing . . . politicians and the media use that as a tool. It's a divisive thing."

Much later, the moderator tested the group's reaction to a race-class story, asking whether they agreed or disagreed that "politicians doing the bidding of corporate interests and big donors intentionally use race to keep us divided and distracted."

One man responded, "I don't think that they're specifically looking to start a race war or anything like that." Nevertheless, he agreed that "politicians will use whatever advantage they can get to keep themselves in office," including by looking at different racial communities and asking "How can I rile them up according to their worst fears to get them to notice me and not the other guy?"

"I agree," came a response. "It's not every one of them that really do it but the ones that do it, there are some where it's to the point where it's blatantly obvious."

The conversation continued along these lines until another participant joined in to summarize the group's thoughts: "By telling us you have to hate the Black man because he does all the bad stuff. That's what they're doing. They're dividing us so they can conquer. If we would all come together the politicians wouldn't have the strength they have."

Before it can move people to collective action, an economic message has to get them over the hump of a structural analysis explaining how government policies ripple through the economy to affect their daily lives. In contrast, the race-class message offers the possibility of traveling an easier road. It takes people along a clear path, from tough times to intentional division to joining together. People can readily grasp purposeful division, as they see it in their families, their workplaces, in community groups, and very much in politics. And they know that coming together is the clear solution.

Including the White Racial Group

Conventional wisdom holds that support for liberal policies craters when race is foregrounded. The thinking is simple: Many whites will support liberal policies when they view themselves or people like them as beneficiaries. If they are reminded that Blacks may benefit—for instance from "Obamacare," a name for the Affordable Care Act invented by the Right to give it a racial cast—support for social welfare often plummets.

We found something strikingly at odds with this consensus. Respondents to our survey were *more enthusiastic* about progressive policies when specifically told that all racial groups would benefit.

We asked people which came closer to their views: a right-wing probusiness story, or a progressive agenda promoting activist government. In doing so, we offered respondents two versions of the progressive message, with and without the italicized text: "To make life better for working people we need to invest in education, create better paying jobs, and make healthcare more affordable for *white, Black, and brown* people struggling to make ends meet."

How did the two versions of the progressive message compare? The race-silent progressive message bested the probusiness message by a margin of 33 points. This result confirms that voters generally prefer progressive over probusiness economic policies.

But what happened when the progressive policy position included the phrase "white, Black, and brown"? The winning margin over the conservative policies increased to 41 points, a significant improvement. Mentioning that all racial groups would benefit drove up support for investing in education, creating better-paying jobs, and making healthcare more affordable. Support for progressive policies did not fall off a cliff when race was mentioned. It dramatically increased when combined with assurances that all racial groups will benefit.

But this is not an argument for inserting race into the conversation in any form.

We also asked respondents their opinions regarding "greedy special interests," offering two alternatives. One message stayed silent on race ("Greedy special interests hold us back, damaging our economy by rigging the rules in their favor"). The other centered on harm to people of color but did not mention whites. ("Greedy special interests hold us back, dividing us against each other by blaming Black and brown people for our problems so they can rig the rules in their favor"). We did not measure these against each other directly, so no head-to-head results are available. Still, compared to when no direct mention of race was made, persuadables responded *less positively* when told that special interests specifically target Black and brown people.

Along similar lines, in another set of questions we contrasted "greedy special interests" and "greedy special interests dividing us by blaming Black and brown people for our problems." Again we found that when Black and brown people were invoked, persuadables were *less likely* to take the progressive position. That is, they found the progressive critique of "greedy special interests" less convincing when warned about efforts to scapegoat Black and brown people.

This combination of results suggests two important insights:

1) People are worried about racial division. They want messages that touch on this, and they respond positively to messages that expressly communicate that all racial groups, whites included, will do better by coming together.

2) What tends to lose the persuadable middle is naming racism solely in terms of harms to communities of color in a manner that implicitly excludes and perhaps even faults whites.

Assuring voters that whites will benefit from activist government proved to be an essential element in generating enthusiasm. Expressly stating that whites benefit seemed to cut against two core themes of the Right's story: that talking about racism really means blaming whites; and that addressing racism reflects concern for people of color but not for whites.

Here's another example where mentioning race—and including whites as among those who benefit—increased support for the progressive message.

We asked respondents which was closer to their opinion, a message of racial fear or a race-class message offered in two different versions. The first named division and coming together in general terms. The second then added a direct mention of racial groups. "We need elected leaders who will reject the divide-and-conquer tactics of their opponents and put the interests of working people first, *whether we're white, Black, or brown.*" The only difference between the two race-class messages was the italicized text, included in one but not the other.

The message that did not specifically mention racial groups *lost* to the dog whistle message. But when the message identified the intended beneficiaries as "working people, whether we're white, Black, or brown," the race-class message *won* against the dog whistle message. Expressly including all racial groups, whites too, among those who gain by fighting racial division produced a net 10-point improvement in the performance of the race-class message.

Clearly the race-class messages work best when they indicate that whites, too, suffer because of racism and stand to gain from cross-racial solidarity and progressive policies. This is the seeming import of the phrase "white, Black, and brown." Most whites now perceive themselves to be a racial group and wonder at least implicitly who threatens their group. The Right's answer is people of color and their liberal enablers. The best Left answer is the billionaires using racism to divide us, white, Black, and brown.

Does the phrase "white, Black, or brown" communicate a lack of concern to Asian Americans, Pacific Islanders, and Native Hawaiians? When surveyed, these groups responded to the phrase "white, Black, and brown" with no notable drop-off in enthusiasm for the race-class message. In contrast, expanding the categories—for instance, to "white, Black, brown, Asian American, Native American, Native Hawaiian, or Pacific Islander"—did diminish support. Perhaps the laundry-list effect undercut the message by making it seem like cynical box-checking.

Naming no more than three groups seems a better approach, not least because messaging research shows that people respond well to groups of three but become befuddled as the numbers rise from there. Among the three, it's unlikely to matter which groups are included so long as whites figure among them. That said, reversing the order to "Black, brown, and white" increased support for the race-class messages from people of color.

A tentative comment on messengers: Commonly, people of color speaking to white audiences must take special care to suppress racial issues—think Barack Obama going out of his way to avoid talking about race. We tested various messages using different messengers. When we tested the racial justice frame, the results seemed to confirm the intuition that people of color should not talk to whites about race. Whites generally disliked the racial justice frame to begin with, and disliked it all the more when delivered by an African American woman compared to a white woman.[9] Along similar lines, political scientist Christopher Stout recently reported that "both black and white voters were substantially less likely to support black candidates who charged racism or otherwise made negative racial appeals."[10] Naming racism in terms of damage to communities of color can be politically costly, especially to messengers of color.

In contrast, we found that whites reacted *more positively* to messengers of color compared to white messengers when they heard a race-class message. The differences were often slight and more research is needed. Still, the results were suggestive. The same race-class messages seemed to gain credibility with persuadables, and with whites in particular, when conveyed by a Latinx woman or an African American man. An invitation to join a multiracial coalition as a welcome ally seemed more persuasive and reassuring when extended by a person of color. For nonwhite politicians and for organizers of color, this is important. It suggests they may gain rather than lose credibility with white audiences by talking about racism, but only when framed as a divide-and-distract weapon against all racial groups, whites included.

Race-Class as Interest Convergence

Naming whites as beneficiaries of cross-racial solidarity also increases support from people of color. Recall that we tested this statement: "We need elected leaders who will reject the divide-and-conquer tactics of their opponents and put the interests of working people first." And then we tested it again, adding at the end "whether we're white, Black, or brown." Looking at the racial breakdown, support for the racially inclusive version went up by 8 points among whites. It shot up by a remarkable 21 points among African Americans.

Why might people of color respond more positively to a message of cross-racial solidarity that emphasizes benefits to whites in addition to themselves? People of color seem to have more confidence in cross-racial solidarity when they understand why whites have their own clear stake to join in coalition.

We asked African Americans in Atlanta to respond to this statement: "Americans deserve to make more than a decent living; we deserve to have a decent life and to get it we must unite and participate in our political system no matter what we look like, how we pray, or where we come from."

"It didn't seem very realistic to me. It seemed more based on ideal, what things could be like ideally," a participant named Dwayne countered (not his real name).

Earlier, the moderator had asked Dwayne a question about uniting Americans: "Dwayne, what about you? Do you think that Americans, that most Americans, want to be united?"

His cynicism was obvious: "I think most people would say that, but they probably wouldn't mean that. I think what everybody wants is what's best for themselves. Individually. And I think it's a convenient thing, especially in this climate, to say that we want unity and less division. But I doubt that most people would actually want that; it's just something to say."

Still probing whether unity was possible, the moderator asked for examples of cross-racial cooperation between whites and Blacks. This came back:

"You know, Abraham Lincoln, he freed the slaves, right? But that was a business deal. It wasn't, 'I feel sorry for Black people. Let me free the slaves.' When he freed the slaves, that was a business deal that worked, I guess, in our benefit, because people were no longer slaves, but . . ."

Like Dwayne, many in the nonwhite focus groups understood that people act out of self-interest, and they wanted to know what whites stood to gain from cross-racial movement.

Their viewpoint reminded me of the "interest convergence" perspective from Derrick Bell that I often share with my racial justice students. Bell took a long view on civil rights and racial progress. Cutting through the fine-sounding language of equality, rights, and freedom, Bell noticed a pattern that by no means was limited to Lincoln and the end of formal slavery. Racial advances for African Americans occurred when racial progress helped major segments of the white community, Bell observed. Bell certainly found inspiration in the courage and strength of moral leaders, and recognized the important role that moral arguments play in energizing people to join justice movements.[11] Nevertheless, he resisted being lulled into supposing that moral appeals could do most of the heavy lifting. Instead, Bell insisted that racial progress was more likely to follow when powerful segments of white society—elites as well as broad numbers—recognized that it served their own interests.

To highlight the role of self-interest is not to suggest that political motives are purely mercenary and never moral. Moral claims play a galvanizing role in moving people to action. Take Rev. William Barber's new fusion movement around racial and economic justice. Rev. Barber is reinvigorating Martin Luther King's Poor People's Campaign from half a century ago. In doing so, he uses moral and spiritual commands as the essential organizing glue that binds people to each other. The first principle of the new Poor People's Campaign tells us: "We are rooted in a moral analysis based on our deepest religious and constitutional values that demand justice for all. Moral revival is necessary to save the heart and soul of our democracy."[12]

Even in the "self-interest" at the heart of interest convergence, notions of morality and values play very important roles. Self-interest is not, for most, a concept analyzed on an Excel spreadsheet that calculates dollars and cents. It's a matter of finances, yes, but also involves providing for one's family and especially one's children; receiving what you merit measured against what others receive and deserve; and self-respect as well as status in the community. In other words, most people do not sharply distinguish between morality and self-interest. Rather, they blend them together, typically in terms heavily influenced by cultural norms.

This means people tend to reject moral claims that run counter to their sense of what helps them and their family. In the midst of the Great Depression, the famed novelist, progressive muckraking journalist, and would-be politician Upton Sinclair wrote, "It is difficult to get a man to understand something, when his salary depends upon his not understanding it!" He might have said as well that it is difficult to show people an injustice when their income depends on not seeing it. To be sure, some remarkable people stand ready to address the immorality of unjust social hierarchies, though it requires that they upend their world to do right. But in general, it is not an especially promising route toward mass mobilization to ask people to sacrifice what they see as essential to their children's future, to give up some of what they believe they deserve, to relinquish some of their status, just because "it's the right thing to do."

The blending of morality and self-interest also means, though, that as people see how something helps them, they become much more open to moral demands pushing in the same direction. It's hugely important that among persuadables there's a widespread belief in progressive racial norms. Once people understand that the greater threats in their lives come from economic titans rather than from other working families, that new understanding quickly finds expression in moral terms. This is not a simple matter of cynically putting a moral gloss on selfishness. The anti-racist values are genuine and add to the impetus to fight racism. Persuadables more fully open themselves to embracing anti-racist values once they see that their and their children's well-being will flow from cross-racial solidarity.

The box on the next page summarizes the case for the Left to merge race and class, emphasizing the aligned interests of the class Left and the race Left.

The Essential Case for the Left to Merge Race and Class

(1) The Right's principal political strategy is to exploit coded racism as a divide-and-conquer weapon.

(2) The Left can unite and build by calling out intentional racial division and urging every racial group to join together to demand that government work for all of us.

(3) All working families, white families included, will be economically better off if a large voting majority believes in cross-racial solidarity and rejects messages of racial menace. This would facilitate the sorts of wave elections that can get government back on the side of working families rather than giant corporations.

(4) State violence against communities of color will not drastically diminish until people stop electing politicians who promise to punish supposedly threatening and undeserving people of color. Electing leaders loyal to a multiracial movement that emphasizes our shared humanity may provide the best chance to shift government from persecuting to helping communities of color.

10

20/20 Vision: Comparing the Left's Possible Responses to Anti-Immigrant Dog Whistling

The dominant Republican threat story in 2018 and most likely in the election circus of 2020 will center on immigrants as dangerous people. How should the Left respond? This concluding chapter explores possible responses as a means to summarize key differences among the messaging and organizing choices faced by the Left.

Pander to Racial Fear and Resentment

One recurrent strain of thought is that Democrats cannot beat the Right's dog whistling and so instead should imitate it by reassuring racially fearful and resentful voters that liberals, too, will protect them from supposedly dangerous and undeserving people of color. Over the life of dog whistle politics, Democrats have been more inclined to take this approach than to seek victory as champions of communities of color. Such reasoning helped Bill Clinton win election twice. Today, advice along these lines crops up repeatedly in the immigration context.

Invoking recent history, Democratic strategists often criticize Hillary Clinton for coming across as wanting "open borders," especially when compared to Barack Obama. Consider a 2017 piece titled "How Immigration Foiled Hillary" by *New York Times* contributor Thomas Edsall. We met him earlier as the co-author of *Chain Reaction*, the 1991 book advancing the "racial justice as liberal charity" version of history that influenced Bill Clinton, and more recently James Traub. In this 2017 article, Edsall highlighted immigration's role in driving Republican turnout. He then contrasted Clinton's progressive immigration policies with Obama's harder line, noting that Obama "stressed policies calling for the deportation of criminals and in fact deported more people than George W. Bush or Bill Clinton."[1] The implication seemed clear: Democrats should jettison progressive positions on immigration reform and get serious about hardening the border lest they once again be "foiled." Edsall in effect urged Democrats to reassure anxious white voters that liberals, too, would guard against perceived racial threats.

But if Obama is to be a role model on immigration, a closer look is required. Tellingly, this takes us back to Bill Clinton. In the 1990s, the Republicans were also agitating voters with dire warnings of the danger posed by "illegals." Democrats responded by adopting the same discourse and offering their own draconian policies. As he had with his "tough on crime" stance against the Black community, Clinton led the way.

Memos recently made public from the Clinton Presidential Library make clear the political calculus at work. Rahm Emanuel was a senior adviser to Clinton. He urged the president to take the immigration issue from Republicans through stunts like increasing the National Guard presence along the border and dramatically halting naturalization proceedings for a month, ostensibly to "review past files for criminal misconduct." But Emanuel knew that press conference posturing requires more than gimmicks. He also urged Clinton to "achieve record deportations of criminal aliens,"[2] and Clinton followed through, drastically increasing appropriations for border security and cracking down on those he, too, called "illegal aliens."[3] Clinton also signed a series of laws targeting immigrants lawfully present in the country.[4]

The Obama administration repeated this gambit, developing a hard line against immigration. Was Emanuel giving the same advice? He certainly had Obama's ear, as his first chief of staff. In addition, Obama named Janet Napolitano head of the Department of Homeland Security. She had been governor of Arizona, and before that, the attorney general in that state, at a time when Joe Arpaio was the elected sheriff of Maricopa County, home to Phoenix. Arpaio was a darling of the Right for his systematic targeting of Latinxs as "illegal aliens," and was ultimately indicted for racist civil rights violations. Throughout her time as Arizona's top law enforcement officer, Napolitano handled Arpaio with kid gloves, earning his endorsement in her own gubernatorial campaign.[5]

Under Napolitano, Homeland Security in the first year of the Obama administration removed roughly 400,000 persons, higher than the highest totals ever reached by the Bush administration.[6] Then it continued this record-setting pace for the next eight years. Virtually all of the immigrants who were deported in 2010—an astounding 97 percent—were Hispanic, a disproportionately high share given that Latinxs accounted for roughly 81 percent of all undocumented immigrants in the United States.[7] Over these years, the number of people seeking to cross the border without authorization was declining, partly because of stepped-up enforcement, but also because of improved economic conditions in Mexico and the 2008 recession in the United States. Nevertheless, the Obama administration kept aggressively deporting people; over eight years it removed 3.1 million individuals, at a rate 1.5 times greater than the Bush administration.[8]

Obama in his first term appeared to have listened to the Democratic strategists urging a tougher stance on immigrants.[9] Once safely reelected, Obama moderated. He created the Deferred Action for Childhood Arrivals (DACA) program, offering limited protections to unauthorized immigrants brought into the country as children. DACA suspended deportation for roughly 800,000 "Dreamers," a reference to the DREAM Act, legislation that would have provided similar protections had it not been blocked by the Republican-controlled Congress in 2010. After the 2014 midterms, Obama was even more emboldened, proposing a parallel program, Deferred Action for Parents of Americans (DAPA), for unauthorized immigrant parents of children who were either citizens or lawfully present. By one estimate, a quarter of Latinx children in the United States have an unauthorized immigrant parent.[10] Texas and twenty-five other states, all with Republican governors, successfully sued to block DAPA. In September 2017, the Trump administration moved to end DACA.[11]

Obama deserves accolades for his efforts to help unauthorized immigrants through DACA and DAPA. The GOP intransigence in Congress, in the states, and among voters demonstrated the pervasive hostility toward immigration reform that his administration faced.

But Obama also deserves the critical nickname pinned on him by immigration activists, "Deporter in Chief." To compete with GOP messages stoking racial fear of immigrants, the Obama administration adopted harsh deportation and detention policies that harmed millions of families.

This strategy did not defang GOP messaging around immigration; it just made it more extreme as the GOP kept upping the ante. Dog whistling works because it promotes falsehoods depicting nonwhites as semihuman. The facts about deportations and border enforcement matter less than the fears dog whistling stokes. Deporting more and more people will not defuse the threat narrative, just as building a wall will make no practical difference in border security. The point is the nightmare, not the reality.

Campaigning against sanctuary cities, migrant caravans, birthright citizenship, and criminal illegal aliens in 2018, Donald Trump accused Democrats of supporting "sanctuary cities of death."[12] Democratic senator Joe Donnelly, running for reelection in Indiana, took the bait. He released an ad with banners proclaiming "Joe Donnelly: Joining with Trump to Build Wall & Protect Our Borders." Likewise, responding to Trump's government shutdown over funding for a border wall, in January 2019 the Democrats stopped just short of caving, offering a billion dollars for "border security"—accepting and advancing the right-wing fear-based frame. How can Democrats expect to compete on that terrain? Do they think that halfhearted support for walls or billions for border security will help them unseat candidates warning about sanctuary cities of death? It didn't work for Donnelly, who lost.

In sum, it seems unlikely that Democrats can win by dog whistling around immigration:

1) Competing with the GOP on dog whistle terms means unleashing state violence against communities of color. This is deeply immoral. It also demoralizes and alienates the communities under siege as well as the Left's advocates and base.

2) Because competing with the Right for support from racially anxious voters becomes a competition, the Right will not stand still but will become even more extreme.

3) The core Democratic voters look very different than in the 1990s, when Bill Clinton successfully imitated dog whistling. There are more people of color. Whites in the party are more liberal on racial issues. There's an activist base that will vociferously challenge this sort of race-baiting.

Because the GOP has effectively cornered the market on tales of horror and threat from immigrants, the only way to compete on immigration is to tell a completely different story. But what should that story look like?

Run Silent Regarding the GOP's Appeals to Racial Panic

Another impulse is to ignore the immigration issue insofar as possible and emphasize instead pocketbook issues like wages or healthcare. As the 2018 midterms approached and dog whistles against immigrant caravans and knife-wielding killers reached a crescendo, two of the most influential think tanks in Democratic politics came together to recommend that approach. In a confidential four-page memo acquired by the *New York Times*, the centrist groups Third Way and the Center for American Progress offered suggestions on how to respond to dog whistles on immigration.

The memo began by confirming what everyone knew: the GOP was amping its base on fears about immigrants. The Right's "attacks pack a punch," the groups warned. The *Times* reported that to counter that, "The strategists who prepared the memo advised [that Democrats] should spend 'as little time as possible' talking about immigration itself, and instead pivot to more fruitful issues for Democrats like health care and taxation."[13] In other words, their advice amounted to this: *The Right's anti-immigrant fear-mongering is really working, so cross your fingers that by pivoting to economics your audience will stop listening to the Right.*

A related effort to avoid naming the Right's racism can be found in advice to focus on the fiscal costs of immigration enforcement. This focus on dollars purposefully avoids spotlighting the scapegoating of immigrants and instead directs attention to the money burned up on prisons and walls, or more broadly on costs to the economy from discouraging immigration. The theory is to appeal to persuadables on pocketbook issues without alienating them by mentioning immigrant bashing.

These race-silent responses frustrate the base as well as the targeted communities, which resent arguments that ask them to prioritize money over lives. Immigrants are people with families who are woven into communities. "They" blend into "us" as loved ones, neighbors, fellow church members, and co-workers. Politicians who don't talk about immigrants as human beings lose credibility with important segments of the Left.

The head-in-the-sand responses also fail to speak directly to what's actually motivating persuadable voters. Part of the problem is the disparity in the messages, dollars versus family safety. It's challenging to convince voters to change the channel to *Washington Week in Review* when they're engrossed watching *Predator*.

A deeper problem comes because the economic messages leave room for the fear narrative to continue to shape the conversation, even in the Democrats' own messaging. The message *worry about the greenbacks being wasted on efforts to keep out brown immigrants* implicitly generates predictable questions: *Well, how much is the* correct *amount to spend protecting the nation from dangerous people? And how much benefit to the economy do we need to make it worthwhile to allow killers, rapists, and terrorists into our country?* Staying silent on racial fear ignores the actual impetus behind the anti-immigrant panic, leaving it uncontested and able to operate even within the economic framework that purports to challenge the Right's anti-immigrant demagoguery.

Condemn the Right's Racism

In 2017, Virginia held a special governor's race. The Republican candidate, Ed Gillespie, was trailing badly in the polls. A former head of the Republican National Committee, he had earlier encouraged the GOP to reach out to voters of color. But down in the polls in the closing months, Gillespie seemingly concluded Trumpism offered his only chance. He began running what became known as his "Kill, Rape, Oppress" television ads, featuring tattooed members of MS-13, a gang associated with immigrants from El Salvador. A voiceover falsely accused his opponent of offering these fearsome figures "sanctuary." [14]

In response, a group called the Latino Victory Fund released their own ad. It showed a white man in a pickup truck with a Confederate flag and a Gillespie bumper sticker, the engine revving and the truck screaming around leafy suburban corners, chasing a frightened group of brown children. In the words of the fund's president, "we wanted to send the message that, by borrowing the lexicon of white supremacists and refusing to disavow racist symbols, Gillespie made his campaign a haven for hate." [15]

The Gillespie campaign quickly responded with its own ad seeking to take advantage of the Latino Victory Fund spot. "LIBERAL ADS PORTRAY GILLESPIE VOTERS AS RACISTS," blared a banner. "Calling people who don't agree with you white supremacists is totally out of bounds," said a person featured in Gillespie's counter-ad.[16] The White House weighed in, with the press secretary accusing the ad of "stoking political racism."

Gillespie was following one of Trump's most important innovations to dog whistling. Like Trump, Gillespie seemed to purposefully incite objections from liberals and the media. The standard dog whistle theater had evolved. Now, the Right dog whistles in an over-the-top manner, with racial imagery and narratives that shock the engaged political middle. Then they weaponize the resulting outrage as supposed attacks on their voters.

It was in this sense that the Latino Victory Fund ad was ill-advised. It did *not* label every Gillespie voter a neo-Nazi nor constitute its own form of racism, as the White House alleged. But it did give Gillespie last-minute ammunition. He still lost the race, but in the closing days, the Latino Victory Fund ad gave him an infusion of energy, allowing him to pose as the victim of scurrilous liberal allegations of personal bigotry and as a populist standing with his supporters against the snooty pencil-necks who think all working people are racists. This was a message that resonated far beyond his base. Even the editorial board of the *Washington Post*, which had endorsed Gillespie's opponent, played into the storyline that it's offensive to forcefully indict a politician's demagoguery. It described the ad as "despicable," "gutter tactics," and "vile," and even criticized Gillespie's Democratic opponent for not being quick enough to denounce it.[17]

Call for Racial Justice

Many activists oppose dog whistle campaigns and practices by employing a racial justice frame. Calls for abolishing Immigration and Customs Enforcement take this approach. Alexandria Ocasio-Cortez, elected to the House in 2018, took a courageous early stance against ICE for what she described as its "barbarism at the border."[18] The strength of this message lay in its power to mobilize the base.[19] In addition, her position helped shift the center of the whole debate. Notice the headline of a *New York Times* story reporting on the New York congresswoman's call to abolish ICE: "Ocasio-Cortez Pushes Democrats to the Left, Whether They Like It or Not."[20]

Nevertheless, calling for abolishing ICE also has the real potential to strengthen the Right's frame. The Right says that liberals protect dangerous people of color and endanger innocent Americans. Trump gleefully invoked denunciations of ICE to prove this point. "Nancy Pelosi and the Democrats want to abolish the brave men and women of ICE," Trump proclaimed. "What I want to do is abolish the killers in ISIS."[21] Even House member Luis V. Gutiérrez of Illinois, one of the leading Democratic voices on immigration reform, acknowledged the peril of the Ocasio-Cortez approach: "I mean, you want to change the conversation from the inhumanity of caging children to abolishing ICE? They must have been jumping for joy at the White House."[22]

So should the Left abandon the racial justice frame? When it came to connecting with people in the political middle, it proved unhelpful to start with racial justice messages that centered harm to people of color and implicitly condemned whites. But in politics the goal is not always to win the next election. Sometimes the aim is to move the whole debate.

The Right frequently talks about shifting the "Overton window." Joe Overton worked for a right-wing think tank, and this term reflects one of his insights.[23] Overton argued that most voters accept only a relatively narrow band of policy ideas as legitimate, and as a consequence, politicians are constrained by their constituents' imagination. But—and here's the key—the window was movable. While the acceptable range turned on what seemed "reasonable" versus what seemed "extreme," these were relative terms rather than fixed points. What seemed plausible and legitimate could be shifted by either side. If a new set of ideas emerged that redefined what was radical, ridiculous, and unthinkable, then by comparison earlier positions—previously rejected as extreme—gained new legitimacy as now relatively less controversial and so more acceptable.

In 2017, *Vox* released a helpful video illustrating Trump's impact on political news coverage in terms of the Overton effect.[24] "Trump's presidency has forced news networks to grapple with conspiracy theories, right-wing trolls, and dishonest government spokespeople—making them a regular fixture of our national political debates," *Vox* observed. In turn, neoconservatives like Bill Kristol, an architect of the Iraq War, were cast in the role of the moderate when they criticized Trump's extremism, the video showed. Trump was shifting the window, not because majorities accepted his lunacy but because his actions became the basis for comparison. What was outrageous before Trump now became moderate when Trump took the previous extremes out to, well, new extremes.

The Left was doing something similar. When debates about reparations erupted in the run-up to the 2016 election, the notion that the country might actually atone for hundreds of years of racist oppression seemed daft. Three years later, almost every leading presidential candidate among the Democrats endorsed reparations.[25] The window had shifted. In a similar dynamic, Sanders in

2016 called for a revolution in the country's economic priorities, earning skepticism and ridicule. Three years later, his economic populism defined the new normal among leading Democratic presidential contenders.

Racial justice advocates have a strong interest in continuing to push into the national conversation seemingly radical ideas like disarming the police, abolishing Immigration and Customs Enforcement, massive investments specifically in communities of color, a huge redistribution of land to American Indians and Native Hawaiians, and so on. These ideas help redefine the national imagination regarding what's possible and legitimate, shifting that window leftward.

But caution: the whole point of the Overton window analysis is that the political center shifts in response to ideas at the margins. The strategy is to create an extreme position that can serve as a tacit reference point. Should politicians running for office campaign on marginal, extreme ideas?

As a first cut, the answer is clearly no. In a close contest, it would seem a poor game plan to brand one's candidacy as extreme. Indeed, Overton developed his thesis as a way to explain the role of think tanks. Groups that are not involved in electoral popularity contests—such as think tanks, grassroots groups, and unions—are ideal candidates to shift the debate by introducing radical demands and visions.

That doesn't mean that every elected official should avoid radical departures. Politicians and political campaigns often have high levels of public visibility. This gives politicians a pronounced ability to strategically challenge conventional wisdom. It helps the whole movement when politicians backed by a loyal base, like Ocasio-Cortez, seize the mic with radical ideas. She can shift the debate and still build greater enthusiasm for her reelection. Likewise, long-shot candidates have a choice to make. Is their agenda to seek victory no matter how unlikely, perhaps to build name recognition for the next cycle? Avoiding extreme positions might help. Or is the goal to raise the public's consciousness and shift the Overton window?

Bottom line: There are good reasons to powerfully condemn racism and to stake dramatic goals. Doing so can move the whole debate, not despite but precisely when radical positions strike many as extreme. Typically, groups not directly involved in electoral politics are in the best position to lead the charge. Because of their platform, however, select politicians have the greatest power to change the conversation. Still, in crafting their public face, advocacy groups and politicians should understand they're invoking a racial justice frame that may shift thinking, thrill activists, and impress the base, but in the short run will likely lose the persuadables and energize committed reactionaries.

A Race-Class Message About Immigration

Encouraging people to see their fates as linked across color lines is critical to defeating dog whistling and its mass violence. The race-class research suggests that efforts to broaden the "we" will be most successful when those not at risk of deportation come to see how fearmongering imperils their own well-being. When people perceive that messages of racial threat are strategic lies that harm them and their families, they're more likely to reject these fear stories entirely and to recognize their shared humanity with those they're told menace them. The following box offers a race-class narrative on immigration.[26] The one after that dissects the message into its component parts, offering a pocket summary of a typical race-class message.

A Race-Class Narrative About Immigration

Regardless of where we come from, what our color is, or how we worship, every family wants the best for their children. But today, certain politicians and their greedy lobbyists are putting all of our families at risk. They rig the rules to enrich themselves and avoid paying their fair share of taxes, while they defund our schools and threaten seniors with cuts to Medicare and Social Security. Then they turn around and point the finger for our hard times at new immigrants—even tearing families apart and losing children. When we reject their scapegoating and come together across racial differences, we can make this a nation we're proud to leave all of our kids—whether we're white, Black, or brown, from down the street or across the globe.

Anatomy of a Race-Class Narrative

Regardless of where we come from, what our color is, or how we worship, every family wants the best for their children.
  Discuss race overtly and as including everyone. Beyond physical features, this can be done by invoking the differences the Right seeks to racialize, including national origin and religion. As a matter of general messaging advice, start with an affirmative value statement rather than a problem.

But today, certain politicians and their greedy lobbyists are putting all of our families at risk.
  Identify the actual source of threat to working families, taking care to explain motives, even through simple terms like "greedy."

They rig the rules to enrich themselves and avoid paying their fair share of taxes, while they defund our schools and threaten seniors with cuts to Medicare and Social Security.
  Highlight the connection between benefits to the economic royalty and hardship for working families.

> Then they turn around and point the finger for our hard times at new immigrants—even tearing families apart and losing children.
>
> Name racial scaremongering as the divide-and-distract weapon of the rich. Connect the inhumanity of the government's actions to political posturing. This makes clear that racial oppression is an ugly strategy rather than a legitimate response to supposedly dangerous people.
>
> When we reject their scapegoating and come together across racial differences, we can make this a nation we're proud to leave all of our kids—whether we're white, Black, or brown, from down the street or across the globe.
>
> Call for people to join together across racial differences. Link joining together to building a government that promotes racial and economic justice for all families. The goal is to show people that defeating the Right's dog whistling is the key to their family's well-being even if they are not the Right's immediate target. When directly naming racial groups, it's important to include whites.

A Final Thought

In the rhetorical chess game of politics, the Right invariably seeks to hijack the Left's messages—as when politicians kick back against accusations of dog whistling with their own charges of racism. But a message of social solidarity will be harder for the Right to coopt, because the notion that some people merit regard while others deserve disdain sits at the core of their worldview. They can shift the lines of division, for instance from one racial group to another, or to immigration or religion. But in a world where they must explain why so many suffer, the Right cannot easily set down the idea that only some but not others fully deserve to thrive.

Thus, "join together" offers the single clearest and most durable crystallization of the competing value systems offered by the Left and Right. It's the center of the progressive worldview and the foundation for building a robust majority.

Yet progressives in the United States often despair. They know that support for activist government depends on high levels of social solidarity. But they also believe the United States cannot build that solidarity because its population is too racially diverse. It's why, people commonly say, Scandinavian countries have robust social welfare systems but the United States does not and cannot: they look alike and feel interconnected, while we are variously colored and socially splintered.[27]

But division is not an unalterable fact. Solidarity, like ideas about race, is a social product. Consider the supposedly homogeneous "white" group that banded together to support the New Deal and the Great Society programs. In reality, racism *between* European communities in the United States flourished through the 1920s—the Klan that Trump's father likely belonged to especially hated European-origin Catholics and Jews. It was the Depression and then World War II that made it imperative for the government and other public-minded groups to proactively foster a sense of unity among "whites," thereby creating the solidarity we take for granted. The white solidarity that seems so natural today is a product of purposeful action undertaken in a distant yesterday to save the country from impending catastrophe.

Likewise, many democracies in Europe and around the world currently face demagogic efforts to turn even subtle social differences into bases for group hatred. European nations feel especially vulnerable because of their changing complexions and the arrival of immigrants with different religions, and sure enough, anti-immigrant fearmongering is building support for authoritarian governments. But these European democracies already know how to meet this emergency. They've done it before, when they formed themselves into nation-states in the first place. Benedict Anderson in *Imagined Communities* demonstrated that promoting perceptions of linked fate *within* emerging European nations— intentionally inventing a sense of national belonging that transcended village and valley—required considerable purposeful work by the new nation-states.[28]

For democracies under demagogic assault, the most effective defense is to vigorously promote social solidarity. Every liberal public-minded institution all over the world—from governments to churches, unions to universities, philanthropic foundations to community groups—must make social solidarity its North Star. In the United States that principally means fighting dog whistle divisions by promoting connections across racial lines.

Is this only about race? No. Race is the appropriate focus in the United States because of its particular history. Other nations have distinct histories that may involve different conceptions of racial division, or divisions rooted in other notions of fixed and natural hierarchy. Also, divide-and-conquer politics typically involves simultaneous attacks on multiple fronts. These almost always involve patriarchy and the aggressive promotion of traditional gender roles. In the United States, strategic racism forms one part of a larger culture-war politics that seeks advantage in stoking many different sorts of social hierarchies.

Can the race-class strategy be extended beyond race? Most likely, yes. While it focuses on racial division as a key driver of American politics, the race-class analysis offers a foundational story about purposeful division and the power of collective alliances that seems more widely applicable. The intuition seems correct that this research might also offer shield and sword against sexist or transphobic dog whistling domestically, for example, or against anti-Muslim agitation in Europe. Still, group hierarchies take various forms in the United States and abroad. Efforts to expand the race-class approach to combat other culture-war divisions will require more research and experimentation.

Nevertheless, there's a practical and moral vision at the heart of the race-class approach that is universal. The call to reject division and join together translates into an affirmative vision of solidarity that encompasses everyone. The ultimate goal—something each generation can use to guide its own efforts—is to come together to move society, government, and the marketplace toward ensuring that every person has the fullest possible opportunity to thrive. In the short run, the race-class approach seeks to build immediate multiracial coalitions and to win upcoming elections. But as a foundational story, the bigger vision is a long-term cultural shift— a shift that continually encourages us to extend to everyone the fundamental values of liberty, equality, and dignity.

Afterword: Darkest Before the Dawn

"The nation is sick. Trouble is in the land. Confusion all around." Martin Luther King Jr. was giving what would be the last sermon of his life, on April 3, 1968, in Memphis, Tennessee.

"But I know, somehow, that only when it is dark enough, can you see the stars. And I see God working in this period of the twentieth century in a way that men, in some strange way, are responding— something is happening in our world. The masses of people are rising up."

The masses of people that King saw rising up included Americans of all races and from every walk of life, pushing for change. King was in Memphis to support a labor strike, part of his shift toward connecting the fight against racism to the struggle to alleviate poverty and economic exploitation, while linking both to ending United States imperialism and militarism.

As I write this, it is April 3, 2019, exactly fifty-one years later. Donald Trump is president. His popularity among Republicans is at record highs. "Trump's Takeover of the Republican Party Is Almost Complete," a headline from the day's *New York Times* declares.[1]

If King were still with us, looking out from that Memphis pulpit, he would see a vista not much different from the scene he described half a century ago: racism, economic exploitation at home and abroad, militarism on behalf of extractive industries, all still trouble the land. And, yes, masses of people are rising up.

More than five decades later, however, we can conclude that King was mistaken, in the darkness of that long-ago night, to think he saw the stars of radical change. It's not that nothing shifted for the better; it would be our mistake to minimize the

fervent hunger for change that King and the civil rights movement stirred. But the fundamental restructuring of society to
lift up the poor and people of color did not occur. Instead, we've
crossed peaks and labored across valleys. We won major advances
in civil rights. We elected a Black president. And yet we stagger
through the war on crime, state disinvestment in the public infra-
structures of civic life, and a rewriting of government economic
rules that leaves most Americans worse off while it grossly rewards
the wealthy top 1 percent.

It's hard not to wonder if, like King, we too are mistaken to
think that in the midst of our own era's deepening darkness there's
a glimmer that might be a new dawn. After all, some of the nation's
most powerful economic and political forces have a vested interest
in public division. And millions of white people seem more committed to the perks of white identity than to joining hands across
the color line to demand a broad and shared prosperity.

A new freedom, if we can build it, won't come easy. But still, I
think there is reason to hope—more reason to hope now than in
decades past, when the civil rights movement achieved much only
to see the racial fearmongering of dog whistle politics take much
away.

Fifty years ago, Rev. King understood the need for multiracial
coalitions. His approach was rooted in a concept that white people could rally around; one that would draw them into the civil
rights movement by emphasizing not just its moral force but its
pragmatic potential to protect them. The threat then was not so
much economic, though many whites remained trapped in poverty. More looming in the minds of most whites was the risk of
metastasizing violence as fury in response to racial oppression sur-
faced and spread.

Nonviolence was the essence of King's theory of social change.
King called for the masses to rise in the name of human brother-
hood. By battling racial hatred with public professions of love,
King telegraphed the comforting message to whites that Black
people were not the enemy. He made "we are all God's children" a

marker of our shared identity and a promise of security and safety. And from that foundation—a fusion of justice and peace—he expanded the movement to embrace broader human rights issues: structural changes to battle entrenched poverty, fair wages for working people, an end to militarism.

Fifty years later, the playbook hasn't much changed. Now, as then, it's not just racism we need to address, but also poverty, fair wages, militarism, plus climate collapse as well. And now, as then, the hard work cannot be done by communities of color alone.

People of color cannot simply sum up all of the different non-white groups and declare ourselves a near numerical majority ready to take power and transform society. It is more than a numbers game. The truth is that whites as a group remain dominant in wealth, power, and status. And anyway, people of color are no more a solid homogeneous bloc than white people are. They hold a mix of reactionary as well as progressive views on race, government, and the marketplace.

Fundamental change requires support from large swaths of the white racial group. In turn, this makes the fulcrum of whether fundamental change is possible what the labor historian David Roediger calls "the wages of whiteness"—the benefits that whites receive from the mere fact of being white.[2]

Roediger adopted and amplified that notion by drawing upon one of the truly great intellectuals in American history, W. E. B. DuBois. DuBois' crowning work of scholarship was the magisterial *Black Reconstruction in America*, a seven-hundred-page tome originally published in 1935, in the early years of the New Deal. The title might suggest a narrow focus on African Americans in the South immediately after the Civil War. Instead, the book surveyed the national conflict between capitalism and labor in the decades before and after that great cataclysm. In this enduring class struggle, waged across industry and agriculture, in the cities of the North, on the plantations of the South, and across the plains of the Midwest, the crucible dividing the masses was racism manufactured by the oligarchy.

"It must be remembered," wrote DuBois, "that the white group of laborers, while they received a low wage, were compensated in part by a sort of public and psychological wage." Focusing in particular on poor southern whites, DuBois emphasized that they were nearly destitute, yet the planter class contrived to pay them in racial pride, making superiority over Blacks compensation for economic straits. "They were given public deference and titles of courtesy because they were white. They were admitted freely with all classes of white people to public functions, public parks, and the best schools," DuBois wrote. "Their vote selected public officials, and while this had small effect upon the economic situation, it had great effect upon their personal treatment and the deference shown them."[3]

The elite manipulation of racism has ebbed and flowed across American history since capitalism invented "white citizens," "Black slavery," and "red savages." Over the subsequent centuries, "races" have persisted and evolved not in response to some instinctive tendency among people to fear strangers. Instead, the primary driving force constantly imbuing the ideologies of racial differences with renewed vigor has been the opportunity for profit. Profit for some of society's wealthiest segments is the hidden-in-plain-sight engine of whiteness.

With profit for the elites as the principal engine, ordinary white people have been shortchanged on the ride. The benefits of being white have never been much more than tidbits compared to the harvest reaped by the rich, white crumbs of the sumptuous meal of white supremacy consumed behind high gates on gilded plates.

DuBois could see this clearly, especially when looking at the largely shared desperation of the great masses of whites and Blacks in the South up through the Great Depression, when he was writing.

Yet even then, when the dividends paid to whites were primarily deference, due regard, and a sense of superiority, there were also concrete material advantages to being white. As DuBois noted, for instance, "White schoolhouses were the best in the community, and conspicuously placed, and they cost anywhere from twice to ten times as much per capita as the colored schools."

Writing in the first half of the 1930s, DuBois chronicled the psychic wages of whiteness at the historical moment the material wages of whiteness were about to explode upward for the majority of whites. The New Deal was gaining steam. Just over the horizon were economic booms that would be fueled by war spending in the 1940s, federal home loans and the suburban expansion of the 1950s, and Social Security and the GI Bill—government programs that would lift millions of families into home-owning middle-class security. By rule, design, and practice, these benefits would accrue in color-coded fashion; overwhelmingly, the families lifted would be white. Over the next few decades after DuBois wrote *Black Reconstruction*, government, unions, and the regulated market would put the vast majority of whites beyond the immediate reach of desperate poverty.

This was the landscape when King stood at that pulpit in Memphis in 1968. Then, as now, the wages of whiteness were the linchpin of change. The power to actually shift society's direction depended on great masses of whites finding common cause with mobilized people of color. It is here that the wages of whiteness matter. If those wages are high, most whites will prefer to defend them and to defend them viciously, rather than sacrifice those benefits for the speculative promises of a different social order.

King called for a radical downward distribution of wealth to address widespread poverty, combined with a sundering of the walls of racism and an end to military mass violence abroad. With hindsight, it's easy to see not just the justice of his vision but the pragmatic salvation it offered for tens of millions of people of every color. But as King found when he went to the neighborhoods of suburban Cicero, south of Chicago, instead many whites heard in his words and demands damnation. They rioted rather than allow housing integration, just as they would throw stones and hurl racist slurs to fight busing and school integration in Boston, and rampage through the streets of Manhattan to protect de facto whites-only union jobs. The rejection of King's vision was not monolithic among white people, but those loud and angry voices carried the day. The wages of whiteness were too high. There would be no mass movement of whites shifting to build common cause with people of color against the interests of elites in maintaining the status quo.

What gives us the idea that today might be different? After all, the Trump rallies look and sound reminiscent of those white mass gatherings of fifty years ago.

But when we pair hopeful cultural changes over the last half century with the ever-more-evident realities of rule by the rich, we can glimpse a ray of hope. What might the wages of whiteness look like for Matt and Tom, the two white men from Ohio we met at the beginning of this book?

For many, the psychic wages of whiteness have been losing value as important cultural shifts impelled by the civil rights movement continue. Inspired originally by the moral demands and courageous actions of civil rights activists, integrationist sentiment has increased sharply. The visibility and cultural stature of Black entertainers, athletes, and public intellectuals has played an enormous role in the mindset shift. So too have the Black politicians elected to ever-more-prominent positions, at once symbolizing the rising status of African Americans and driving it further. The nation elected and reelected a Black president, and through Barack Obama and his family people of every color came to see the absurdity of racist stereotypes.

Demographic changes and the rising visibility of many different racial groups have also reformed America's historically racist culture. Civil rights reforms went beyond formally prohibiting racial discrimination in employment and housing, to ending express racial barriers in immigration, opening the country's doors to millions of new Americans without direct family ties to Europe. The presence of new faces, languages, foods, and customs has spurred a cosmopolitan culture of curiosity and fusion.

On the material side, the decline in the wages of whiteness

is more equivocal. The canyon between African Americans and whites has remained wide in rates of employment, home ownership, income, and health outcomes. It's still far better from a material point of view to wear white rather than nonwhite skin.

But the overall material position of whites has worsened significantly since Rev. King's last sermon. This is the story of surging wealth inequality, declining jobs and pensions, hollowed-out cities, broken rural towns, and the Great Recession. This is the narrative of deaths of despair from suicide and opioid abuse spreading across the country.

With rare exceptions, we tend to discuss these trends in economic terms divorced from race. But the economic crises confronting the vast majority of whites is very much connected to whiteness. Dog whistle politics has made the majority of white voters unwitting co-conspirators in their own economic calamity. It is largely whites voting their racial anxieties who empower the politicians engineering surging inequality. Worsening economic insecurity is the true material wage of whiteness paid over the last half century.

Donald Trump's election connects to these larger trends. His ardent supporters hear in "make America great again" the promise of restored racial status. Fifty-four percent of whites voted for Trump in 2016, many in response to rising racial resentment spurred by Obama's victories and the very societal changes just described. Trump's base also feels the tightening vise of economic desperation. They are squeezed in the market by worsening pay and evaporating benefits, and squeezed in the public sphere by eroding schools, crumbling roads and levies, and a disintegrating safety net.

Still, four in ten whites in 2016 rejected crude race-baiting appeals. And there's reason to believe an energized Left can drive those numbers much higher, precisely because of Trump.

Trump exemplifies the personal disaster of clutching to the myth of white superiority. Over decades, the nation has been moving toward the conviction that racial chauvinism is morally bankrupt. Dog whistling encourages whites to reject this progress—but in doing so makes plain the ugly character of racial pride. Trump's appeals to white fear and vanity carry him into lies, cruelty, braggadocio, mockery, sexism, xenophobia, and boorishness. The racial rage he encourages pops up on our phones in frightening tableaus: images of torch-bearing marchers yelling racist slurs, massacres at the speed of automatic gunfire, the slow processions of funeral marches. Trump illustrates on the national stage the individual destitution of racial supremacism.

Trump also personifies the economic costs for most whites of clinging to whiteness. His supporters make a Faustian bargain. Seeking false salves to their sense of imperiled white identity, they foreclose the possibility of decent livelihoods. They vote for border walls and Muslim bans, but get a White House cabinet of corrupt billionaires bent on looting the country for themselves and their titan friends. Trump's election shows the collective disaster of using white pride to paper over class warfare. Trump epitomizes the connection between white racial spite and widespread economic ruination.

This is not how most whites see things—not the larger trajectory of the country, nor the horror of Trumpism. Nor is it exclusively white persons who fail to perceive this reality. Many people of color also accept and internalize the core stories woven by the Right about who deserves respect and who does not, about whether to trust the economic royalty or instead to build power collectively. The wreckage around us does not pile neatly into a giant arrow everyone can follow for the way forward.

But today's crises do present a moment when an energized Left can seize the country's imagination to achieve radical change.

Now may be the best opportunity in the long history of this society to break the weightiest chains of racial hierarchy. For the first time, it may be possible to convince the majority of whites—not nearly all, but at least a solid majority—that providing for their families requires relinquishing their attachment to supposed white superiority. This may also be the best chance to build cross-racial solidarity among nonwhites, a task ever more pressing as the country's racial composition complexifies. Our research has shown that a huge chunk of the electorate straddles the progressive-reactionary line, and many are likely to merge left if economic and racial issues are appropriately and comprehensively intertwined.

The persuadable middle may not be persuadable for much longer. The curtain may be lowering day by day. Trends among whites threaten the solidarity necessary for democracy's survival. The current president and the political party that leans on, learns from, and protects him see great benefits in stoking racial fear and resentment. With our next national election little more than a year away, either we seize the day with an inclusive message of racial solidarity, or we risk letting white nationalists aligned with economic elites drag us backward toward a replay of some of the ugliest chapters in our country's history.

We're deep in the chasm of the latest reaction against racial progress right now. It's not clear we can dig out. It's not certain we've reached the nadir. And many of us are still wondering how the country was dragged over this cliff. Yet the shock of the present might be the jolt that impels us to reach forward with renewed strength for a hopeful future. When racial communities of every color embrace cross-racial solidarity and government that is truly of, by, and for *all* the people, then we will take another firm step toward becoming the America our ideals proclaim.

I wish the advice and analysis in this book could offer a quick fix, but obviously nothing can. Changing the country's direction will take powerful social movements and a radically transformed Democratic Party, human rights campaigns that build solidarity across many unjust social hierarchies, and aggressive litigation plus street agitation to restore voting rights and drive dark money out of politics. It will require hundreds of millions of dollars in donations small and large, plus an army of citizen-activists (whatever their formal citizenship status), their shoe soles worn bare by door knocking and protest marching.

Still, I believe this book and those convinced by it can offer yet more shoulders leaning into the shared task of building for all of us dignity and the practical opportunity to thrive. I hope the darkness of this current moment may herald the coming dawn.

ACKNOWLEDGMENTS

Hope comes from community, and while the errors here are mine, this book would not exist without a marvelous community of family, friends, and fellow travelers.

The continuity between *Merge Left* and my prior book, *Dog Whistle Politics*, includes those who made both possible. My daughter Chelsea and granddaughter Lennea provided sounding boards with their own perspectives on racial justice, and my wife, Debbie, to whom this book is dedicated, both endured its writing and also made it immeasurably better through her keen editing. Asad Rahim, a research assistant on the prior book, offered critical feedback on a draft of this one. Claudette Silver helped promote *Dog Whistle Politics* and proved indispensable to *Merge Left*, fostering the connections that would develop into the race-class narrative project and also offering very helpful insights and probing questions in response to multiple drafts.

With *Dog Whistle Politics*, I developed many new relationships, and in particular learned a great deal from working with the AFL-CIO. I especially benefited from the insights of my fellow co-chairs of the Advisory Council on Racial and Economic Justice, Ana Avendaño and Dorian Warren, as well as from the support of AFL-CIO president Richard Trumka. Among others, these union leaders notably pushed forward the race and class conversation: United Food and Commercial Workers president Marc Perrone, United Steelworkers executive vice president Fred Redmond, International Union of Painters and Allied Trades president Kenneth Rigmaiden, International Union of Bricklayers and Allied Craftworkers president James Boland, and Canada's Building Trades Unions director Bob Blakely. I also greatly benefitted from conversations with Carmen Berkley, Tefere Gebre, Jon Hiatt, Lisa Jordan, Tiffany Loftin, Katherine McFate, Kelly Fay Rodríguez, Damon Silvers, and Robin Williams.

AFL-CIO political director Mike Podhorzer deserves special mention. He played a key role in jump-starting and guiding the race-class narrative project, and battled through three complete drafts of the book, generously sharing insights and raising challenging questions. This book would have been further improved had I realized the friendship would have survived my imposing the next three drafts as well.

The race-class narrative team provided research, insights, conversations, and thoughtful pushback that shaped this book. Anat Shenker-Osorio took the lead on research, coordinated with the pollsters, offered tutorials on narrative strategy, raised funds, rocked colorful shoes, and helped rescue an early draft of this book. Heather McGhee, an early supporter of *Dog Whistle Politics*, was the other principal partner and offered her own keen insights on the tricky intersection of race and class and also, through her presidency of Demos and DemosAction, provided the race-class project an initial home. Other key contributors at Demos and DemosAction included Liz Doyle, Tamara Draut, Anika Fassia, Adam Lioz, Rodney McKenzie, and Causten Rodriguez-Wollerman.

The Service Employees International Union under the leadership of international president Mary Kay Henry and secretary-treasurer Gerry Hudson constituted a key partner in the race-class narrative project. The SEIU's Racial Justice Center, including Tinselyn Simms, Liz Grez, Kerry Jones, and Bernard Moore, joined as an initial partner and continue to promote and develop the research. I'm also grateful to SEIU Healthcare Minnesota, as well as Faith in Minnesota, for allowing me to use the flyers they created for their canvassing test of the race-class message.

The race-class narrative project drew on two primary pollsters, Cornell Belcher of Brilliant Corners, assisted by Dee Brown, and Celinda Lake of Lake Research Partners. I'm exceptionally grateful to Celinda for insights before and after the research, and to

Lake Research partner Jonathan Voss, who did much of the heavy lifting for the project, and also very generously responded in detail to an early draft and helped create the graphics for *Merge Left*. I and the entire race-class team are also tremendously grateful to the many anonymous activists and scholars who agreed to serve as intellectual resources for the project.

Funding for the race-class narrative project came from many sources. I'm uniquely grateful to The California Endowment and Alexandra Desautels and Sandra Witt for the crucial first dollars in, as well as to the Open Society Foundations and Alvin Starks for the bulk of the funding.

In the narrative and political organizing world broadly construed, I learned from so many people I hesitate to name individuals, yet with apologies to others I've inadvertently omitted, let me acknowledge the insights of Lorena Chambers, Eve Ensler, Kimberlé Crenshaw, Glenn Harris, Doug Hattaway, Alfred Ironside, Deepa Iyer, Saru Jayaraman, Alan Jenkins, Van Jones, Jee Kim, Richard Kirsch, Naomi Klein, Eddie Kurtz, Amber Phillips, Steve Phillips, Art Reyes, Rashad Robinson, Frank Sharry, Jonathan Smucker, and Miya Woolfalk.

I drew heavily on the goodwill of Berkeley Law and our inspirational dean, Erwin Chemerinsky, for the time and the resources to write. Berkeley also provided a willing (or at least captive) set of readers. This included my colleagues at a faculty workshop as well as the students in the fall 2018 social justice writing seminar I co-taught with Kathy Abrams. In addition, the extraordinary/irreverent students in my spring 2019 race and American law seminar productively critiqued, debated, and satirized the book: my thanks to Candace Graff, Vanessa Hernandez, Tori Larson, Alex Mabanta, Peta Oxholm, Alexis Payne, Amed Prado, Anna Rodriguez, Dylan Saba, Kristina Steinmetz, Emily Storms, Genesis Tejeda, and Farrah Vazquez.

At Berkeley, I also benefited greatly from my colleague David Oppenheimer's steady encouragement and many ideas, as well as from the critiques offered by Shaun Ossei-Owusu, a former student and now a law professor. Very helpful comments and research came from several students outside my classes, including Nadim Houssain, Melissa McCall, EJ Toppin, and Gus Tupper. Thanks also to Alejandro Ceballos for his excellent and upbeat administrative assistance. Finally, thanks go to Berkeley's Haas Institute for a Fair and Inclusive Society and its remarkable collection of activist-scholars, especially its director, john powell, as well as Olivia Araiza, Taeku Lee, Gerald Lenoir, Julie Nelson, Stephen Menendian, and Richard Rothstein.

Thank you, too, to Rick Banks at Stanford Law School for inviting me to workshop a few chapters in his race and law seminar, and also for introducing me to his sister, Sandy Banks, who carefully edited and vastly improved the manuscript.

I'm indebted to The New Press, and to its funders who gave it the leeway to publish a book that many commercial presses shied from. New Press executive director Diane Wachtell first encouraged me to write *Dog Whistle Politics* so it was a nice closing of the circle to work with her on this project, and editorial director Carl Bromley through his steady interventions prodded the book closer toward intelligibility. My agent, Andrew Stuart, thoughtfully responded to my evolving ideas about how best to write back against Donald Trump's election, and in this way not only helped find a home for *Merge Left* but shaped it from the outset.

In addition to those already listed, many other friends also contributed directly. Michelle Anderson provided unstinting encouragement as well as incisive comments on two drafts, and also trenchant advice on the craft of writing, only crudely followed, I'm afraid. A regular dinner crew—Rosa-Linda Fregoso, Herman Gray, Aída Hurtado, and Craig Haney—leavened food and wine with sharp political insights that have found their way into *Merge Left*. Rey Rodríguez helped me keep in perspective the reasons I was writing and the sacrifices required to do so. Al Lepp, who has provided extensive editorial assistance over the years, this time begged off but did offer the tooth marks of his new toddler on an initial printout. Marcy Kates cheered an early draft, as did my neighbor, Carole Ramsey. Melissa Daar was a creative gem, brainstorming with me about key insights and metaphors, and enlisting her network into the effort as well. My thanks—and apologies—to the many other friends who tolerated excessive book talk with good humor.

For me, authoring these two books has involved many passages. Most painfully, in the years preceding *Dog Whistle Politics*, I lost both my brother and my dad. In the years since, while writing *Merge Left*, my brother's best friend, Danny O'Sullivan, also passed on, and so did my father's best friend, Bob Miller. As the youngest child, I knew both my whole life and both acted like older brothers to me. Danny's generosity, humility, joshing, and laughter made the world better and lighter. Millers (for no apparent reason we always added the "s") helped inspire my law career as well as a passion for justice, and in turn politics. His family—wife Stephanie, and children Sarah and Stephen—closed his memorial program with a favorite quote from his personal hero, Robert F. Kennedy: "make gentle the life of this world." Millers fervently believed in this mission—and also in the need to fight like hell to make it so. I hope this book carries something of his spirit.

Notes

Preface

1. Ian Haney López, *Dog Whistle Politics: How Coded Racial Appeals Have Reinvented Racism and Wrecked the Middle Class* (2014).

2. Derrick Bell, "*Brown v. Board of Education* and the Interest-Convergence Dilemma," 93 *Harvard Law Review* 518, 523 (1980).

3. Frank Luntz, *Words That Work: It's Not What You Say, It's What People Hear* (2007).

4. Luntz, *Words That Work*, 164–65, 173.

5. Christopher Cadelago and Ted Hesson, "Why Trump Is Talking Non-stop about the Migrant Caravan," *Politico*, October 23, 2018.

6. For Shenker-Osorio's thoughts on messaging around the economy, see Anat Shenker-Osorio, *Don't Buy It: The Trouble with Talking Nonsense about the Economy* (2012). For a helpful summary of her advice around messaging, see Anat Shenker-Osorio, *Messaging This Moment: A Handbook for Progressive Communicators* (Center for Community Change, 2017).

7. Matt Broomfield, "Women's March Against Donald Trump Is the Largest Day of Protests in US History, Say Political Scientists," *Intercept*, January 23, 2017.

8. Pew Research Center, "For Most Trump Voters, 'Very Warm' Feelings for Him Endured," August 2018. For a thoughtful investigation of dog whistling along gender lines, see Wendy Davis, "Wolf Whistle Politics: Taking Back the Conversation to Advance Women's Rights," in *Wolf Whistle Politics: The New Misogyny in America Today,* xvii (Diane Wachtell, ed. 2017).

Introduction

1. Robin DiAngelo, "White Fragility," *International Journal of Critical Pedagogy* 54, 57, 60–61 (2011).

2. *Economist*/YouGov Poll, Item 77, October 31, 2016.

3. Ben Steinnov, "In Class Warfare, Guess Which Class Is Winning," *New York Times*, November 26, 2006.

4. Jane Mayer, *Dark Money: The Hidden History of the Billionaires Behind the Rise of the Radical Right*, xvi–xvii (2017).

5. David Frum, "An Exit from Trumpocracy," *Atlantic*, January 18, 2018. See generally Thomas E. Mann & Norman J. Ornstein, *It's Worse than It Looks: How the American Constitutional System Collided with the New Politics of Extremism* (2012).

6. Lake Research Partners, "Race-Class Narrative Anchor Project: Dial Survey Report," October 2018. Conducted in September 2018, this poll interviewed roughly 800 Asian Americans, Native Hawaiians and Pacific Islanders, and Native Americans, split about evenly between the groups. The data regarding Native American views was too equivocal to warrant folding them in as "people of color" in terms of their attitudes. More research is warranted here.

1. Yes, It's Still Dog Whistling. That's a Good Thing Because the Alternative is Far Worse

1. Paul Krugman, "Trump's Supreme Betrayal," *New York Times*, July 30, 2018.

2. Greg Sargent, "Trump's Cruelty and Hate Are Creating a Defining Moment for Democrats," *Washington Post*, July 13, 2018.

3. Thomas B. Edsall, "Trump Has Got Democrats Right Where He Wants Them," *New York Times*, February 1, 2018.

4. Pew Research Center, "For Most Trump Voters, 'Very Warm' Feelings for Him Endured," August 2018.

5. Gallup, Presidential Approval Ratings—Donald Trump, March 2019.

6. This discussion draws on Christopher N. Lasch, "Sanctuary Cities and Dog-Whistle Politics," 42 *New England Journal of Criminal and Civil Confinement* 159 (2016).

7. Jeremy Stahl, "The Exploitation of 'Beautiful Kate,'" *Slate*, August 10, 2017.

8. Ashley Parker and Steve Eder, "Inside the Six Weeks Donald Trump Was a Nonstop 'Birther,'" *New York Times*, July 2, 2016.

9. David Frum, "The Problem with Downplaying Immigrant Crime," *Atlantic*, July 29, 2015.

10. Lasch, "Sanctuary Cities and Dog-Whistle Politics."

11. Mary Ellen Klas and Emily L. Mahoney, "Why Richard Corcoran Failed in His Bid for Florida Governor," *Tampa Bay Times*, May 9, 2018.

12. Tim Marcin, "Ron DeSantis Tells Floridians Don't 'Monkey This Up' by Electing Andrew Gillum, First Black Nominee for Governor," *Newsweek*, August 28, 2018.

13. Deirdre Shesgreen and Eliza Collins, "Exclusive: Immigration Dominates GOP Candidates' TV Ads in House Contests Across the Country," *USA Today*, May 29, 2018. See also Catherine E. Shoichet, "No, You're Not Crazy. There Are Way More Campaign Ads About Immigration This Year," *CNN*, October 15, 2018. For a larger history of immigration politics and racial fearmongering, see Eric Kaufmann, *Whiteshift: Populism, Immigration, and the Future of White Majorities* (2019).

14. Kemp for Governor, "So Conservative," posted to YouTube, May 9, 2018.

15. Lindsey Bever, "'Make America White Again': A Politician's Billboard Ignites Uproar," *Washington Post*, June 23, 2016.

16. Mary Bowerman, "Outrage over Candidate's 'Make America White Again' Sign," *USA Today*, June 22, 2016.

17. Ken Nicholson, "UPDATE: 'Make America White Again' Campaign Signs Removed," *WRBCtv*, June 27, 2016.

18. FiveThirtyEight.com, "Chuck Fleischmann," last checked, April 16, 2019.

19. Eugene Scott, "Former Ku Klux Klan Grand Wizard David Duke Running for Senate Seat in Louisiana," *CNNPolitics*, July 23, 2016; Gideon Resnick, "David Duke Plans to Run for Congress," *Daily Beast*, July 12, 2016.

20. Quoted in David Harsanyi, "David Duke: A Question for Republicans," *National Review*, July 29, 2016.

21. Heather Caygle, Sarah Ferris, and John Bresnahan, "Steve King Stripped of Committee Seats—with More Punishment Coming," *Politico*, January 14, 2019.

22. Glenn Thrush, "Eager to Court Jews (and Fracture Democrats), Republicans Push Bills on Anti-Semitism," *New York Times*, March 24, 2019.

23. Philip Bump, "Of Course Trump's Outrage at the NFL Protests Had to Do with Race," *Washington Post*, September 25, 2017.

24. *Economist*/YouGov Poll, October 30–November 1, 2016, 94. See also Chris Cillizza, "57% Think Donald Trump Is a Racist. So . . ." *CNN*, March 2, 2018 (noting that calling someone a "racist" may just be an insult, rather than a substantive judgment).

25. "Trump Speaks at Manchester, New Hampshire, Rally; Clinton to Speak in Reno, Nevada," *CNN Transcripts*, August 25, 2016.

26. For a thoughtful essay regarding Trump's exploitation of the political correctness frame, see Moira Weigel, "Political Correctness: How the Right Invented a Phantom Enemy," *Guardian*, November 30, 2016.

27. Rowland Evans and Robert Novak, "Future 'White Man's' Party," *St. Petersburg Times*, June 25, 1963, 9-A.

28. Tali Mendelberg, *The Race Card: Campaign Strategy, Implicit Messages, and the Norm of Equality* 103 (2001). Within five years, doubts emerged whether simply making race evident was enough to strip dog whistling of its power. Gregory Huber and John Lapinski, "The 'Race Card' Revisited: Assessing Racial Priming in Policy Contests," *American Journal of Political Science* 421 (2006).

29. Nicholas Valentino, Fabian Guy Neuner, and L. Matthew Vandenbroek, "The Changing Norms of Racial Political Rhetoric and the End of Racial Priming," *Journal of Politics*, November 2016 (reporting on experiments conducted from 2010 to 2012).

30. Valentino, Neuner, and Vandenbroek, "Changing Norms." See also Sean McElwee, "Combating Racism Is Crucial to Revitalizing American Politics: It's Not Easy, but It Can Be Done," *Salon*, December 25, 2016.

31. Michael D'Antonio interview, "The Choice 2016," *Frontline*, September 27, 2016; Maggie Haberman and Alexander Burns, "Donald Trump's Presidential Run Began in an Effort to Gain Stature," *New York Times*, March 12, 2016.

32. "America Deserves Better," www.youtube.com/watch?v=TIKz216 YDPw.

33. Niels Lesniewski, "Exclusive: Republicans Launch Willie Horton–Style Attack on Kaine," *Roll Call*, October 3, 2016.

34. Asawin Suebsaeng, "RNC Brags About 'Willie Horton' Attack That Was So Racist Its Creator Disavowed It," *Daily Beast*, October 3, 2016.

35. Louis Nelson, "Clinton Ad Ties Trump to KKK, White Supremacists," *Politico*, August 25, 2016.

36. Abby Ohlheiser and Caitlin Dewey, "Hillary Clinton's Alt-right Speech, Annotated," *Washington Post*, August 25, 2016.

37. Nelson, "Clinton Ad."

38. Ian Haney López, *Dog Whistle Politics: How Coded Racial Appeals Have Reinvented Racism and Wrecked the Middle Class* 134 (2014).

39. Cristiano Lima, "Hillary Clinton Walks Back 'Basket of Deplorables' Remark," *Politico*, September 9, 2016.

40. Eugene Scott, "Ron DeSantis's Campaign Claims It's 'Absurd' to Say 'Monkey' is a Racial Dog Whistle. It's Not," *Washington Post*, August 30, 2018.

41. Eugene Scott, "Trump Said It Is 'Racist' to Ask Him about His Nationalism. Here's Why It's Necessary," *Washington Post*, November 8, 2018.

42. Quoting the political scientist Ashley Jardina, Thomas Edsall wrote in 2018 that "Trump 'does potentially benefit from accusing his opponents of playing the race card.' The danger 'of this new era, in which the new political strategy is to accuse elites of falsely making charges of racism,' Jardina argues, is that it may be increasingly difficult, if not impossible, to effectively condemn politicians when they do in fact attempt to race bait, or when they express views that are racist or support policies that are detrimental to racial and ethnic minorities." Thomas B. Edsall, "Don't Feed the Troll in the Oval Office," *New York Times*, June 28, 2018.

43. Wendy Davis, "Wolf Whistle Politics: Taking Back the Conversation to Advance Women's Rights," xvii, xxii–xxiii, in *Wolf Whistle Politics: The New Misogyny in America Today* (Diane Wachtell, ed. 2017).

44. Sheryl Gay Stolberg, "Two Years and Hundreds of Inflammatory Ads Later, the G.O.P. Is the Party of Trump," *New York Times*, November 6, 2018.

45. Nia-Malika Henderson, "Blacks, Whites Hear Obama Differently," *Politico*, March 3, 2009.

46. Nate Cohn, "Demise of the Southern Democrat Is Now Nearly Complete," *New York Times*, December 4, 2014.

47. Philip Bump, "When Did Black Americans Start Voting So Heavily Democratic?" *Washington Post*, July 7, 2015.

48. Linwood Holton, "An End to the Southern Strategy?" *New York Times*, December 23, 2002.

49. Amy B. Wang, "One Group Loved Trump's Remarks about Charlottesville: White Supremacists," *Washington Post*, August 13, 2017.

50. For a more detailed discussion of racial views among Trump's supporters, see chapter 8.

51. Cassandra Santiago and Saeed Ahmed, "Merriam-Webster Redefines 'Troll' and 'Dog Whistle' to Conform to the Times," *CNN*, September 19, 2017.

52. Jamelle Bouie, "The Trouble with Biden," *New York Times*, March 11, 2019.

53. Cristiano Lima, "Boehner: 'There Is No Republican Party. There's a Trump Party,'" *Politico*, May 31, 2018.

2. Testing Racial Fear

1. The survey allowed respondents to state if they agreed with the material on the left side of the flyer but not the material in the middle.

2. Slightly fewer people of color also disagreed or strongly disagreed, compared to whites (21 percent compared to 24 percent). The main difference was the far greater number of respondents of color who identified themselves as "neutral" toward, or who agreed with some but not other parts of, the Republican flyer (42 percent of the respondents of color, versus 30.5 percent of white respondents).

3. Steve Phillips, *Brown Is the New White: How the Demographic Revolution Has Created a New American Majority* (2016).

3. The Right Consistently Links Race, Class, and Government

1. Pew Research Center, "For Most Trump Voters, 'Very Warm' Feelings for Him Endured," August 2018.

2. Daniel Cox, Rachel Lienesch, and Robert P. Jones, "Beyond Economics: Fears of Cultural Displacement Pushed the White Working Class to Trump," PRRI/*Atlantic*, May 9, 2017. In general, there was much less concern about economic fairness among Republicans than Democrats. Pew Research Center, "The Partisan Divide on Political Values Grows Even Wider," October 2017.

3. John Sides, Michael Tesler, and Lynn Vavreck, *Identity Crisis: The 2016 Presidential Campaign and the Battle for the Meaning of America* 2, 93 (2018).

4. See Brian F. Schaffner, Matthew MacWilliams, and Tatishe Nteta, "Explaining White Polarization in the 2016 Vote for President: The Sobering Role of Racism and Sexism," paper prepared for presentation at the Conference on the U.S. Elections of 2016: Domestic and International Aspects, January 8–9, 2017, IDC Herzliya Campus; Michael Tesler, "The Education Gap among Whites This Year Wasn't about Education. It Was about Race," *Washington Post*, November 16, 2016; Jon Greeny and Sean McElwee, "The Differential Effects of Economic Conditions and Racial Attitudes in the Election of Donald Trump," *Perspectives on Politics* 35 (forthcoming 2019). Further debunking the economic stress arguments, some studies showed that political views regarding economic policy followed from, rather than drove, partisan affiliation and support for Trump. David C. Wilson and Darren W. Davis, "Appraisals of President Obama's Economic Performance: Racial Resentment and Attributional Responsibility," 55 *Electoral Studies* 62–72 (2018); Robert Griffin and Ruy Teixeira, "The Story of Trump's Appeal: A Portrait of Trump Voters," Democracy Fund Voter Study Group, June 2017. Relatedly, a major study found that areas negatively impacted by trade agreements were no more likely to support Trump. Discussed in Max Ehrenfreund and Jeff Guo, "A

Massive New Study Debunks a Widespread Theory for Donald Trump's Success," *Washington Post*, August 12, 2016.

5. John Hudak, "A Reality Check on 2016's Economically Marginalized," Brookings Institution, November 16, 2016; Valerie Wilson, "People of Color Will Be a Majority of the American Working Class in 2032," Economic Policy Institute, June 9, 2016.

6. Liz Hamel, Elise Sugarman, and Mollyann Brodie, "Kaiser Family Foundation/CNN Working-Class Whites Poll," September 23, 2016.

7. Cox et al., "Beyond Economics."

8. Joan Neff Gurney and Kathleen J. Tierney, "Relative Deprivation and Social Movements: A Critical Look at Twenty Years of Theory and Research," 23 *Sociological Quarterly* 33 (1982).

9. Sides, Tesler, and Vavreck, *Identity Crisis*, 7, 8.

10. Paul Krugman, "The Angry White Male Caucus," *New York Times*, October 1, 2018. See also Rebecca Traister, "Fury Is a Political Weapon. And Women Need to Wield It," *New York Times*, September 29, 2018; and Michael Kimmel, *Angry White Men: American Masculinity at the End of an Era* x–xi, 233 (2013, 2017).

11. Justin Gest, *The New Minority: White Working Class Politics in an Age of Immigration and Inequality* 101, 135, 165 (2016).

12. Cox et al., "Beyond Economics."

13. Arlie Russell Hochschild, "I Spent 5 Years with Some of Trump's Biggest Fans. Here's What They Won't Tell You," *Mother Jones*, September/October 2016. See generally Arlie Hochschild, *Strangers in Their Own Land: Anger and Mourning on the American Right*, chapter 9 (2016). See also Catherine Cramer, *The Politics of Resentment: Rural Consciousness in Wisconsin and the Rise of Scott Walker* (2016).

14. Lyndon B. Johnson, "War on Poverty" (1964).

15. Ronald Reagan, "Radio Address to the Nation on Welfare Reform," February 15, 1986, online transcript by Gerhard Peters and John T. Woolley, American Presidency Project.

16. Carmen DeNavas-Walt and Bernadette D. Proctor, U.S. Census Bureau, "Income and Poverty in the United States: 2014," U.S. Government Printing Office 12 (2015).

17. Ira Katznelson, *When Affirmative Action Was White: An Untold History of Racial Inequality in Twentieth-Century America* (2005).

18. Matthew Frye Jacobson, *Roots Too: White Ethnic Revival in Post–Civil Rights America* (2006).

19. "'Welfare Queen' Becomes Issue in Reagan Campaign," *New York Times*, February 15, 1976; Josh Levin, "The Welfare Queen," *Slate*, December 19, 2013.

20. Kaaryn S. Gustafson, *Cheating Welfare: Public Assistance and the Criminalization of Poverty* 34–35 (2011).

21. Gustafson, *Cheating Welfare*, 36.

22. Dan T. Carter, *From George Wallace to Newt Gingrich: Race in the Conservative Counterrevolution, 1963–1994*, at 64 (1996).

23. "Did Nancy Reagan Make 'Racist' Remark?" *Chicago Tribune*, March 1, 1980.

24. George Lakoff, *Don't Think of an Elephant: Know Your Values and Frame the Debate*, 7–14 (2004).

25. Frederick Mayer, *Narrative Politics: Stories and Collective Action* 3, 105 (2014).

26. Elliott Woods, "Fear: How the NRA Sells Guns in America Today," *New Republic*, April 16, 2018.

4. How the Right's Core Narrative Shapes the Political Landscape: Base, Persuadables, and Opposition

1. Pew Research Center, "For Most Trump Voters, 'Very Warm' Feelings for Him Endured," August 2018.

2. Stephanie McCrummen, "Judgment Days," *Washington Post*, July 21, 2018.

3. Mike Podhorzer, Weekend Reading—August 12 and 19, 2018, emails to author and hundreds of others, citing Pew Research Center, "For Most Trump Voters."

4. Katherine Stewart, "God's Red Army," *New York Times*, November 2, 2018.

5. Pew Research Center, "For Most Trump Voters."

6. Michael Tackett, "White Evangelical Women, Core Supporters of Trump, Begin Tiptoeing Away," *New York Times*, March 11, 2018.

7. Robert P. Jones, *The End of White Christian America* 56, 106 (2016).

8. Jones, *The End of White Christian America*, 171.

9. Marjorie J. Spruill, *Divided We Stand: The Battle Over Women's Rights and Family Values That Polarized American Politics* 304 (2017). For the argument that support for authoritarianism around the world finds its greatest commonality

in the backlash against women's equality, see Peter Beinart, "The Global Backlash Against Women," *Atlantic*, January 2019.

10. Jones, *The End of White Christian America*, 86, 167–68.

11. Jones, *The End of White Christian America*, 86.

12. Jones, *The End of White Christian America*, 92.

13. Kevin M. Kruse, *One Nation Under God: How Corporate America Invented Christian America* xiv (2015).

14. Podhorzer, Weekend Reading.

15. Podhorzer, Weekend Reading.

16. Pew Research Center, "For Most Trump Voters."

17. Amy Walter, "Getting to Know White Voters," *Cook Political Report*, August 29, 2018. Walter observes that, among whites, identifying as evangelical is a more powerful predictor of supporting Trump than gender or education. "The gap between white voters who approve and disapprove of Trump by gender was 25 points. By education (college versus non-college) it was about the same at 26 percent. But the gap in perceptions of the president between white voters who are evangelical and those who aren't was a whopping 60 percent!"

18. Stephen Hawkins, Daniel Yudkin, Míriam Juan-Torres, and Tim Dixon, "Hidden Tribes: A Study of America's Polarized Landscape," *More in Common*, October 2018, 6.

19. Hawkins et al., "Hidden Tribes," 5, 11. It's worth adding that the report's naturalistic imagery of "tribes" is dangerous. It implies that our differences are somehow rooted in and thereby fixed by nature, rather than generated by society and therefore more open to change. It also imports a subtle racial element, bringing race into the conversation without addressing thoughtfully and directly the actual work race does in American politics.

20. On factors that trigger a sense of anxiety among whites about declining group dominance, for instance, see the work of Jennifer Richeson, discussed later in this chapter.

21. Kinder and Kalmoe conclude that there is "little reason to regard moderation as an ideological category." Donald R. Kinder and Nathan P. Kalmoe, *Neither Liberal nor Conservative: Ideological Innocence in the American Public* 159 (2017).

22. We asked whether people agreed with this statement: "People of color who cannot get ahead in this country are mostly responsible for their own condition." The base resoundingly rejected this claim, giving it a mean agreement rating of 2.6 on a ten-point scale. The opposition widely accepted it, with a mean agreement rating of 6.7. African Americans split the difference (4.7). Latinxs were much

closer to the opposition (5.9), and indeed expressed the same level of agreement with this statement as did whites in general.

23. Arthur Delaney and Michael McAuliff, "Paul Ryan Wants 'Welfare Reform Round 2,'" *HuffPost*, March 20, 2012.

24. Carol Anderson, *One Person, No Vote: How Voter Suppression is Destroying Our Democracy* (2018).

25. Pew Research Center, "For Most Trump Voters, 'Very Warm' Feelings for Him Endured," August 2018.

26. Jens Manuel Krogstad and Mark Hugo Lopez, "Black Voter Turnout Fell in 2016, even as a Record Number of Americans Cast Ballots," Pew Research Center, May 12, 2017.

27. Overall, roughly 20 percent of Latinxs voted for Trump in 2016, and approximately 24 percent voted Republican in the 2018 congressional elections. Collaborative Multi-Racial Post-Election Survey (CMPS) 2016—Topline Results by Race (March 2017), 7; Latino Decisions, "American Election Eve Poll 2018—Latino Voters," November 7, 2018. Exit polls put the number of Latinxs voting Republican in 2018 congressional races at 30 percent. Jens Manuel Krogstad, Antonio Flores, and Mark Hugo Lopez, "Key Takeaways about Latino Voters in the 2018 Midterm Elections," Pew Research Center, November 9, 2018. About half of Latinxs consider themselves white, and these individuals are roughly twice as likely to identify as Republicans. Laura Gómez, *Manifest Destinies: The Making of the Mexican American Race* 167 (2nd ed. 2018).

28. Maria Abascal, "Us and Them: Black-White Relations in the Wake of Hispanic Population Growth," 80 *American Sociological Review* 789 (2015). See also Dave Seminara, "Liberals Say Immigration Enforcement Is Racist, but the Group Most Likely to Benefit from It Is Black Men," *Los Angeles Times*, March 16, 2018 ("African Americans favor reducing legal immigration more than any other demographic group."); and Nicolas C. Vaca, *The Presumed Alliance: The Unspoken Conflict Between Latinos and Blacks and What It Means for America* (2004).

29. Sean McElwee, "The Rising Racial Liberalism of Democratic Voters," *New York Times*, May 23, 2018.

30. Pew Research Center, "The Partisan Divide on Political Values Grows Even Wider," October 5, 2017, 33.

31. McElwee, "Rising Racial Liberalism." See also Eric Kaufmann, "Americans Are Divided by Their Views on Race, Not Race Itself," *New York Times*, March 18, 2019. Some scholars advise caution, noting that partisanship may be playing a role. The evidence on this is mixed, however, and at most might account for a small

fraction of the changes documented by the survey data. Peter K. Enns, "Clarifying the Role of Racism in the 2016 U.S. Presidential Election: Opinion Change, Anti-Immigrant Sentiment, and Vote Choice," paper prepared for presentation at the 2018 meeting of the American Political Science Association, 17; Andrew W. Engelhardt, "Racial Attitudes through a Partisan Lens," August 24, 2018.

32. Robert P. Jones, "Hidden Racial Anxiety in an Age of Waning Racism," *Atlantic*, May 12, 2014.

33. Maureen A. Craig and Jennifer A. Richeson, "More Diverse Yet Less Tolerant? How the Increasingly Diverse Racial Landscape Affects White Americans' Racial Attitudes," 40 *Personality and Social Psychology Bulletin* 750, 758 (2014).

34. Maureen A. Craig and Jennifer A. Richeson, "On the Precipice of a 'Majority-Minority' America: Perceived Status Threat from the Racial Demographic Shift Affects White Americans' Political Ideology," 25 *Psychological Science* 1189, 1191–92, 1196 (2014). For updates to their work, see Maureen Craig and Jennifer Richeson, "Information about the US Racial Demographic Shift Triggers Concerns about Anti-White Discrimination among the Prospective White 'Minority,'" forthcoming, *PLoS One*.

35. Craig and Richeson, "On the Precipice," 1196.

36. Quoted in Brian Resnick, "White Fear of Demographic Change Is a Powerful Psychological Force," *Vox*, January 28, 2017. A similar study confirmed that information about increasing racial diversity produced rightward political shifts among whites, and that "party affiliation did not significantly moderate the effects." Brenda Major, Alison Blodorn, and Gregory Major Blascovich, "The Threat of Increasing Diversity: Why Many White Americans Support Trump in the 2016 Presidential Election," *Group Processes and Intergroup Relations* 1, 8 (2016).

37. Craig and Richeson, "On the Precipice," 1193; Resnick, "White Fear."

38. Ryan D. Enos, "How Segregation Leads to Racist Voting by Whites," *Vox*, November 28, 2017.

39. Jones, "Hidden Racial Anxiety."

40. Quoted in William Wan and Sarah Kaplan, "Why Are People Still Racist? What Science Says about America's Race Problem," *Washington Post*, August 14, 2017.

5. Should the Left Lead with Racial Justice?

1. Ed Pilkington, "Bill Clinton: Mass Incarceration on My Watch 'Put Too Many People in Prison,'" *Guardian*, April 28, 2015.

2. Michelle Alexander, "Why Hillary Clinton Doesn't Deserve the Black Vote," *The Nation*, February 10, 2016.

3. Anne Gearan and Abby Phillip, "Clinton Regrets 1996 Remark on 'Super-Predators' after Encounter with Activist," *Washington Post*, February 25, 2016.

4. Liz Fields, "Bill Clinton Yells at Black Lives Matter Protesters, Defends Violent Crime Bill," *Vice News*, April 7, 2016.

5. Dara Lind, "#BernieSoBlack: Why Progressives Are Fighting about Bernie Sanders and Race," *Vox*, July 20, 2015.

6. Casey Tolan, "Nancy Pelosi Leaves Press Conference after Being Shouted Down by Undocumented Immigrants Protesting Talks with Trump," *San Jose Mercury News*, September 18, 2017.

7. Sean McElwee, "The Future of the Party: A Progressive Vision for a Populist Democratic Party," online report, April 2018, 6.

8. Harry Enten, "Registered Voters Who Stayed Home Probably Cost Clinton the Election," *FiveThirtyEight*, January 5, 2017.

9. Quoted in Thomas B. Edsall, "Democrats Are Playing Checkers While Trump Is Playing Chess," *New York Times*, October 12, 2017.

10. Quoted in Naomi Klein, *No Is Not Enough: Resisting Trump's Shock Politics and Winning the World We Need* 125 (2017).

11. Keeanga-Yamahtta Taylor, *From #BlackLivesMatter to Black Liberation* 80–92, 142–44 (2016).

12. Patrisse Khan-Cullors and asha bandele, *When They Call You a Terrorist* 5 (2017).

13. In California, the racial justice message was presented by two different messengers, an African American woman and a white woman. The number here represents that for the African American woman. For more regarding messengers, see chapter 9.

14. Kathy Kiely and Jill Lawrence, "Clinton Makes Case for Wide Appeal," *USA Today*, May 8, 2008; Adia Harvey Wingfield and Joe R. Feagin, *Yes We Can? White Racial Framing and the Obama Presidency* 60 (2nd ed. 2013).

15. Joe Conason, "Was Hillary Channeling George Wallace?" *Salon*, May 9, 2008.

16. Kiely and Lawrence, "Clinton Makes Case."

17. Steve Phillips, "Move Left, Democrats," *New York Times*, February 21, 2017; Jens Manuel Krogstad and Mark Hugo Lopez, "Black Voter Turnout Fell in 2016, Even as a Record Number of Americans Cast Ballots," Pew Research Center, May 12, 2017.

6. Can Democrats Build a Supermajority While Staying Silent About Racism?

1. Jonah Goldberg, "No, Liberals, Not Everything Is 'Racist,'" *New York Post*, November 16, 2016.

2. Robert Kuttner, "Steve Bannon, Unrepentant," *American Prospect*, August 16, 2017.

3. Gabriel Sherman, "'I Have Power': Is Steve Bannon Running for President?" *Vanity Fair*, December 21, 2017.

4. Chuck Schumer, "Chuck Schumer: A Better Deal for American Workers," *New York Times*, July 24, 2017.

5. Miles Kampf-Lassin, "The Democrats' New Agenda Is Everything That's Wrong with the Party," *In These Times*, July 28, 2017.

6. Abby Phillip, Thomas Gibbons-Neff, and Mike DeBonis, "Trump Announces That He Will Ban Transgender People from Serving in the Military," *Washington Post*, July 26, 2017. For a thoughtful repudiation of Trump's ban on military service by transgender persons, see *Karnoski v. Trump,* Order Granting in Part and Denying in Part Plaintiffs' and Washington's Motions for Summary Judgment; Granting in Part and Denying in Part Defendants' Motion for Partial Summary Judgment (United States District Court, Western District of Washington, Case 2:17-cv-01297-MJP, Document 233, April 13, 2018).

7. Mathew Rozsa, "Donald Trump at Ohio Rally: Immigrant Gang Members Will Torture and Kill Teenage Girls," *Salon*, July 26, 2017.

8. Kelly Swanson, "Trump Tells Cops They Should Rough People Up More during Arrests," *Vox*, July 28, 2017.

9. Mark Lilla, "The End of Identity Liberalism," *New York Times*, November 18, 2016.

10. Mark Penn and Andrew Stein, "Back to the Center, Democrats," *New York Times*, July 6, 2017.

11. Graham Vyse, "What Bernie Sanders Meant to Say About Identity Politics," *New Republic*, November 22, 2016.

12. See, for example, Todd Gitlin, "The Left, Lost in the Politics of Identity," *Harper's Magazine*, September 1993.

13. Christopher Achen and Larry Bartels, *Democracy for Realists: Why Elections Do Not Produce Responsive Government* 4 (2016).

14. James Traub, "The Party of Hubert Humphrey," *Atlantic*, April 7, 2018.

15. Traub, "The Party," emphasis added.

16. Traub, "The Party," quoting Thomas Byrne Edsall and Mary D. Edsall, *Chain Reaction: The Impact of Race, Rights, and Taxes on American Politics* (1991).

17. Michael Brenes, "The Once and Forever Liberal," *American Prospect*, January 31, 2018.

18. Bill Moyers, *Moyers on America: A Journalist and His Times* 167 (2004). There is also the apocryphal story that, upon signing the bill, Johnson turned to an aide and lamented, "we have lost the South for a generation." Clay Risen, "How the South was Won," *Atlanta Journal-Constitution*, April 30, 2006.

19. Eric Schickler, *Racial Realignment: The Transformation of American Liberalism, 1932–1965,* at 285–86 (2016).

20. Ira Katznelson, *Fear Itself: The New Deal and the Origins of Our Time* (2013).

21. From the beginning of the twentieth century, the radical left grasped "the political idea that black people reside in the eye of the hurricane of class struggle," observes Robin Kelley. Robin D.G. Kelley, *Freedom Dreams: The Black Radical Imagination* 38 (2002). The McCarthyist expulsions of radicals from the labor movement, in turn, effectively expelled from unions those elements most committed to anti-racism. As Manning Marable notes, "The purge of communists and radicals from organized labor from 1947 to 1950 was the principal reason for the decline in the AFL-CIO's commitment to the struggle against racial segregation." Manning Marable, *Race, Reform, and Rebellion: The Second Reconstruction in Black America, 1945–1990,* at 28 (1991).

22. Schickler, *Racial Realignment,* 285–86.

23. Eric Schickler, "Debunking the Myth that 'Identity Politics' Is Bad for the Democratic Party," *Vox*, April 21, 2018.

24. For a more critical appraisal of Joe Biden, see Jamelle Bouie, "The Trouble with Biden," *New York Times*, March 11, 2019.

25. Angela P. Harris, "Race and Essentialism in Feminist Legal Theory," 42 *Stanford Law Review* 581, 585 (1990).

26. Kimberlé Crenshaw, "Demarginalizing the Intersection of Race and Sex: A Black Feminist Critique of Antidiscrimination Doctrine, Feminist Theory, and Antiracist Politics," 1989 *University of Chicago Legal Forum* 139 (1989).

27. Black Lives Matter, What We Believe, https://blacklivesmatter.com/about/what-we-believe/

28. J. D. Vance, *Hillbilly Elegy: A Memoir of a Family and Culture in Crisis,* 190–91 (2016).

29. Vance, *Hillbilly Elegy*, 139.
30. Vance, *Hillbilly Elegy*, 146.
31. Vance, *Hillbilly Elegy*, 7.
32. Sarah Jones, "J.D. Vance, the False Prophet of Blue America," *New Republic*, November 17, 2016.
33. Charles Murray, *Losing Ground: American Social Policy, 1950–1980* (1984).
34. Vance, *Hillbilly Elegy*, 144.
35. Charles Murray & Richard Hernstein, *The Bell Curve: Intelligence and Class Structure in American Life* (1994).
36. Charles Murray, *Coming Apart: The State of White America, 1960–2010*, at 282 (2012).
37. Murray, *Coming Apart*, 300 (emphasis added). Murray describes the above claim as something he thinks that "neuroscientists and geneticists will prove over the next few decades."
38. Nancy Isenberg, *White Trash: The 400-Year Untold History of Class in America* xvi (2016).

7. When Economic Populists Talk About Racial Justice

1. Tom LoBianco, "Sanders: Trump Channeling Americans' Anger toward Minorities," *CNNPolitics*, March 29, 2016.
2. Robert Reich, "Robert Reich: How to Prevent Future Trumps," *Salon*, July 7, 2018.
3. Ian Haney López and Robert B. Reich, "The Way Forward for Democrats Is to Address Both Class and Race," *Nation*, December 12, 2016. See, for instance, the proposals offered in Robert B. Reich, *Saving Capitalism: For the Many, Not the Few* (2016).
4. Louis Jacobson, "Bernie Sanders Says 'Real Unemployment' Rate for African American Youth is 51 Percent," *PolitiFact*, July 13, 2015.
5. "Bernie Sanders Has a Direct Answer on Reparations at Iowa Forum," *FusionTV*.
6. Sanders also mentioned the need to address mass incarceration, but he did not focus on this. Nevertheless, his website offered a comprehensive plan to address this. "Issues: Racial Justice," berniesanders.com, https://berniesanders.com/issues/racial-justice/.
7. Ta-Nehisi Coates, "The Case for Reparations," *Atlantic*, June 2014.
8. William A. Darity Jr., "How Barack Obama Failed Black Americans," *Atlantic*, December 22, 2016.

9. Devah Pager, *Marked: Race, Crime, and Finding Work in an Era of Mass Incarceration* (2007).

10. Pager was instrumental in the "Ban the Box" movement, promoting state laws that prohibit employers from including a box on job application forms that asks about criminal convictions. Dara Linddara, "Ban the Box: President Obama's Plan to Help Ex-Prisoners Get Jobs, Explained," *Vox*, April 29, 2016.

11. Kathleen Geier, "Bernie's Greatest Weakness," *The Nation*, January 22, 2016.

12. Philip Bump, "Bernie Sanders Gains on Hillary Clinton in a New Poll," *Washington Post*, January 19, 2016.

13. Ta-Nehisi Coates, "Why Precisely Is Bernie Sanders Against Reparations?" *Atlantic*, January 19, 2016.

14. Sam Sanders, "'This Is Not 2016': What People Don't Get About Bernie Sanders and Race," *Politico*, March 9, 2019; James Hohmann, "The Daily 202: Will supporting reparations become a new litmus test for Democrats in 2020?" *Washington Post*, February 22, 2019.

15. Danielle Kurtzleben, "2020 Democrats Wrestle with a Big Question: What Are Reparations?" *National Public Radio*, March 1, 2019.

16. National Public Radio, Point Taken, "Reparations for Slavery in the United States?" May 2016.

17. "Bernie Sanders Has a Direct Answer."

18. For example, we asked respondents to choose between two statements, indicating which came closer to their opinion. One emphasized activist government ("To make life better for working people we need to invest in education, create better paying jobs, and make healthcare more affordable for people struggling to make ends meet"). The other tarred government as the problem ("To make life better for working people we need to cut taxes, reduce regulations, and get government out of the way of business"). Overall, more than twice as many people preferred the progressive agenda of investing in education, creating jobs, and making healthcare affordable, 62 percent to 32 percent. It was a slam dunk for the progressive base, winning support from nine out of ten people (89 percent to 9 percent). The progressive economic agenda also dominated among persuadables, winning support from more than six in ten (63 percent to 29 percent).

19. For an overview of Americans' progressive economic views, see Benjamin Page and Lawrence Jacobs, *Class War? What Americans Really Think About Economic Inequality* (2009).

8. The "Merge Right" Chapter, Or How Trumpism Mines and Fuels Dangerous Trends Among Whites

1. Mike Pear, "All the Evidence We Could Find About Fred Trump's Alleged Involvement with the KKK," *Vice*, March 10, 2016; Linda Gordon, *The Second Coming of the KKK: The Ku Klux Klan of the 1920s and the American Political Tradition* (2018). Asked about his father's probable arrest by the *New York Times* in a 2015 interview, Donald Trump responded, "It never happened. And they said there were no charges, no nothing. It's unfair to mention it, to be honest, because there were no charges." The lack of charges became a recurring defense. "By the way," Trump continued, "did you notice that there were no charges? Well, if there are no charges that means it shouldn't be mentioned." Jason Horowitz, "In Interview, Donald Trump Denies Report of Father's Arrest in 1927," *New York Times*, September 22, 2015.

2. Richard Rothstein, *The Color of Law: A Forgotten History of How Our Government Segregated America* (2017).

3. David Cay Johnston, *The Making of Donald Trump* 34 (2017).

4. "Klan race thought mirrored the principles of eugenics, accepted in the 1920's as state-of-the-art science," writes the historian Linda Gordon. "From this pseudo-science it logically followed that those of northern European ancestry ruled because they were superior and deserved to rule." Gordon, *The Second Coming of the KKK*, 22.

5. *Frontline*, "The Choice 2016," September 27, 2016.

6. Phil Han, "Donald Trump: I Have the Genes for Success," *CNN*, February 11, 2010.

7. Marina Fang and J. M. Rieger, "This May Be the Most Horrible Thing That Donald Trump Believes," *Huffington Post*, September 28, 2016.

8. Jonathan Mahler and Steve Eder, "'No Vacancies' for Blacks: How Donald Trump Got His Start, and Was First Accused of Bias," *New York Times*, August 27, 2016.

9. David W. Dunlap, "1973 | Meet Donald Trump," *New York Times*, July 30, 2015, quoting "Major Landlord Accused of Antiblack Bias in City," *New York Times*, October 16, 1973, A1.

10. Mahler and Eder, "'No Vacancies' for Blacks."

11. Mahler and Eder, "'No Vacancies' for Blacks."

12. Michael Kruse, "How Gotham Gave Us Trump," *Politico Magazine*, July/August 2017.

13. Oliver Laughland, "Donald Trump and the Central Park Five: The Racially Charged Rise of a Demagogue," *Guardian*, February 17, 2016. See also German Lopez, "Donald Trump's long History of Racism, from the 1970s to 2018," *Vox*, January 14, 2018.

14. Donald Trump, "Donald Trump: Central Park Five Settlement Is a 'Disgrace,'" *Daily News*, June 21, 2014.

15. "READ: Donald Trump's Advocate Interview Where He Defends Gays, Mexicans," *Advocate*, September 28, 2015.

16. Eleanor Clift, "Pat Buchanan: Donald Trump Stole My Playbook," *Daily Beast*, June 6, 2016.

17. Maggie Haberman and Alexander Burns, "Donald Trump's Presidential Run Began in an Effort to Gain Stature," *New York Times*, March 12, 2016.

18. Ashley Parker and Steve Eder, "Inside the Six Weeks Donald Trump Was a Nonstop 'Birther,'" *New York Times*, July 2, 2016.

19. Michael D. Shear, "With Document, Obama Seeks to End 'Birther' Issue," *New York Times*, April 27, 2011; Stephanie Condon, "Poll: One in Four Americans Think Obama Was Not Born in U.S.," *CBS News*, April 21, 2011.

20. Maggie Haberman, "The Donald Rising: Trump Tied for 1st," *Politico*, April 12, 2011.

21. Gabriel Sherman, "Operation Trump: Inside the Most Unorthodox Campaign in Political History," *Atlantic*, April 3, 2016.

22. Editorial Board, "A Chance to Reset the Republican Race," *New York Times*, January 30, 2016.

23. David Brock and Ari Rabin-Havt, *The Fox Effect: How Roger Ailes Turned a Network into a Propaganda Machine* 38 (2012); John Koblin, Emily Steel, and Jim Rutenberg, "Roger Ailes Leaves Fox News, and Rupert Murdoch Steps In," *New York Times*, July 21, 2016; Jeffrey Toobin, "Campaign Tips from the Man Who Has Done It All," *New Yorker*, June 2, 2008; Geoff Pender, "Donald Trump Jr. Speaks at Neshoba Fair," *Clarion-Ledger*, July 26, 2016.

24. Paul Begala, "Begala: Donald Trump Is No 'Idiot.' He's Something Worse," *CNN*, May 2, 2018.

25. John Sides, Michael Tesler, and Lynn Vavreck, *Identity Crisis: The 2016 Presidential Campaign and the Battle for the Meaning of America* 2 (2018).

26. Alana Semuels, "No, Most Black People Don't Live in Poverty—or Inner Cities," *Atlantic*, October 12, 2016.

27. Amber Phillips, "Chris Christie Says Hillary Clinton 'Started' This Whole 'Bigot' Thing. Actually, Donald Trump Did," *Washington Post*, August 28, 2016.

28. Aaron Blake, "Donald Trump Doesn't Seem to Know What a 'Bigot' Is," *Washington Post*, August 26, 2016.

29. Transcripts, "Trump Speaks at Manchester, New Hampshire, Rally; Clinton to Speak in Reno, Nevada. Aired 2:30-3p ET," *CNN*, August 25, 2016.

30. Jenna Johnson and Abigail Hauslohner, "'I Think Islam Hates Us': A Timeline of Trump's Comments about Islam and Muslims," *Washington Post*, May 20, 2017.

31. Allegra Kirkland, "Halperin: Trump Attack on 'Mexican' Judge 'Not Racial,' Mexico 'Not a Race,'" *TalkingPointsMemo*, June 4, 2016.

32. Karen E. Fields and Barbara J. Fields, *Racecraft: The Soul of Inequality in American Life* (2014).

33. See Edward W. Said, *Orientalism* 9–12 (1978). See also Deepa Kumar, "Framing Islam: The Resurgence of Orientalism During the Bush II Era," 34 *Journal of Communication Enquiry* 254, 260 (2010); Zareena Grewal, "The 'Muslim World' Does Not Exist," *Atlantic*, May 21, 2017; Khaled Beydoun, *American Islamophobia: Understanding the Roots and Rise of Fear* 1–5 (2018); Yaser Ali, "Shariah and Citizenship—How Islamophobia is Creating a Second-Class Citizenry in America," 100 *California Law Review* 1027 (2012); Neil Gotanda, "The Racialization of Islam in American Law," 637 *Annals of the American Academy of Political and Social Science* 184 (2011).

34. Khaled A. Beydoun, "Between Muslim and White: The Legal Construction of Arab American Identity," 69 *N.Y.U. Annual Survey of American Law* 29, 38 (2013).

35. Walter Ewing, Daniel E. Martínez, and Rubén G. Rumbaut, "The Criminalization of Immigration in the United States," American Immigration Council Special Report, July 13, 2015. See also M. Kathleen Dingeman and Rubén G. Rumbaut, "The Immigration-Crime Nexus," 31 *University of La Verne Law Review* 363 (2010).

36. Leo R. Chavez, *The Latino Threat: Constructing Immigrants, Citizens, and the Nation* (2008); Otto Santa Ana, *Brown Tide Rising: Metaphors of Latinos in Contemporary American Public Discourse* (2002).

37. Gabriel Thompson, "How the Right Made Racism Sound Fair—and Changed Immigration Politics," *Colorlines*, September 13, 2011; Lawrence Downes, "What Part of 'Illegal' Don't You Understand?" *New York Times*, October 28, 2007; Charles Garcia, "Why 'Illegal Immigrant' Is a Slur," *CNN*, July 6, 2012; and Mónica Novoa, "Open Letter from Drop the I-Word to *The New York Times*," October 1, 2012.

38. Antonio Flores, "How the U.S. Hispanic Population Is Changing," Pew Research Center, September 18, 2017; Gustavo López, Kristen Bialik and Jynnah Radford, "Key findings about U.S. immigrants," Pew Research Center, November 30, 2018.

39. Adrienne LaFrance, "Fox Got It Wrong with '3 Mexican Countries,' but It Also Got It Right," *Atlantic*, March 31, 2019.

40. On the reactionary hijacking of colorblindness in the legal context, see my articles "Intentional Blindness," 87 *N.Y.U. Law Review* 1179 (2012), and "'A Nation of Minorities': Race, Ethnicity, and Reactionary Colorblindness," 59 *Stanford Law Review* 985 (2007).

41. Ashley Elizabeth Jardina, "Demise of Dominance: Group Threat and the New Relevance of White Identity for American Politics," 51 (PhD diss., University of Michigan, 2014). See also Ashley Jardina, *White Identity Politics* (2019).

42. Ashley Jardina, "White Identity Politics Isn't Just about White Supremacy. It's Much Bigger," *Washington Post*, August 16, 2017.

43. Jardina, "Demise of Dominance," 172.

44. Eric Knowles and Linda Tropp, "Donald Trump and the Rise of White Identity in Politics," *Conversation*, October 20, 2016.

45. Brenda Major, Alison Blodorn, and Gregory Major Blascovich, "The Threat of Increasing Diversity: Why Many White Americans Support Trump in the 2016 Presidential Election," 1 *Group Processes and Intergroup Relations* 8 (2016).

46. Jardina, "Demise of Dominance," 37, 38.

47. Jardina, "White Identity Politics." See also Jardina, *White Identity Politics*, 81.

48. Derek Black speaking with Terry Gross on *Fresh Air*, "How a Rising Star of White Nationalism Broke Free from the Movement," September 24, 2018.

49. William Saletan, "What Trump Supporters Really Believe," *Slate*, August 29, 2017. See also Philip Bump, "Of Course Trump's Outrage at the NFL Protests Had to Do with Race," *Washington Post*, September 25, 2017.

50. Cited in Saletan, "What Trump Supporters Really Believe."

51. Bob Woodward, *Fear: Trump in the White House* 8 (2018).

52. Jane Mayer, "The Reclusive Hedge-Fund Tycoon Behind the Trump Presidency," *New Yorker*, March 27, 2017.

53. Woodward, *Fear*, 9.

54. Paul Blumenthal and J. M. Rieger, "This Stunningly Racist French Novel Is How Steve Bannon Explains The World," *Huffington Post*, March 4, 2017.

55. Jonathan Martin, Jim Rutenberg, and Maggie Haberman, "Donald Trump Appoints Media Firebrand to Run Campaign," *New York Times*, August 17, 2016.

56. Woodward, *Fear,* 23.

57. Woodward, *Fear,* 14.

58. Sarah Posner, "How Donald Trump's New Campaign Chief Created an Online Haven for White Nationalists," *Mother Jones*, August 22, 2016.

59. Richard Spencer, "The Conservative Write," *Taki's*, August 6, 2008.

60. Quoted in Adrian Florido, "The White Nationalist Origins of the Term 'Alt-Right'—and the Debate Around It," *NPR*, November 27, 2016.

61. "Richard Bertrand Spencer," Southern Poverty Law Center, accessed October 2017.

62. Graeme Wood, "His Kampf," *Atlantic*, June 2017.

63. Southern Poverty Law Center.

64. Evan Osnos, "The Fearful and the Frustrated," *New Yorker*, August 31, 2015 (emphasis added).

65. Allum Bokhari and Milo Yiannopoulos, "An Establishment Conservative's Guide to the Alt-Right," *Breitbart*, March 29, 2016.

66. Joseph Bernstein, "Here's How Breitbart and Milo Smuggled Nazi and White Nationalist Ideas into the Mainstream," *BuzzFeed*, October 5, 2017.

67. Bokhari and Yiannopoulos, "An Establishment Conservative's Guide."

68. Adam Serwer, "America's Problem Isn't Tribalism—It's Racism," *Atlantic*, November 7, 2018.

69. Wil S. Hylton, "Down the Breitbart Hole," *New York Times*, August 16, 2017. See Yochai Benkler, Robert Faris, and Hal Roberts, *Network Propaganda: Manipulation, Disinformation, and Radicalization in American Politics* (2018).

70. "For the record" a *New York Times* journalist notes, "Richard Spencer says he is not a Nazi." Liam Stack, "Attack on Alt-Right Leader Has Internet Asking: Is It O.K. to Punch a Nazi?" *New York Times*, January 21, 2017.

71. Daniel Lombroso and Yoni Appelbaum, "'Hail Trump!': White Nationalists Salute the President-Elect," *Atlantic*, November 21, 2016.

72. Nahal Toosi, "Inside Stephen Miller's hostile takeover of immigration policy," *Politico*, August 29, 2018.

73. Peter Baker, "'Use That Word!': Trump Embraces the 'Nationalist' Label," *New York Times*, October 23, 2018.

9. The Race-Class Approach

1. Among persuadables, using the mean convincing rating, 4 race-class messages were more convincing than colorblind economic populism, 2 tied that message, and 3 were one point less convincing. We also used a dial test to measure performance. By that metric, all 9 race-class messages received a higher rating than colorblind economic populism. Color-blind economic populism rated behind the opposition message when measured by dial testing.

2. Among whites, the most convincing race-class message had a mean convincing rating 5 points ahead of the colorblind economic populism message (70 to 65). The margin was plus 4 points for African Americans (81 to 77) and plus 5 points for Latinxs (79 to 74). The more significant difference between racial groups comes from comparing the mean convincing rate for the race-class message versus the opposition message. The gap for whites is plus 4 for the race-class message (70 to 66). Among African Americans, it's a much greater plus 18 (81 to 63), and among Latinxs it's a comparable plus 17 (79 to 62).

3. RuralOrganizing.org, "POLLING BRIEF | 2018 National Rural Survey," http://ruralorganizing.org/polling-brief-2018-national-rural-survey.

4. Latino Decisions, "Battleground Districts July 2018 Midterm Survey—Immigration Policy Attitudes," 5–6, July 2018.

5. Matthew Stolle, "DFLers Say 'We Are Greater than Fear' in Final Rochester Campaign Stop," *Post Bulletin*, November 1, 2018. The "Greater than Fear" messaging guide is available at greaterthanfear.us/guide (last checked April 16, 2019).

6. Ian Haney López, "The Most Important Part of Day One That No One Is Focusing On," *BillMoyers.com*, July 26, 2016.

7. Available for viewing beginning at minute 15 at www.facebook.com/NetrootsNation/videos/10156411312139827/?v=10156411312139827.

8. Keeanga-Yamahtta Taylor, *From #BlackLivesMatter to Black Liberation* 251, 216 (2016).

9. In California, the racial justice message received an average convincing rating among persuadables of 60 when presented by an African American woman; the comparable convincing rating rose to 64 when the messenger was a white woman. By way of comparison, the opposition message received an average convincing rating from persuadables in California of 62.

10. Christopher T. Stout, "Black Candidates Know They Have to Be Careful in Talking about Race. Here's What the Research Suggests," *Washington Post*, February 19, 2019. Stout found, in contrast, that promising to specifically help

communities of color produced positive responses from voters of color, while neither gaining nor losing support from white voters.

11. Derrick Bell, *Ethical Ambition: Living a Life of Meaning and Worth* (2002).

12. Poor People's Campaign: A National Call for Moral Revival, Fundamental Principles. On the central role of moral arguments in social movement mobilization, see Marshall Ganz, *Why David Sometimes Wins: Leadership, Organization, and Strategy in the California Farm Worker Movement* (2010).

10. 20/20 Vision: Comparing the Left's Possible Responses to Anti-Immigrant Dog Whistling

1. Thomas B. Edsall, "How Immigration Foiled Hillary," *New York Times*, October 5, 2017.

2. Erin Carlson, "White House Memos Reveal Emanuel's Agenda on Immigration, Crime," *NBCChicago.com*, June 20, 2014.

3. Gabriel Thompson, "How the Right Made Racism Sound Fair—and Changed Immigration Politics," *Colorlines*, September 13, 2011.

4. Douglas S. Massey, "Racial Formation in Theory and Practice: The Case of Mexicans in the United States," 1 *Race and Social Problems* 12, 19 (2009).

5. Tom Zoellner, "Partners in Pink Underwear," *Slate*, November 24, 2008; Joe Hagan, "The Long, Lawless Ride of Sheriff Joe Arpaio," *Village Voice*, August 2, 2012; Tom Jackman, "How Ex-Sheriff Joe Arpaio Wound Up Facing Jail Time before Trump Pardoned Him," *Washington Post*, August 25, 2017.

6. Muzaffar Chishti, Sarah Pierce, and Jessica Bolter, "The Obama Record on Deportations: Deporter in Chief or Not?" Policy Beat, Migration Policy Institute, January 26, 2017.

7. Julia Preston, "Latinos Support Obama, Despite Deportation Policies," *New York Times*, December 28, 2011.

8. Chishti et al., "The Obama Record."

9. Thompson, "How the Right Made Racism Sound Fair."

10. Wyatt Clarke, Kimberly Turner, and Lina Guzman, "One Quarter of Hispanic Children in the United States Have an Unauthorized Immigrant Parent," National Research Center on Hispanic Children & Families, October 2017.

11. Will Wilkinson, "The Immigration Debate Is about Whether Latinos Are 'Real Americans,' Democrats Debate Policy as Trump Pursues a Radical Ethnonationalist Agenda," *Vox*, February 22, 2018.

12. Julie Hirschfeld Davis, "G.O.P. Finds an Unexpectedly Potent Line of Attack: Immigration," *New York Times*, October 14, 2018.

13. Hirschfeld Davis, "Unexpectedly Potent Line of Attack." See also CAP Action Fund and Third Way: Battleground Immigration Survey, https://cdn .americanprogressaction.org/content/uploads/sites/2/2018/08/22090028/Battle ground-Sanctuary-Cities-Survey-House-Battleground-Deck-D08.22.18.pdf.

14. Thomas B. Edsall, "The Trumpification of Ed Gillespie," *New York Times*, November 2, 2017.

15. Cristóbal Alex, "My organization's anti-Gillespie ad provoked a backlash. But I won't stop defending Latinos," *Washington Post*, November 7, 2017.

16. Fenit Nirappil, "Gillespie ad attacks Latino Victory Fund commercial; Northam ad ties him to Trump," *Washington Post*, November 2, 2017.

17. Editorial Board, "An ad that had no place in Va.'s governor's race," *Washington Post*, October 31, 2017.

18. David Weigel, "Democrats Visit Detention Centers to Attack 'Zero Tolerance' Immigration Policy," *Washington Post*, June 23, 2018.

19. Sean McElwee, "The Power of 'Abolish ICE,'" *New York Times*, August 4, 2018.

20. Shane Goldmacher, "Ocasio-Cortez Pushes Democrats to the Left, Whether They Like It or Not," *New York Times*, January 13, 2019.

21. Robert Draper, "The Democrats Have an Immigration Problem," *New York Times*, October 10, 2018.

22. Quoted in Draper, "The Democrats Have an Immigration Problem."

23. Nathan J. Russell, "An Introduction to the Overton Window of Political Possibilities," Mackinac Center for Public Policy, January 4, 2006.

24. Carlos Maza, "How Trump Makes Extreme Things Look Normal: Why We Should Worry about the 'Overton Window,'" *Vox*, December 21, 2017.

25. James Hohmann, "The Daily 202: Will Supporting Reparations Become a New Litmus Test for Democrats in 2020?" *Washington Post*, February 22, 2019.

26. This message reflects a conversation Anat Shenker-Osorio and I had with Frank Sharry, head of America's Voice, a leading progressive immigration advocacy group. It draws on a message the race-class project tested, but this message itself was not tested on a survey. See Shenker-Osorio's memo, "Words that Work on Immigrant Rights." See also Frank Sharry, "As the GOP Revs Up Its 'Divide and Distract' Strategy, How Should Democrats and Progressives Respond?" *Medium*, September 11, 2018.

27. Alberto Alesina, Edward Glaeser, and Bruce Sacerdote, "Why Doesn't the United States Have a European-Style Welfare State?" Brookings Papers on Economic Activity, 187, 189 (2001) ("America's troubled race relations are clearly a major reason for the absence of an American welfare state").

28. Benedict Anderson, *Imagined Communities: Reflections on the Origin and Spread of Nationalism* (1983).

Afterword: Darkest Before the Dawn

1. Alexander Burns and Jonathan Martin, "Trump's Takeover of the Republican Party Is Almost Complete," *New York Times*, April 3, 2019.

2. David Roediger, *The Wages of Whiteness: Race and the Making of the American Working Class* (1991). See also David Roediger, *Class, Race, and Marxism* (2017).

3. W. E. B. DuBois, *Black Reconstruction in America*, 700–701 (1935; reprint, 1998).

Index

About the Author

Ian Haney López is a law professor at the University of California, Berkeley, where he teaches in the areas of race and constitutional law. He co-founded the Race-Class Narrative Project, and also co-chaired the AFL-CIO's Advisory Council on Racial and Economic Justice. He holds an endowed chair as the Earl Warren Professor of Public Law at UC Berkeley and lives in Richmond, California.

ALSO BY IAN HANEY LÓPEZ

Dog Whistle Politics: How Coded Racial Appeals Have Reinvented Racism and Wrecked the Middle Class

Racism on Trial: The Chicano Fight for Justice

White by Law: The Legal Construction of Race

EDITED BY IAN HANEY LÓPEZ

After the War on Crime: Race, Democracy, and a New Reconstruction (with Jonathan Simon and Mary Louise Frampton)

Race, Law and Society